AFRICA FIRST!

1st edition 2021
© 2021 Berg & Feierabend Verlag, Berlin
All rights reserved

Editor: Bert Hoppe
Translation: Joy Hawley, Elizabeth Oertel
Typesetting: artwork-factory.com
Set with DIN and Minion
Cover design: Peter Feierabend and Frank Behrendt
Set with DIN
Printing: PrintMediaNetwork

ISBN 978-3-948272-14-2

Printed in Europe

www.bergundfeierabend.de

Martin Schoeller · Daniel Schönwitz

AFRICA FIRST!

Roadmap for a joint future

BERG & FEIERABEND

Table of Contents

Foreword Dr. Gerd Müller   7
Preface Dr. Antonella Mei-Pochtler   11
Foreword   17
Invest instead of sending aid – the Spice Route 2.0   21

Section I: The Facts   39
   Chapter 1: Poverty, hunger and social insecurity   41
   Chapter 2: Climate crisis, civil wars and mass emigration   53
   Chapter 3: Birth rates and population growth   65
   Chapter 4: Economy, infrastructure and trade   71
   Chapter 5: Investments, the Silk Road, and mountains of debt   79

Section II: The Key Statements   87
   Key Statement 1: Africa and Europe share a common destiny with enormous potential   89
   Key Statement 2: Unregulated capitalism has failed across the board in Africa   97
   Key Statement 3: Neither "free" nor "fair" trade can defeat poverty   103
   Key Statement 4: Africa needs the social market economy   111
   Key Statement 5: Minimum wages and insurance for the unemployed play a key role   123
   Key Statement 6: Fair wages and social reforms lower birth rates—and trigger an "upward spiral"   141
   Key Statement 7: Social-ecological market economy: The world is ready for "prosperity for all"   151

Section III: The Agenda   **161**

Europe can demand and support reform—
and thus spark change   162

Tool 1: Infrastructure financing—
Let's build a European Silk Road to Africa!

Tool 2: Development aid—Why we need an
upgraded Marshall Plan   179

Tool 3: Trade—Let's put an end to
"Europe First" for good!   193

Outlook: The new EU-Africa Pact is the opportunity
of the century   203

Appendix   **213**

Executive Summary: Our key points and
recommendations in overview   213

Our answers to biases and sweeping judgements   219

Bibliography and references   226

The authors   232

Foreword Dr. Gerd Müller

Shaping the future with the reform partnerships

Only a few months ago, we could say it without a doubt: Africa is on its way up. At the beginning of the Covid-19 pandemic, our neighboring continent was home to six of the ten fastest growing economies. The annual growth rate in internet usage was over 20 percent. Africa's soils harbor significant quantities of raw materials such as gold, platinum and coltan. And there is a huge potential for generating renewable energy. In Ouarzazate in the Moroccan desert, one of the most modern solar power stations in the world has been built with German support. Building on this experience, we will use solar power to invest in the production of green hydrogen and methanol.

How the legacy of the Covid-19 pandemic will impact the African continent is as uncertain as the situation in Europe. However, one thing is already clear: the economic effects threaten to wipe out long-standing development successes. Closed borders, tourism at a standstill, disrupted trade flows and supply chains mean immediate existential hardship for many people in Africa. Social security systems are often weak or even completely non-existent; hardly any of the 85% of informal workers on the African continent have any savings. The health crisis quickly turns into a hunger crisis. In Niger and South Sudan for example, millions of people are dependent on food aid.

All the more topical and urgent is the demand of the two authors of this book to establish and expand social security systems. Even before Covid-19, too few people in Africa were benefiting from the natural wealth of their continent, from international trade or economic growth. Added to this is population growth. It is both an opportunity and a challenge that Africa's population will double by 2050. 20 million new jobs must be created every year for the young generation by 2030 alone to give them a sufficient income to live on and decent prospects.

Investments are urgently needed to meet the needs of the growing population, in particular to provide clean water, sanitary facilities, schools, hospitals and transport infrastructure. Moreover, 600 million people, half the population, continue to live without electricity. The challenges we face are considerable and we must tackle them together.

The days of the old-style "development aid" are long gone. As early as 2015, the African Union adopted its own ambitious vision for development, Agenda 2063. We have reorganized our development cooperation with Africa on the basis of this; away from the donor/recipient model and towards a partnership as equals, oriented on the respective reform agenda of our African partners.

Our Marshall Plan with Africa, launched in 2017, initiated this paradigm shift. German state development aid is not spread too thinly, but is intended to act as a catalyst for private sector investment, and thus activate sustainable, inclusive and self-sustaining economic development that benefits all.

We have developed a new model for development cooperation to allow us to achieve this: the reform partnerships. We provide targeted support to governments that are making progress in their countries in establishing the rule of law and resolutely fighting corruption. In this way, we help to improve the structural framework for the involvement of the private sector and thus create new jobs and generate more income.

In addition, we have developed instruments to make it more attractive for German and European companies to invest in African countries. We are supporting such responsible investments through the Development Investment Fund and complementing these with advice and networking.

The Covid-19 pandemic has made us aware that we live in a global village where everything is interconnected. We must consider social and ecological issues in combination with one another to make globalization fairer: these include health, education, gender equality, ecological and social standards in global supply chains, and also the preservation of natural resources. This is what Agenda 2030 with its 17 sustainable development goals set out to do when it was adopted by all member states of the United Nations.

Each individual country will develop in its own particular way. What is certain, however, is that we can only move forward through the joint efforts of governments, business and every single member of society. The same applies to Africa as to Germany.

That is why I am pleased that we can count on committed and responsible entrepreneurs like Martin Schoeller, who puts his heart and soul into his work for our neighboring continent. Dear readers, I hope he sets an example that will inspire further entrepreneurial commitment to Africa and to sustainable development worldwide!

Dr. Gerd Müller
German Federal Minister of Economic Cooperation and Development

Preface Dr. Antonella Mei-Pochtler

Africa First, but not alone.

Admittedly, when some readers see the title *Africa First*, they may automatically think of well-known examples of isolationist foreign and economic policy, and they might start to make appropriate comparisons. In this case, however, the choice of words is quite justified, although the context is fundamentally different.

Early man took his first steps on African soil, where he learnt skills like how to use fire and sophisticated techniques with tools. It was from here that other continents were settled. Two million years later, we once again find ourselves in a scenario in which the continent known as the cradle of mankind will permanently assume an important role, and a decisive one for Europe, in a changing world order, and rightly so.

65 percent of the more than 1.2 billion people who make up the African population are younger than 35 years old, and 40 percent of them are even younger than 15. The average age on this continent is 19.5, the lowest in the world. If we compare this with the average age in Europe, which is around 42.5 years, the term "Africa: A Continent of Opportunities", which has been too often dismissed in the past, gains an entirely new meaning. If the forecasts prove to be true, by 2035 Africa will become the continent with the world's largest working population; by that time almost a quarter of the globe's population of working-age adults will live there. Incidentally, the population of Africa is expected to double by 2050, and by 2100 the continent will have about 40 percent of the world's births, unless the birth rate is reduced due to education and wealth.

This has crucial implications for the urgently needed transformation at the individual, social, economic and political level.

With this in mind, there is no need to further explain that the facts presented in the first part of the "Agenda for our common future" do not only concern Africa. In the long run, the effects of a lack of education, poverty, social insecurity, a lack of jobs, locally occurring climate disasters and famine, armed conflict, migration, population growth, declining economic growth and mountains of debt will by no means be confined to the continent—on the contrary, the effects will be felt worldwide! To ignore these risks would be to fail to recognize that Africa is a fundamental and firmly integrated part of today's networked world.

Austria lived up to its well-established role as an arena for dialogue and bridge-building when it hosted the high-level Africa-Europe Forum on the topic of "taking cooperation to the digital age" during its EU Council Presidency in 2018, which aimed at promoting a new and effective form of entrepreneurial cooperation on an equal footing.

Not only are numerous economists aware that the classic model of development aid has become obsolete, it is also clearly visible to everyday people. During the forum, more than 50 official delegations from member states of the African Union and the EU networked with nearly 1,000 innovators and start-ups from Africa and Europe as well as with established companies to discuss issues of prosperity and growth. All participants were aware that many of the great challenges of our time can only be solved by leveraging vision, technology and entrepreneurship. Digitization cannot be given enough importance—whether in the sectors of agriculture, health or mobility, the most effective concepts use the approach "digital first".

Entrepreneurship is the norm in Africa. According to the African Development Bank, Africa has the highest figure worldwide. Around 22 percent of the working population start a business—with one of the highest rates of women in the world.

If necessity is the mother of invention, too much necessity can also paralyze; but for Africa to be able to fully exploit its great potential, further prerequisites are needed, such as resilience in the face of humanitarian, economic and health crises. Europeans have created such an environment for their own continent over the last 150 years—in large surges and in many small, practical steps. Take, for example, the dual vocational training system successfully established in Germany and Austria to train the skilled workers that are needed everywhere.

It is important to share this experience, not least in order to keep well-educated Africans in their home countries or to win them back after their education outside of Africa. Entrepreneurial education projects, such as Sebastian Thrun's online academy Udacity, which is run in cooperation with Egypt and offers a broad training in programming for everyone, are going in the right direction. It is also important to further strengthen the role of women—there is much to learn from the Scandinavian countries in particular. The World Economic Forum predicts that around 15 to 20 million "increasingly trained" young Africans will enter the labor market every year over the next three decades. The creation of quality jobs is therefore fundamental to leveraging the continent's demographic dividend as much as possible.

The European Union and Austria can and must act as catalysts on both a large and small scale, as partners working on an equal footing towards the necessary transition in these important areas, to jointly develop intelligent entrepreneurial solutions and bring their potential to the streets. Or into the air—this is how the disruptively innovative US company Zipline has just started its business in Africa and developed it to such an extent that it is now being used in other parts of the world.

Their mission is to provide "vital, on-demand delivery for the world", for example by establishing the primary blood plasma supply chain via drone deliveries. A genius, cost-effective infrastructure solution in order to guarantee the delivery of life-saving products in rural areas at exactly the right time, to exactly the right place, in a safe and reliable manner and across national borders. Piloted in Rwanda, scaled in Ghana and now also implemented in the USA, Zipline's solution is a perfect example of "Africa first, but not alone".

Now the Europeans must not hide their light under a bushel. With its core product WADI, an inconspicuous device that uses solar power to disinfect water, the Austrian company Helioz—Future Economy has developed an innovative and accessible solution that is needed by 660 million people worldwide who still lack access to clean water. Currently 2,000 children worldwide die every day from diseases caused by contaminated water. This is another example of "Africa First, but not alone".

The list of inspiring examples, including the Austrian companies Andritz in the energy sector and Vamed in the health sector, is long, but not long enough, because right now we need a combination of courageous disruptors and innovative specialists to develop entrepreneurial solutions in and for Africa in the sectors of infrastructure, health, energy, mobility and agriculture.

That is why this book comes at exactly the right moment, from the right intellectual pioneers and entrepreneurs who are executing these projects, as Martin Schoeller and his team wrote. At the end of the day, however, it is Africans who will have to take matters into their own hands. In the words of former US President Barack Obama in 2009: "Africa's future is up to Africans"—and that means "Africa first, but not alone".

Dr. Antonella Mei-Pochtler
Special Representative of the Chancellor of Austria
Head of the Strategy Department of ThinkAustria

Foreword

Peace, freedom and prosperity through a social market economy—an impulse for establishing a European-African economic area

German Federal Minister for Economic Cooperation and Development Gerd Müller's new Africa policy is a major step forward: We are moving away from the blanket approach—and towards partnerships on an equal footing with selected states that are willing to reform. This creates incentives for the rule of law and at the same time more attractive conditions for the private sector. But that is not enough. In this book, we recommend that reform states also receive decisive support to invest in infrastructure. Innovative financing concepts and safeguards make it possible to do this without raising taxes and placing an excessive burden on existing national budgets. And if we make reforms which move towards towards a social market economy a prerequisite for this support, we are laying the foundations for the effective fight against poverty and the creation of broad-based prosperity.

The agenda we present for discussion in this book therefore focuses on infrastructure investments in Africa. The proposed initiative would be more of an initial catalyst, rather than pouring Europe's money down the drain. After all, an economic upturn in Africa would also create millions of jobs here, which are needed more urgently than ever after the Covid-19 crisis. Moreover, in the long term, the continent can thus become the new growth engine of the global economy.

And let's not kid ourselves: if extreme poverty continues to shape the continent in the future and the population continues to grow rapidly (with 4 billion inhabitants in the next 60 years, according to UN forecasts), then human rights and peace will also be in danger in Europe.

On the other hand, the race has begun: the Chinese and the Russians have long since been busy staking out their claims. Europe cannot stand by idly or halfheartedly if it wants to continue to play a shaping role in world politics.

In terms of freedom, peace, human rights and more widely distributed wealth, Europe is the most successful region in the world. Over the past 70 years we have proven that a model of society based on reciprocity works. Europe is the world's financially strongest economic power with a gross national product similar to that of the USA, but with significantly lower debts and deficits. And in the Covid-19 crisis, the European Union has demonstrated its joint financial and operational strength.

As the USA and China are currently competing for global influence with a less than cooperative approach in each case, Europe with its social model based on reciprocity has an almost unique selling point. That is why I am convinced that we have the strength and the resources to create the largest market in the world, the growth region of the future and broad prosperity with a European-African economic area.

As long as the US says "America First", they disqualify themselves from partnerships that are naturally based on the win-win principle. This opens a window of opportunity for peace and freedom through the social market economy, i.e. the European Economic Model.

I have been involved in Africa for many years as Consul of Togo and a family entrepreneur with activities in many countries in the southern hemisphere. I am working to make Togo, one of the small and very poor countries of the continent, a model for other developing countries. I have been interested in the question of how to implement social standards and create broad-based prosperity since the beginning of my professional life in Brazil.

In the course of my 40 years of working as an entrepreneur, I have come to the conclusion that only the social market economy can end extreme poverty.

Martin Schoeller
Pullach, October 2020

NOTE OF THANKS

Numerous people from my personal and professional life have contributed to this book. They have told me about interesting developments and publications, questioned my reasoning and helped me to sort my thoughts and organize my writing for this book. I would like to thank them all very much.

Also on behalf of my co-author Daniel Schönwitz, I would especially like to thank Martin Schaffrinna, who dug deep into databases and statistics and compiled valuable figures, tables and graphics.

My thanks also go to numerous knowledgeable discussion partners for exciting ideas, valuable hints and well-founded assessments. These include George Soros, former WTO President Pascal Lamy, the long-standing EU Trade Commissioner Karel de Gucht and ESM President Klaus Regling. Johannes Singhammer, a long-standing member of the German Bundestag and current BMZ Special Advisor for West Africa, Antonella Mei-Pochtler, advisor to the Austrian Chancellor, and Professor Robert Dussey, Foreign Minister of Togo, have also been of great help to me.

Investing instead of sending aid—the Spice Route 2.0

Why Africa needs the social market economy, what soccer has to do with it—and how we can use Europe's financial power for an unprecedented infrastructure plan

It is a mind-boggling humanitarian catastrophe: almost 300 million people in Africa suffer from severe food insecurity, more than three million young children die there year for year, also due to the effects of malnourishment. Seen from a distant Europe, we often perceive this reality merely as cold numbers that do not concern us personally. But we should remember that they stand for countless human tragedies that words cannot adequately describe.

Therefore, we must overcome the classic human reflex of denial. We must take action now, otherwise we will be faced with future generations asking us: "What did you do about it?" And we will not be able to talk our way out of it with our ignorance. In a globalized world, one can no longer claim not to have been aware of poverty, hunger and their dramatic consequences.

The time for excuses is over; especially since the situation is becoming more acute and its effects could affect us as well. If population growth continues at an unabated rate, Africa will no longer be home to just 1.3 billion people, but to more than 4 billion people by the end of the century, many of whom will live in extreme poverty. You don't have to be a prophet to predict that by then, at the latest, Africa's problems will also become Europe's problems. Even now, millions of Africans want to escape the misery at home to the Global North.

VAST PROBLEMS, AND A TREMENDOUS POTENTIAL

In light of these difficulties and major risks, we often overlook that the continent is both a source of impressive success stories and holds tremendous opportunities. A number of countries such as Ghana, Rwanda and Ethiopia prove that Africa is anything but a lost cause; in some regions, the rates of poverty and hunger are falling significantly.

This should be an incentive for us, especially since we have to keep the following in mind: while the downside scenario is pessimistic, the upside potential could not be greater; the same applies to Europe, too. After all, Africa is a promising market at an early stage of development, with a purchasing power similar to that of China 30 years ago. Europe has the opportunity to do more than prevent a mass exodus to the Global North: Together with Africa, we can create the largest economic area in the world—in a partnership as equals.

That is why we need to act. And the good news is that we can do it too. After presenting an intensive analysis of the status quo (see Section I: The Facts), this book presents seven key statements on why previous development concepts have not eliminated extreme poverty and on what basis sustainable and inclusive growth can be achieved (see Section II: Key Statements). We will conclude by considering which concrete steps are now necessary in order to reach this goal (see Section III: The Agenda).

This book is based on extensive experience in Africa and other developing countries as well as research and countless discussions with political and economic decision-makers in Africa and Europe. Proposing a policy that is organized both systematically and practically, the book demonstrates how Europe can kick start the development of Africa; also in order not to leave the continent to China's interests in resources alone.

THE EUROPEAN FORMULA FOR PEACE

First of all, it is important to recognize that the unregulated market economy and unrestricted global trade are not enough to defeat poverty and create widespread prosperity (see Key Statements 2 and 3). In contrast to South America and Asia, where hundreds of millions of people have joined the middle class in the last 30 years, development in the countries of sub-Saharan Africa in particular has been characterized by stagnation for a variety of different reasons. It has yet to profit from globalization.

The collapse of the Soviet Union and the GDR prove that even communism and socialism do not offer solutions to eradicate poverty—and countries such as Cuba, North Korea, and Venezuela demonstrate this even today.

The winner in the competition between the systems is clearly the social market economy, which belongs to the heart of the European brand. We therefore speak of the "European Economic Model" (it is astonishing that there is still no established translation in English for the German term). It is a coherent social and economic model that has proven itself to be more successful than communism (which fails to create incentives) and turbo-capitalism (which does not protect against extreme poverty).

According to the free market economy, as Adam Smith once stated, the ambition and egoism of the individual ultimately benefits the common good as well. We now know that this ideal can falter due to the phenomenon of abuse of power and partial market failure. However, soccer is an impressive example of how rules of the game make fair play possible when they are enforced. The game demonstrates how the human ambition to compete, the energy and the desire to win can lead to fair, sporting competition worldwide.

These principles can also be applied to the economy. Here too, participants have the motivation and desire to win the competition—but at the same time they are willing to comply with the rules as long as they apply to everyone and are enforced by a referee system. The European Economic Model essentially rests on four pillars—social, ecological, antitrust and anti-corruption standards.

These core rules have paved the way for the creation of an unprecedentedly broad unprecedentedly broad distribution of wealth on our continent. Over the past 70 years, Europe has demonstrated that a social model based on reciprocity can indeed work with the formula "Market + rules = peace + prosperity." In many respects, it is more successful than the less cooperative approaches with which the USA and China are competing for global influence. Africa therefore also needs the social market economy (see Key Statement 4).

THE SOCIAL MARKET ECONOMY IS THE WINNER, BUT IT HAS NOT YET ARRIVED IN AFRICA

The most important goal for poor countries is first and foremost: those who work must be able to feed a family. And whoever loses their job, must not fall into destitution. This is what Pope Francis means when he speaks of "the three T's": *Terra, Techo, Trabajo*—people need a piece of land, a roof over their heads and work.

Many African countries are far from this. Unskilled workers in particular often have no bargaining leverage to negotiate for a wage that would also make them consumers. If a commodity such as unskilled labor is available in abundance, and this is the case without functioning social systems because everyone needs money to survive, then the market fails and rules are necessary.

A decisive step is therefore the establishment of robust social security systems. They decisively strengthen the bargaining position of workers because they offer an alternative to underpaid work, at least temporarily. Therefore, this can ultimately lead to the enforcement of higher wages and the observance of a legal minimum wage threshold (see Key Statement 5).

FAIR WAGES ARE IN THE INTEREST OF THE ECONOMY

It may seem astonishing to read such things from the perspective of an entrepreneur, but a look at emerging markets shows that when workers receive fair wages thanks to the rules of the social market economy, they consume more, and this in turn increases domestic demand, the gross domestic product and production facilities run at a higher capacity. This in turn lowers unit costs, which can compensate for wage increases from the perspective of entrepreneurs. So the minimum wage and the resulting increase in production creates a self-financing effect, since productivity increases at the same time.

Henry Ford once put the connection between mass consumption and economic growth in a nutshell: If only the CEO can afford a car, then I don't need to build a factory. Higher wages are therefore also in the interest of the economy. This leads to the conclusion that wage increases benefit all players (which is only counter-intuitive at first glance).

HALT POPULATION GROWTH, STIMULATE GROWTH FORCES

With regard to Africa, it is particularly important to note that a significant increase in wages would be a decisive step towards halting population growth. For with higher average per capita income, the birth rate declines (see Key Statement 6). And it is statistically proven that starting at around $250 to $300 per month, the birth rates approach the equilibrium of two children per woman.

If population growth comes to a standstill, distribution conflicts and in turn the associated risks would be reduced, while the chances of receiving a "demographic dividend" would increase. Just as we have to bring the world into balance, the population must also achieve a balance. For then economic growth will finally translate into increased prosperity for broad sections of society; and that is the best foundation for human rights and peace.

Figure 1: From an agrarian state to a social market economy
As wages rise, birth rates decrease

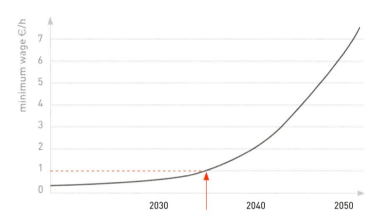

If the minimum wage increases by 15 percent per year, this means a...
...quadrupling in 10 years
...six-fold increase in 30 years
When we reach 1€/h, the population stabilizes thanks to a decreasing birth rate

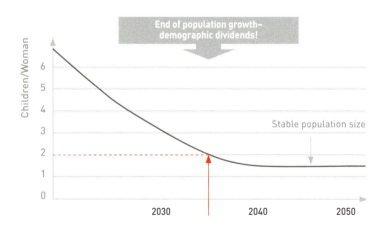

Contrary to what pessimists assume, this increase in prosperity does not necessarily lead to an ecological catastrophe. In specialist publications and books it has long been proven that sustainable qualitative growth is possible (see Key Statement 7).

It would already be a huge step towards reducing poverty and population growth if minimum wages were to reach just one-tenth of the European level—in other words, the equivalent of just under 1 per hour. To achieve this, the current wages in sub-Saharan Africa must increase tenfold. This growth can be attained organically with a growth rate of 15 percent per year within 15 years or even faster. The aim of this book is to show a new way to bring the minimum wage from 10 cents per hour to this level for the majority of Africans, and at the same time stop the population growth, which will otherwise intensify conflicts over scarce resources.

INVESTING IN INFRASTRUCTURE TO BOOST GROWTH
A modern infrastructure is the basis for an industrial and social policy that leads to higher wages. I like to compare it to a platform: only on this foundation can a market economy based on the division of labor develop. China has demonstrated this to the world with its breathtaking race to catch up to become a modern industrial nation: China's first step on this journey was to build a comprehensive infrastructure, largely using its own financial resources. This was the initial spark, so to speak. Now Africa needs one too.

This brings us to the crucial shortcoming in current development policy: many efforts by the European Union, Germany and international institutions are primarily focused on attracting private investors from Europe to invest in Africa. This should boost growth and, somehow or other, lead to an established economy based on the European model at some point. Anyone who talks to entrepreneurs in Africa or is active there themselves will recognize that a sufficient amount of private investment can only come if the right infrastructure is in place and a minimum level of the rule of law and governance (the latter two factors are already the focus of European policy).

We can thus only hope for increased entrepreneurial involvement in Africa if the continent's infrastructure is resolutely established and expanded. This is comparable to the development of building land: construction can only begin once the roads, cables and water pipes are in place. This would create the aforementioned platform on the basis of which poor countries can develop in three further phases into modern industrial and service-based economies with fair wages:

» the phase of private investment,
» the phase of refining raw materials as well as wage-intensive processing (shoes, textiles etc.) for export and
» the phase of growing internal consumption.

Figure 2: The path to prosperity for all in the social market economy

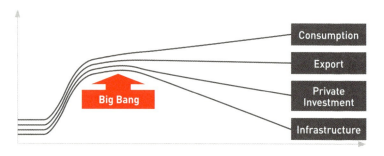

High investment in infrastructure (I) triggers private investment (II), which leads to an increase in exports (III) and consumption (IV). In this way, the agrarian state matures into a modern industrial and service society, supported by exports and consumption. *Private investment and infrastructure initiatives are no longer required to the same extent*

Figure 3: The four-phase growth model for developing countries

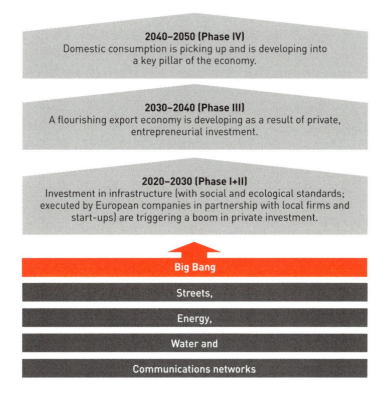

HOW EUROPE IS PARTNERING WITH AFRICA TO MOBILIZE CAPITAL FOR AFRICA'S DEVELOPMENT

This is where our concept comes in (see Section III: The Agenda): We advocate supporting those countries that are pushing ahead with reforms in the spirit of the social market economy with fair infrastructure loans. This can also be done exclusively through European or German guarantees for privately placed bonds. Poor countries are confronted with a decisive obstacle: they do not have sufficient resources, and in some cases they lack the know-how to handle such investments and projects on their own.

We therefore propose that Europe, similar to what Germany did in the former GDR, should finance or even guarantee investments in Africa on a large scale—with the help of development banks such as the European Investment Bank (EIB), the European Bank for Restructuring and Development (EBRD), the Kreditanstalt für Wiederaufbau (KfW) and the African Development Bank. Through Africa Bonds, these institutions could mobilize capital from European investors and pass it on in the form of fair loans. Our concept (see Tool 1) would neither involve tax increases nor unbearable risks of loss. After all, European credit ratings and the link to reforms ensure that the bonds retain their value and remain liquid at all times. Citizens who buy the bonds therefore keep their money—and yet infrastructure is being built in Africa at the same time.

Europe would thus use its creditworthiness and financing power to mobilize money for the reconstruction of Africa. In this way we would, so to speak, replace the citizens of Africa who are not (yet) in a position to invest broadly in the common infrastructure. We are convinced that there would be great interest in Africa Bonds on the market because investors today can no longer obtain government bonds at attractive conditions. Private investors would therefore quickly absorb placements of securities.

WHAT MAKES EUROPEAN OFFERS MORE ATTRACTIVE

It is important, however, that European financing proposals are more attractive to reform-oriented African politicians and governments than offers from the Far East. China often demands high interest rates, insists on relatively short maturities and allows ownership of the financed investment to be transferred at maturity. In return however, China decides to award the funds quickly and without bureaucracy, while the EU often takes an agonizingly long time. The Foreign Minister of Togo, Prof. Robert Dussey, described this problem very clearly at the Munich Security Conference.

Since Beijing can obtain ownership of the infrastructure that has been financed through its credit if problems arise with repayment, there is already talk of the "diplomacy of the debt trap". Many African states have now become heavily dependent on China (see Chapter 5). Moreover, it is obvious that many infrastructure projects primarily serve China's interests—and less those interests of the countries themselves.

Here Europe can compete with loans at lower interest rates, with longer terms and with standards that promote prosperity in the region. In many cases, guarantees would suffice to enable a country to issue its own bonds at lower interest rates. Europe does not want privileged access to resources, but rather partnerships that would be mutually beneficial. After all, we too would benefit in the long term from the construction of infrastructure and, in particular, from the subsequent increase in trade relations and lower numbers of refugees.

BIG RESULTS WITH MODEST SUMS

Sums of money that are inconsequential in the European context are sufficient to make a big difference in Africa. For example, the infrastructure program (Plan National de Développement) proposed for Togo by the Tony Blair Institute for Global Change has a budget of $6 to 7 billion, which corresponds to around $1,000 per inhabitant. This is a negligible amount compared to the sums invested in East Germany since reunification. For Togo, however, it represents a fortune, because it will help to give the country a big and possibly decisive boost. If the project in Togo is successful, it could become an exemplary beacon for many African countries.

With this in mind, a thought experiment: $1,000 per capita, as in Togo, extrapolated to the whole of Africa, would mean around $1,300 billion. This is roughly the amount that China, according to estimates, intends to invest in its Silk Road initiative until 2027.

We are convinced that Europe can mobilize 100 billion per year for Africa through Africa Bonds, without burdening national budgets and thus taxpayers. This would correspond to 0.5 percent of our gross national product, would boost the regional economy and create millions of jobs. If we were to cover the annual interest on the infrastructure loans—for example in the context of innovative development cooperation programs—that would correspond to a burden of one cent per day for every EU citizen. Moreover, if we use existing development aid budgets by reallocating them wisely, the amounts could be financed from existing tax revenues and would not have to be additionally raised.

At current exchange rates, the sum of $100 billion would, incidentally, roughly correspond to the funding shortfall for the expansion of infrastructure in Africa, which the African Development Bank estimates at up to $108 billion per year. Just to make the comparison absolutely clear: for Europe the national debt would increase from €13 trillion to €13.1 trillion, for Africa it would fundamentally transform life. And if we work with guarantees, these would not even factor into debt calculations as per current accounting standards.

An incredible amount could be achieved in Africa with guarantees or sums that Europe could raise without having to pinch any pennies. And let's remember, the money would be repaid multiple times over in the form of a flourishing European-African economic area, which would also create millions of jobs in Europe. This is more important than ever in view of the increasing geopolitical competition with China and the USA, but also because of the lasting impact of the Covid-19 crisis, which has destroyed millions of jobs.

Low interest rates mean that investors all over the world are desperately looking for alternative investments; according to a recent study, global assets have risen to a record value of almost €195 trillion despite the Covid-19 crisis. With just €1 trillion of this, we can transform Africa into a booming region. Low interest rates, which are primarily attributable to inherent overcapacity in mature industrial societies, thus offer us the opportunity of a lifetime to achieve great things with modest commitments.

LET'S BUILD A EUROPEAN SILK ROAD – THE SPICE ROUTE 2.0!
We therefore strongly advocate tapping into the potential of the capital markets, investing courageously and supporting financing through guarantees. In view of low debt levels—especially in comparison with the USA—and with intelligent financing concepts, it is economically and technically feasible for Europe to mobilize €1 trillion for Africa within ten years without being forced to economize in other areas (especially since investments in Africa could accelerate the transition to sustainable energies).

In a nutshell: with this book we want to make it clear that more funding is required, that we can afford the outlay and that we must link support to the standards of the social market economy to end extreme poverty.

By doing this, we can improve the lives of hundreds of millions of people (and their descendants) in a sustainable way. Assuming a turnover factor of three for investments in infrastructure, this could lead to annual growth rates of 10 to 15 percent, such as China also achieved.

In this way, we would ultimately be continuing a great tradition. Ever since Vasco da Gama, the Spice Route has connected Europe with Africa and India—three regions that are today home to around half of humanity. By reviving this connection via a "Spice Route 2.0", Europe can lay the foundation for a flourishing economic area and counter the Chinese "New Silk Road" with something substantial—minus the colonial attitude. With the long-term goal of creating a European-African-Indian economic area, half of humanity could eventually benefit from the European Economic Model.

Certainly, calling for reforms in accordance with the social market economy could be interpreted as paternalism. But anyone who has talked to political decision-makers in Togo, for example, knows that reformers there have also come to the realization that legal and social standards are of vital importance if growth is to benefit the poor. Moreover, intra-African competition already encourages the use of best practices as a marker of a modern state willing to reform. We can also avoid framing our demands from a position of assumed European superiority by invoking the "17 Sustainable Development Goals" (SDGs) of the United Nations as inspiration. Because a large number of the SDGs can be achieved simultaneously if we eliminate extreme poverty through social standards and higher wages.

As such, there is a congruence of interests between reform-oriented decision-makers and, for once, the impoverished, who usually go unheard. In any case, they failed to benefit from previous reform agendas, such as the Washington Consensus, because the social dimension of the market economy was neglected.

DEEPER DEVELOPMENT PARTNERSHIPS, FAIRER TRADE

In addition to infrastructure financing, our agenda therefore provides for two further instruments to promote reforms. We urgently recommend that the social market economy be made the cornerstone of our trade and development relations with Africa—in a spirit of partnership and taking into account the special characteristics and traditions of developing countries. Development cooperation and deepened trade partnerships should therefore also be linked to the introduction of standards in accordance with the European Economic Model, as per the principle of "support and challenge" (see Tool 2).

These standards ensure fair play at all levels and can be demanded and introduced gradually over the course of cooperation between Africa and Europe. The ongoing negotiations on a new EU-Africa treaty (the so-called Cotonou follow-up agreement) offer a once-in-a-lifetime opportunity for this. We must use it! To this end, we have drawn up a concrete proposal for a supplement to the agreement and presented it to those responsible in the German Federal Ministry for Economic Cooperation and Development (see Appendix).

It is clear that the unconditional elimination of all kinds of trade barriers has not helped in the fight against poverty. We are now entering the Globalization 2.0 phase, in which trade underpinned by clear rules will be a catalyst for the social market economy. As such, we must offer reform-minded states new, fair trade agreements (see Tool 3).

FIGHTING CORRUPTION WITH INNOVATION
We have already made great strides in development aid thanks to the new Africa policy promoted by Minister Gerd Müller. Germany's new reform partnerships in Africa are underpinned by an understanding that standards are only met when there are arbitrators, such as anti-corruption authorities, cartel watchdogs, courts of law or arbitration institutions. The establishment of such institutions is rightly an important cornerstone of development cooperation. It helps progress the fight against corruption, which many see as the decisive obstacle to greater corporate involvement in Africa.

Moreover, a technological innovation can help here. Therefore, we propose that both the conclusion of contracts and their procedural execution in the field of development cooperation and infrastructure financing be carried out using blockchain technology. This means that no side can unilaterally change contracts or processes. In addition, international auditing firms could monitor to ensure that the individual steps are carried out correctly.

This underlines that we cannot allow prejudices to guide our thoughts and actions. Africa is, on many levels, much further than many observers seem to realize. With investments, innovations and intelligent financing concepts, we can achieve great things together, for the benefit of both continents.

SECTION I

THE FACTS

CHAPTER 1

POVERTY, HUNGER AND SOCIAL INSECURITY

The situation is drastic: while more and more people in Asia and South America join the ranks of the middle class, hundreds of millions of Africans continue to suffer from extreme poverty and hunger; with an upward trend. This makes Africa a loser of globalization.

WHILE THE REST OF THE WORLD IS ESCAPING POVERTY
Generalizing about Africa as one unit is a risky move, considering the diversity of the continent. But in comparison with the other continents there are several trends that illustrate Africa has by far the biggest problems—and is currently the undisputed "loser" of globalization.

According to current figures, the 14 poorest countries in the world are all in Africa. Their respective economic output is less than $2,000 per capita per year; in some cases three out of four people live in "absolute poverty". This means that they have to get by on less than $1.90 a day (converted into local purchasing power in each case, see Figure1). In the Democratic Republic of Congo alone, this affects nearly 65 million people.

In total, according to the World Bank report *Accelerating Poverty Reduction in Africa* (2019), around 413 million Africans suffer from extreme poverty; in 1990 it was 278 million people. In the course of the strong population growth, the rate fell from 54 to 41 percent, but in view of the dramatic increase in absolute numbers, this is of little consolation.

If the trend continues, the World Bank predicts that by 2030 almost nine out of ten "extremely poor" people in the world will live in central and southern Africa. This is because other regions are making progress in the fight against poverty;

above all Asia and Latin America. Whereas in 1990, 1.9 billion people outside Africa were still living below the poverty line, the latest figure was 736 million. This means that in the rest of the world today, around 1.1 billion fewer people live in absolute poverty than 30 years ago.

According to figures from the World Bank, the poverty rate in East Asia is now 1.3 percent and in Latin America 4.4 percent. Even southern Asia, with a rate of 16.1 percent in absolute poverty, is far better off than most African countries. One of the most impressive rising powers, besides China, is Vietnam. In the early 1990s, more than half of the people living there were still extremely poor. Today the figure is 1.9 percent.

In Africa, on the other hand, the eradication of poverty, which the United Nations proclaimed as an essential goal in the 2015 Sustainable Development Goals, is still a long way off; the percentage of people living in abject poverty is declining at an agonizingly slow pace, and the absolute number has recently risen even further.

Table 1: The 14 poorest countries are all in Africa

		Economic Performance per capita / year[1]	Proportion of "absolute poor" (in %)[2]
1	Burundi	**730**	38.6
2	Central African Republic	**730**	66.3
3	DR Congo	**870**	77.1
4	Niger	**990**	45.5
5	Liberia	**1,160**	38.6
6	Malawi	**1,180**	70.9
7	Mozambique	**1,210**	68.7
8	Sierra Leone	**1,500**	52.3

		Economic Performance per capita / year[1]	Proportion of "absolute poor" (in %)[2]
9	Madagascar	**1,510**	77.8
10	Gambia	**1,660**	45.3
11	Guinea-Bissau	**1,700**	67.1
12	Togo	**1,720**	49.1
13	Burkina Faso	**1,800**	43.4
14	Uganda	**1,820**	41.6
15	**Haiti**	**1,830**	**24.9**
16	Ethiopia	**1,890**	33.5
17	Chad	**1,920**	38.4
18	**Afghanistan**	**1,980**	no data
19	Rwanda	**1,990**	60.4
20	Mali	**2,160**	49.3
21	Zimbabwe	**2,210**	21.4
22	Guinea	**2,230**	35.3
23	Benin	**2,260**	49.8
	(...)		
27	Comoros	**2,760**	17.7
28	Tanzania	**2,920**	49.1
	(...)		
30	Kenya	**3,250**	33.6
31	Lesotho	**3,290**	59.7
32	Senegal	**3,360**	38.0
	(...)		
35	Cameroon	**3,640**	24.0
	(...)		
38	Cote d'Ivoire	**3,820**	27.9
39	Zambia	**3,890**	57.5
40	Mauretania	**3,890**	5.9
	(...)		
43	Ghana	**4,280**	13.6

		Economic Performance per capita / year[1]	Proportion of "absolute poor" (in %)[2]
	(...)		
46	Sudan	**4,480**	14.9
	(...)		
48	Republic of Congo	**4,920**	37.0
	(...)		
52	Nigeria	**5,700**	53.5
	(...)		
60	Angola	**6,440**	30.1
	(...)		
62	Cape Verde	**6,640**	8.1
	(...)		
70	Morocco	**8,060**	3.1
	(...)		
82	Namibia	**10,300**	22.6
	(...)		
86	Egypt	**11,360**	1.4
87	Tunisia	**11,530**	2.0
	(...)		
97	South Africa[3]	**13,090**	16.6

[1] Measured by gross national product, in dollars, converted into local purchasing power
[2] Percentage of residents living on less than $1.90 (converted into local purchasing power)
[3] Not among the 100 poorest countries: Algeria, Botswana, Gabon, among others, Libya / not included: Djibouti, Sao Tomé, among others
Source: World Bank (https://data.worldbank.org/, accessed 2019

ALMOST 300 MILLION AFRICANS GO HUNGRY

The most immediate and serious consequence of poverty is hunger. In its report *State of Food Security and Nutrition in the World* 2019, the Food and Nutrition Organization found that

277 million people in Africa suffer from severe hunger. This corresponds to a rate of 19.9 percent. So one in five people have to go without food for whole days at a time. In 2015, the rate was still 18.1 percent; so it has not fallen as hoped, but increased. If we look at sub-Saharan Africa, it has even increased from 20.9 to 22.8 percent. Among the main drivers of this development are armed conflicts, for example in Sudan, Mali and the Central African Republic. The situation is particularly dramatic in the latter country: according to the World Hunger Index, 61.8 percent of the population is undernourished—by far the highest figure in the world. According to Welthungerhilfe, the rate is over 40 percent in numerous other African countries, including Madagascar, Zimbabwe and Uganda. By way of comparison, in Latin America the rate of starving people is just under 7 percent. The figures show: The UN's goal of largely eliminating hunger by 2030 (Zero Hunger Challenge) will be very difficult to achieve in Africa.

Roughly estimated, 50 percent of starving people are small farmers, 20 percent are agricultural workers, 20 percent inhabitants of urban slums and 10 percent are cattle breeders and fishermen. And, along with the (supposed) breadwinners, their families are also starving.

Many adolescents, in particular, are affected by hunger in Chad, Sudan and Djibouti, where around 15 percent of children suffer from life-threatening emaciation (i.e. wasting). This leads to high rates of child mortality: South of the Sahara alone, around 3.2 million children under the age of five die every year. That is about half of all deaths worldwide in this age group. On average, one in nine children in sub-Saharan Africa die before their fifth birthday.

Table 2: World Hunger Index
Ratios in selected African countries (data partly estimated)

	Malnourished Inhabitants in %	Emaciated (Children over 5 years in %)	Mortality (Children under 5 years in %)
Angola	23.9	4.9	8.3
Ethiopia	21.4	9.9	5.8
Djibouti	19.7	16.7	6.4
Guinea-Bissau	26.0	6.0	8.8
Congo	37.5	8.2	5.4
Liberia	38.8	5.6	6.7
Madagascar	43.1	8.4	4.6
Mali	6.0	13.5	11.1
Niger	14.4	10.9	9.1
Rwanda	36.1	2.0	3.9
Zambia	44.5	6.3	6.3
Sierra Leone	25.5	9.4	11.4
Sudan	25.2	16.3	6.5
Somalia	50.6	15.0	13.3
Chad	39.7	13.0	12.7
Uganda	41.4	3.6	5.3
Central African Rep.	61.8	9.2	12.4
Zimbabwe	46.6	3.2	5.6

Source: Global Hunger Index (2019), Welthungerhilfe

These figures reveal that when people go hungry, the youngest are hit particularly hard. And in addition to life-threatening emaciation, millions of adolescents have stunted growth for their age due to inadequate nutrition. According to UN figures, this affects 149 million children worldwide, 90 percent of whom live in Africa and Asia. Outside Africa, the situation is particularly dire in Bangladesh, where almost 15 percent of pre-school children are "emaciated" according to the World Hunger Index. In addition to stunted growth, malnutrition can have other serious consequences, ranging from the breakdown of the respiratory muscles and cardiac arrhythmia to a weak immune system and a correspondingly high susceptibility to infections. One consequence of hunger is therefore recurring severe illnesses.

Apart from armed conflicts, high food prices and droughts are among the main factors hindering progress—with the climate crisis playing a central role because it is already hitting Africa particularly hard (see Chapter 2). In Kenya, for example, as a result of global warming, more and more water is evaporating from Lake Turkana, causing it to become increasingly salty. As a result, farmers have considerable problems irrigating their fields around the lake. This exacerbates food shortages and raises prices. At the same time, conflicts over fertile land are intensifying.

Climate change is hitting small farmers, in particular, with full force. In addition, agribusinesses and investors from abroad are securing land with particularly high yields for themselves. According to the World Agriculture Report, they have acquired around 10 million hectares in Africa since the turn of the millennium. This is an area larger than the German states of Bavaria and Hesse combined. These areas are primarily used to grow crops and grain for export, which means that they are largely unavailable for food production for the local population.

ONLY ONE IN FIVE IS INSURED BY SOCIAL SECURITY SYSTEMS
Most Africans cannot hope to rely on the state when they become unemployed, sick or old. According to calculations by the International Labour Organization (ILO), on average just under 18 percent of the inhabitants of African states are covered in such

cases: whether through government transfer payments or social insurance benefits. Even in the "most social" state, South Africa, only 48 percent of the population benefits from social security systems. In Lesotho, Cameroon, Burkina Faso, Gambia, Nigeria and Uganda, the rate is well below 10 percent.

Figure 4: Little protection from poverty
Proportion of residents paying into a social insurance scheme or receiving social benefits (in %)

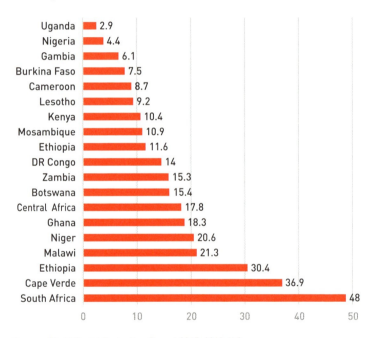

Source: World Social Protection Report 2017–2019, ILO

The most widespread are pension insurance policies. Almost 30 percent of Africans who reach country-specific age limits receive a pension. In Botswana, Mauritius and the Seychelles it is even 100 percent. In countries such as Sierra Leone, Chad, Malawi, Mali and Burkina Faso, on the other hand, less than three percent of the elderly receive money from the state. Often, however, beneficiaries are dependent on additional support from their families because the pension alone is not enough to live on.

Other types of social security are even less developed. For example, the ILO estimates that only 5.6 percent of Africans receive some form of unemployment benefits after losing their job.

Figure 5: Unemployed? The state does not offer support
Rate of adults without jobs receiving unemployment benefits (in %)

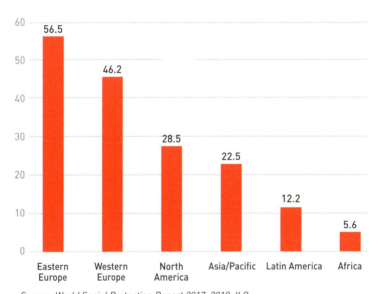

Source: World Social Protection Report 2017–2019, ILO

South of the Sahara, the rates are much lower. By way of comparison, according to the ILO, the rate in Western Europe is 46.2 percent and 56.5 percent in Eastern Europe. Moreover, Europe usually has additional security systems, so that relatively few people fall through its social safety net.

Africans are also poorly insured in the event of illness. Few benefit from statutory health insurance, which takes effect in case of emergency. According to the ILO, three out of four Africans have no legal right to health protection, whether through health insurance or the right to medical care. In Asia and Latin America, the percentage of those not covered is significantly lower in every case.

Figure 6: Helpless in case of illness

Percentage of people not entitled to health protection (in %)

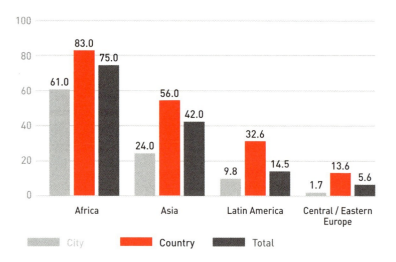

Source: World Social Protection Report 2017-2019, ILO

CHAPTER 2

Climate crisis, civil wars and mass exodus

The climate crisis is hitting Africa particularly hard. It has been intensifying armed conflicts and triggering acute hunger crises, which are driving more and more people to flee their homes—and a large proportion of them are moving north. Numerous people die on their way to securing a better life.

Global warming is already leading to an increasing incidence of heat waves and "temperature anomalies" in Africa. This will trigger further civil wars and migration movements on the already conflict-ridden continent, as demonstrated by the current study *Climate, Conflict and Forced Migration* by the Vienna University of Economics and Business Administration, Shanghai University and the University of East Anglia.

The experts explain the connection between periods of drought and wars by using Syria as an example. In Syria, a long period of drought led to crop failures, which caused farming families to flee to urban areas and thus cause overpopulation in the cities. According to the study, which was published in 2019, this intensified the already severe social tensions during the dictatorship and was thus a driver for political unrest, civil war and the subsequent mass exodus to Europe.

The study shows similar findings "for the Sub-Saharan countries of Africa": in the Sahel zone for example, the increasing drought has already driven millions to flee. Above all, the people in the region around Lake Chad in the border area between Nigeria, Chad and Cameroon have not only suffered atrocities committed by terrorist groups. Droughts and poor harvests are also causing them to leave their homes in droves, desperately hoping for a better life. The climate crisis and armed conflicts are thus intertwined in a devastating way.

Paradoxically, however, the fight against climate change could initially hit African countries hard due to indirect effects. After all, countries like Algeria, Nigeria and Sudan are still heavily dependent on oil. If demand and prices were to fall or even collapse in the course of switching to alternative energy sources in the medium term, these countries could be faced with considerable problems—and violent conflicts.

The signs were already apparent in 2019: declining revenues from the oil business were the main trigger for the revolts that shook Algeria and Sudan because they increased discontent. Nigeria wants to prevent anything similar by introducing a "Zero Oil Plan", which intends to increase the share of state revenues not generated through the oil business fivefold. The government wants to boost exports of "strategic products" such as cocoa, soybeans, rubber and leather in order to reduce dependence on oil.

FAMINE DUE TO CIVIL WARS AND CROP FAILURES

Current statistics show that the climate crisis is a decisive factor contributing to the exacerbation of acute famine. "Climate shocks" and natural disasters plunged around 23 million people in 20 African countries into acute emergency situations in 2018, according to the Food and Agriculture Organization's *Global Report on Food Crises 2019*. In 2017, as many as almost 30 million people suffered from climate-related crop failures and hunger crises:

Table 3: Hunger crises due to climate shocks
Number of people affected (percentage of total population)

	Number of people Affected	Percent of entire population
Ethiopia	8.5 Mio.	10 %
Malawi	5.1 Mio.	27 %
Zimbabwe	4.1 Mio.	42 %
Bangladesh	3.4 Mio.	31 %
Kenya	3.4 Mio.	25 %
Mozambique	3.1 Mio.	25 %
Pakistan	2.7 Mio.	50 %
Haiti	2.3 Mio.	31 %
Uganda	1.6 Mio.	5 %
Madagascar	1.5 Mio.	51 %
Swaziland	0.4 Mio.	39 %
Lesotho	0.3 Mio.	24 %
Djibouti	0.1 Mio.	46 %

Source: Global Report on Food Crises (2018), UN

It is already clear that climate change will continue to impact millions of Africans in the coming years. Expert analyses show that Africa will suffer most from global warming. According to the *Global Adaptation Index* of the University of Notre Dame (USA), the five countries with the lowest score, i.e. the highest vulnerability to climate risks, are all located in Africa (see Table 4). Another 27 countries on the continent also belong to the group of 40 countries with high climate risks. Overall, more than half of the 53 African countries are therefore at high risk.

Table 4: Devastating droughts
The five countries most threatened by climate change

Position	Country	Score
177	DR Congo	29.6
178	Central African Republic	27.5
179	Eritrea	26.2
180	Chad	25.6
181	Somalia	20.2

Source: Global Adaption Index (2017), University of Notre Dame

Further conflicts that cause or exacerbate hunger crises are thus foreseeable—particularly in the Sahel zone, which borders the Sahara in the south. There it is apparent "that global warming is also becoming a fuel for wars," wrote *Der Spiegel* in January 2020. The region is heating up one and a half times faster than the world average. According to the article, too many people are forced to gather "on less and less fertile land", which exacerbates conflicts. For example, the Darfur war in Sudan is considered to be the first climate conflict of our time; droughts and ethnic tensions led to fierce clashes there.

Yet clashes are also increasing in other parts of the region. In Mali, for example, nomads are increasingly forced to drive their herds across fields and pastures in search of grazing land. Some local farmers are fiercely resisting this, resulting in repeated cases of severe violence. In many places, anglers are fiercely fighting over the best fishing grounds, for example in Lake Chad, where climate-induced siltation is increasingly causing islands to form that make fishing difficult.

When it rains, the precipitation is often more intense than usual. Recently, for example, heavy rainfall boosted the reproduction rate of desert locusts in East Africa, which attacked the fields in huge swarms in spring 2020. This further worsened the already precarious food supply in many places.

100 MILLION CLIMATE REFUGEES?
Millions of Africans are already fleeing civil wars, hunger crises and poverty every year. And experts assume that this number will increase rapidly in the coming years—and that most of them will probably continue fleeing to neighboring countries. Minister Gerd Müller, for example, warned as early as 2017 that up to 100 million Africans might set out on their journey to the Global North. "If we continue as we have been doing up to now, people in many parts of Africa will have no other chance than to set out on their journey to our countries," said the CSU politician.

However, it is not only those who have no other choice who will leave their homes; many people with promising futures and top performers are also likely to seek their fortunes elsewhere—especially since globalization and digitization are making it possible for them to find out increasingly quickly and accurately how well we Europeans are doing. "Broadband internet and smartphones have completely changed the world," explained World Bank President Jim Yong Kim in an interview with the *Handelsblatt* at the end of 2018. "By 2025 at the latest, people in every corner of the world will be able to see how people live elsewhere. This has led to measurably higher expectations of people in poor countries. They can no longer tolerate their lack of prospects, but are setting off to new pastures."

The concept of "Fortress Europe" is thus facing a crucial test: if the EU wants to seal itself off, it will have to make highly controversial decisions, particularly with regard to human rights. The contradiction will become increasingly obvious: although we want to deter people, at the same time we want to remain true to our values.

Agreements with transit countries in North Africa are at the core of current EU migration policy. The European Union has pledged a total of 46 million to Libya to support its coast guard, which has been carrying out stricter controls and tracking down smugglers for around three years. According to unanimous reports from human rights organizations and the United Nations however, many of the refugees detained end up in prisons or camps run by militias, where inhuman conditions prevail—and sometimes even torture is used.

THOUSANDS DROWN IN THE MEDITERRANEAN SEA

Nevertheless, from the perspective of the EU, the stricter controls are serving their purpose: according to the United Nations International Organization for Migration (IOM), the number of refugees who arrive in Italy or Malta, having taken the central Mediterranean route via Libya, has fallen significantly from 181,460 in 2016 to around 15,000 in 2019. Although many Africans are switching to the Western Mediterranean route via Morocco, the number has recently declined again. After more than 58,000 in 2018, the authorities in Spain recorded only 25,731 new arrivals in 2019, according to the IOM.

However, many do not make it to the safe shores. Hundreds of people still die every month in the Mediterranean, and the number of people confirmed as dead or missing amounted to 1,283 in 2019, according to the IOM. Since 2014, at least 19,164 refugees have drowned in the Mediterranean Sea.

Figure 7: Number of people who died in the Mediterranean Sea
Month after month hundreds of refugees drown

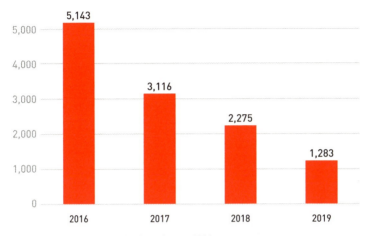

Source: Global Migration Analysis Center, IOM

In truth, there are probably many more people who die every year. Time and again, ships carrying refugees disappear without a trace, reports the IOM—especially since Europe restricted its rescue missions in 2017. Experts worry that many of the missing boats did not reach Europe, but sunk without trace and all their passengers with them.

This fear is supported by the fact that the rate of people who do not survive the passage has risen significantly according to the United Nations High Commissioner for Refugees (UNHCR). The experts estimate that one in 36 refugees died in 2017, while in 2018 it was one in 14. This is probably due to the "restriction of search and rescue missions". The debate about rescue at sea by private initiatives already shows the social tensions that are causing exclusion and isolation in Europe: critics accuse private sea rescue services of supporting the business of human traffickers, at least indirectly.

Yet the Mediterranean is probably not the most dangerous death trap. The UNHCR estimates that "at least twice as many people die en route to the Mediterranean as in the Mediterranean itself." However, according to Vincent Cochetel, who serves as UNHCR special envoy for the Mediterranean and Libya, the number could "also be much higher". In November 2019, he told the *Welt am Sonntag* that because of the high number of unreported cases, nobody could offer more precise figures, but that a tragedy was certainly taking place. The main transit country is Niger, which consists largely of desert and borders Algeria and Libya in the north.

THE CONSEQUENCES OF THE BRAIN DRAIN
Despite diverse hurdles, thousands of refugees and immigrants make it from Africa to Germany each year. According to the Federal Office for Migration and Refugees (BAMF), last year more than 9,000 Nigerians made their first application for asylum in this country. A good 3,500 applicants came from Somalia and Eritrea respectively.

Table 5: Where do our refugees come from?
Initial applications 2019

Country of origin	Amount
Syria	39,270
Iraq	13,742
Turkey	10,784
Afghanistan	9,522
Nigeria	**9,070**
Iran	8,407
Unclear	3,727
Somalia	**3,572**
Eritrea	**3,520**
Georgia	3,329

Source: Asylgeschäftsstatistik (2019), BAMF

The newcomers can be roughly divided into two categories: Some have fled civil wars, famine and extreme poverty—in other words, out of sheer necessity. The others would have survived in their homeland, but they lacked the prospect of a better life. Since these motives are sometimes interlinked, the two groups cannot be clearly separated, but one thing is clear: Among those who leave Africa there are many highly qualified people with promising futures. This is demonstrated by the study *Migration and the Economy* published in 2018, which was written by experts from the US bank Citi in collaboration with Oxford professor Ian Goldin.

Figure 8: Brain drain
Rate of university graduates who emigrate (in percent)

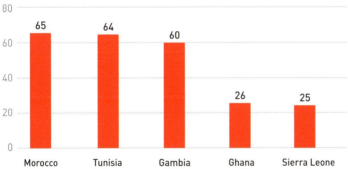

Source: Migration and the Economy (2018), Goldin u.a.

"Immigration has considerable financial and social costs for many developing countries," the authors warn. Brain drain has a particularly negative impact in sub-Saharan Africa, where the average proportion of university graduates is only 4 percent in the first place. In an interview with the *Handelsblatt* in 2018, Wolfgang Schäuble (CDU party), President of the German Bundestag, pointed out that Africa's potential could not be unleashed if "the most capable would rather flee to Europe".

Indeed, there are many indications that well-educated people in particular are leaving their home countries. After all, thanks to digitization and the internet, they can see what is going on here in Europe and due to their education, they can take advantage of opportunities that are available elsewhere in the world. According to the above-mentioned study, developing countries with high unemployment rates suffer the highest rates of brain drain. This supports the hypothesis that many well-educated people leave their homes because they would otherwise be "unproductive" there, the authors write. Refugees and migration are, thus, on the one hand enormous obstacles to development for many countries, but on the other hand, they cannot be stemmed if no new jobs are created there.

Another obstacle to development are the so-called remittances: After emigration, the "hardworking" people often send a portion of their income back home to support those who stayed at home. However, such remittances "reduce participation in the labor market and increase the proportion of informal employment," warn four economists from the International Monetary Fund (IMF) in an analysis entitled *Are Remittances Good for Labor Markets?*

The IMF economists consider the main problem to be the following: that the payments create dependency and false incentives. For those who can rely on remittances from abroad are less likely to create other sources of income, for example establishing a company, through apprenticeships or further training. This hinders economic development. In turn, the IMF analysis shows that remittances sent back home have a hindering effect on the average income and the growth in productivity in developing countries.

This particularly affects sub-Saharan Africa, where these money transfers make up a large percentage of the gross domestic product and are an important driving force for emigration. The highest percentage of the GDP is 27.1% in Liberia, followed by 21% in Comoros, and 20.8% in Gambia, according to World

Bank statistics. In Nigeria, remittances make up "only" 5.6 percent of the gross domestic product, but add up to US $22 billion annually:

Figure 9: Remittances sent to Africa
in 2017 (in billion dollars)

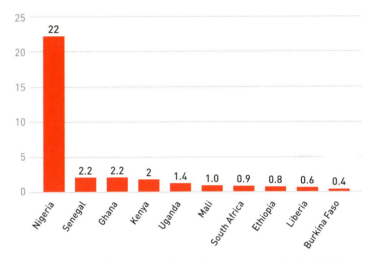

Source: Migration and Remittances: Recent Developments and Outlook (2018), World Bank

Anyone who believed that refugee movements would tend to be positive for African countries because unemployment rates would fall and additional remittances could be expected needs to reconsider: brain drain is dangerous and reduces our chances of eradicating poverty and hunger. The development economist Raúl Delgado Wise, UNESCO coordinator for migration and development, therefore considers migration ultimately to be a "subsidy for the global North provided by the global South". The northern hemisphere benefits from numerous qualified immigrants, whose education is paid for by their country of origin.

CHAPTER 3:

Birth rate and population growth

Despite mass emigration, the population in Africa is growing rapidly. In 30 years, more than 2.5 billion people are expected to live on the continent; twice as many as today. The high birth rates intensify the struggle for scarce resources and are one of the greatest obstacles in the fight against poverty and hunger.

Around 1.3 billion people already live in Africa. And the number is rapidly increasing despite the large number of refugees and emigrants leaving the continent. The African population is growing twice as fast as in the rest of the world; in the past decade alone, the growth rate averaged a good 2.5 percent per year. According to a study by the Institute of the German Economy (IW), in 15 African countries the growth rate was even more than 3 percent. Equatorial Guinea is the frontrunner, with 4.4 percent.

The United Nations estimates that more than 2.5 billion people will live in Africa in 2050. By the turn of the century, this figure could reach 4.47 billion—almost as many as in Asia and nearly seven times as many as in Europe:

Table 6: Unchecked growth in Africa
Population forecast (in billions)

	2018	2030	2050	2100
World	7.62	8.55	9.77	11.18
Africa	**1.29**	**1.70**	**2.53**	**4.47**
Asia	4.55	4.95	5.26	4.78

	2018	2030	2050	2100
Europe	0.73	0.74	0.72	0.65
South America	0.65	0.72	0.78	0.71
North America	0.36	0.40	0.44	0.50
Oceania	0.04	0.05	0.06	0.07

Source: World Population Prospects (2018), UN, own research

A look at birth rates reveals the causes of this dynamic: African women give birth to an average of 4.7 children; in Niger it is as high as 7.2 (see Table 7). And this is only changing slowly. According to a UN prognosis, the birth rate in sub-Saharan Africa will not fall below three children per woman until 2054. The tendency to have large families is also particularly pronounced in West Africa, where, in contrast to North Africa, birth rates have declined only slightly in recent decades despite intensive efforts.

Table 7: Up to seven children per woman
Birth rates in African countries (2017)

Country		Country	
Niger	7.2	Nigeria	5.5
Somalia	6.2	Gambia	5.4
DR Congo	6.0	Burkina Faso	5.3
Mali	6.0	Mozambique	5.2
Chad	5.8	Tanzania	5.0
Angola	5.6	Benin	4.9
Burundi	5.6	Zambia	4.9
Uganda	5.5	Cote d'Ivoire	4.8

Source: World Bank (https://data.worldbank.org, abgerufen 2018)

POVERTY AND INSECURITY DRIVE INCREASING BIRTH RATES
The reasons for the high birth rates are manifold. In many places, traditions associated with large families, a low level of education or a lack of access to contraception methods play a role. One key factor, however, is the precarious economic situation and lack of social security. In many regions, people rely on their children and grandchildren as co-earners. They are often the only chance adults have to be provided for in old age.

"Paradoxically, especially in insecure situations, people tend to want large families," found two researchers from the German Institute for International and Security Affairs (SWP) in 2014 in their study *Population Growth, Fertility and the Wish to have Children*. Growing prosperity, on the other hand, is usually accompanied by "a preference for smaller families". The SWP experts point out that high birth rates entail "considerable risks for individuals and society," ranging from a low labor force participation rate among women and high youth unemployment to fierce battles over scarce resources. This creates a negative spiral: poverty and insecurity drive up birth rates, which in turn exacerbate the problem for society as a whole.

This can also be illustrated by the example of education: extreme poverty is often accompanied not only by high birth rates, but also by poor access to education. Limited education in turn fuels birth rates, making it increasingly difficult to escape poverty. Breaking out of this negative spiral is a major challenge. Literacy rates reveal how low the level of education is on the continent: according to a UNESCO survey, the five countries with the world's highest illiteracy rates are all in Africa.

Table 8: How many inhabitants* can read and write?
The five countries with the lowest literacy rates are in Africa

For comparision: Germany	› 99.9%
Central African Republic	36.8%
Burkina Faso	36.0%
South Sudan	31.9%
Guinea	30.4%
Niger	19.1%

* from 15 years of age, excluding people with dyslexia;
Source: World Education Report (2018), UNESCO

Another effect of poverty is child labor: according to a UNICEF study, 72 million children are affected by poverty in Africa. Over two thirds of them work in the family group, helping their parents with the harvest and looking after the animals. The rest work for foreign employers—for example on cocoa plantations in Ghana and Cote d'Ivoire, in gold mines in Burkina Faso or as servants in private households.

Particularly worrying is the fact that sub-Saharan Africa is the only region where no improvement is in sight. In June 2019, on the occasion of the World Day Against Child Labor, the United Nations Children's Fund (UNICEF) warned that child labor appears to have "increased again in recent years". The main reasons, apart from the sluggish economic development, are natural disasters and conflicts: "In times of displacement and need, the danger of children having to work instead of going to school increases."

INTENSIFIED FIGHT FOR RESOURCES
These developments dramatically show that, while it may make sense from the point of view of individual families to bring

more children into the world, this trend involves serious economic and social risks. Societies with high birth rates "generally devote a relatively large share of their resources to children," writes the Berlin Institute for Population and Development, a renowned think tank. One of these resources is the labor force of mothers, or, more generally, the skills and earning potential of the female population. In addition to nourishment, children need schools and vocational training, which poses great challenges for poor countries and can exacerbate distribution conflicts.

According to numerous experts, high population growth therefore hinders progress in the fight against poverty. Indeed, the Institute for Security Studies, an independent EU think tank, it notes with concern in its study *Fertility, Growth and the Future of Aid in Sub-Saharan Africa* that many countries will "likely remain poor" for the foreseeable future because of high birth rates.

CHAPTER 4:

Economy, infrastructure and trade

Some African countries report high growth rates. However, in many places, because the population is also growing rapidly, there is not nearly enough growth to enable people to escape poverty more widely. The greatest obstacles to growth include poor infrastructure, corruption and unfair trade agreements.

Africa has a problem with economic growth. Although most African economies are growing steadily, per capita income is stagnating in several places because the population is simultaneously growing rapidly. In 2017, the IW study *Africa's Divergent Economic Potentials* showed that the annual average growth in per capita income over the last decade slipped below the 1 percent mark at times—and in the particularly weak year 2016, it was even lower than in the rest of the world.

In addition, the poor in Africa often do not benefit from high growth rates: in 2019, only one third of the countries attained "inclusive growth", which, as defined in the *African Economic Outlook*, written by the experts at the African Development Bank, means that both the proportion of the poor and inequality are reduced.

This group includes Cote d'Ivoire, Rwanda and Togo. In its 2019 study *Accelerating Poverty Reduction in Africa*, the World Bank also pointed out that even high growth rates often do not benefit the poorest. If the trend of recent years continues, the African Development Bank predicts that the number of "extremely poor" will only drop by 8 million by 2030. And even that is likely to be difficult. The Covid-19 crisis has also hit Africa hard—the forecast in the *African Economic Outlook*, according to which economic growth should increase to around 4 percent in 2020 and 2021, can thus already be thrown out of the window.

THE ECONOMY IS HARDLY GROWING FASTER THAN THE POPULATION—AFRICA IS MAKING LITTLE PROGRESS

If the Covid-19 downturn turns into a sustained decline, it would be devastating for Africa. For only recently, the continent had a phase of several years in which it made an agonizingly slow economic recovery. Compared to the previous ten-year period, the average growth rate from 2014 onwards has fallen from 5 to 3 percent, writes the African Development Bank. This was only slightly above the rate of population growth. In 2019, the African economy will have grown by 3.4 percent, say experts in the *African Economic Outlook*, but even before Covid-19, the growth rate remained well below historic highs.

At times, the gap between Africa and the other continents in terms of prosperity did not diminish, but actually increased—Africa became even poorer in relative terms. Numerous African countries, as the IW stated in its study *Africa's Divergent Economic Potentials*, suffered from "a very low gross domestic product per capita and weakly growing, sometimes even shrinking economic output". In this context, the African Development Bank points out the numerous weather and climate shocks; it estimates that these factors will be accompanied by a growth decline of two percentage points.

Even though seven of the 15 economies that have grown the most in the last five years are in Africa (including Ethiopia, Côte d'Ivoire and Senegal), there is simply no evidence of a broad-based race to catch up. Taken together, Africa's national economies have recently achieved an economic output of just about $2.3 trillion. By way of comparison, Germany's economic output was the equivalent of around $4 trillion.

CORRUPTION AND POOR INFRASTRUCTURE DETER INVESTORS
Among the causes for the widespread sluggish growth are, in addition to civil wars and climate shocks, poor institutional conditions for entrepreneurs. For example, African countries occupy 11 of the last 20 places on Transparency International's (TI) *Corruption Perceptions Index*, which compares the situation in 180 countries, including Angola, Guinea-Bissau, Eritrea, Sudan and Chad. Somalia comes in last place.

Table 9: The problem of corruption

Position	Country	Position	Country
161	Cambodia	171	North Korea
161	Congo	171	Equatorial Guinea
161	DR Congo	171	Guinea-Bissau
161	Tajikistan	171	Libya
165	Chad	175	Sudan
166	Eritrea	175	Jemen
167	Angola	177	Afghanistan
167	Turkmenistan	178	Syria
169	Iraq	179	South Sudan
169	Venezuela	180	Somalia

Source: Corruption Perceptions Index of 180 countries (2018), TI

The *Corruption Perceptions Index* is the world's best-known indicator in this area and combines 13 individual indices from 12 independent organizations. These include the Country Policy and Institutional Assessment, for which the African Development Bank Group closely monitors and analyzes the laws and institutions in 54 African countries.

The criteria include transparency in the awarding of government contracts, legal certainty for entrepreneurs and the quality of public administration. In many places in Africa, there are considerable shortcomings in these areas, allowing politicians to continue to award contracts to their families and officials to demand generous bribes. This is deadly for entrepreneurial commitment.

At the same time, however, several countries are making progress in the fight against corruption. For example, the African Development Bank confirms progress in Rwanda, Senegal and Ethiopia. In addition, blockchain technology is opening up new, effective ways of preventing corruption (see page 36). Another central problem is infrastructure. A recent survey by the research institute Afrobarometer showed that one-third of Africans still have no access to a stable power supply in more than 30 countries on the continent. An analysis by the World Bank substantiates these findings: according to this study, just as much electricity is produced in sub-Saharan Africa (800 million inhabitants) as in Spain (45 million).

The transport infrastructure is also inadequate in many places. According to the Afrobarometer survey, only half of Africans live near paved roads. The rail network is also patchy, and even the comparatively good digital infrastructure requires considerable investment. "It is estimated that a 10-percent increase in digital coverage would lead to an increase of around 1 percent in African gross domestic product," claimed a recent paper by the EU Commission on development policy on the continent, according to the *Spiegel*.

Although infrastructure is one of the expressly stated priorities of political decision-makers in Africa, most African countries invest too little in roads, railroads, power lines, water pipes, digital networks and other infrastructure projects—the African Development Bank estimates that the continent needs to invest $130 to 170 billion a year in infrastructure. According to a recent analysis by its experts, this leaves a financing gap of between $68 to 108 billion. Of this amount, $56–66 million are needed for water supply and sanitation, and around $40 billion each are necessary for the energy and transport networks. Digital networks, on the other hand, would only require an additional $4–7 billion per year.

With regard to the transport network, the African Development Bank specifies that 80 percent of the missing budget would be used to maintain or modernize existing infrastructure. 20 percent would have to be invested in new roads, railroads, train stations, airports and harbors. The experts also point out that investment in African infrastructure declined in the 1980s and 1990s—in part because the international community pushed for reduced state involvement in the economy in the wake of the Washington Consensus (see Key Statement 2). As a result, Africa has fallen far behind, even though the continent was at a similar starting level to Asia and Latin America in 1960. The expansion of the infrastructure is still proceeding at a much slower pace.

FOREIGN TRADE IS STAGNATING

Another obstacle to growth is weak exports. According to the Federal Statistical Office (Destatis), Germany imports goods worth $22.5 billion from Africa every year. By comparison, the volume of imports from Asia was 20 times as high (see Figure 10). The trade in goods with Africa thus plays a subordinate role for German foreign trade. According to Destatis, it accounts for between 2 and 3 percent of the total volume of trade, even though 17 percent of the world's population lives in Africa. Even among former colonial powers, the situation is not significantly different. In France, a mere 4.6 percent of the import volume comes from Africa, in Great Britain it is just 2 percent.

Figure 10: Africa in the throes of defeat
Where does Germany source its imports? (2018, value of imports in bil. euros)

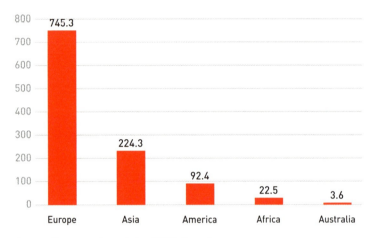

Source: Foreign trade statistics (2019), Destatis

Africa's weakness in terms of exports has various underlying causes, including controversial trade agreements. For example, developing countries in Africa have been hit particularly hard by the protectionist tendencies that have characterized U.S. policy since Donald Trump's presidency. Africa is "much more dependent on overseas trade than Europe, where 63 percent of trade takes place in the region," warned Dirk Kohnert of the nstitute for African Affairs in the 2018 *Review of African Political Economy*. In Africa, by contrast, continental domestic trade has so far offered few opportunities.

The Trump administration not only pursues its "America First" policy vis-à-vis strong trading partners such as China and the EU; it has also not shied away from asserting its economic interests vis-à-vis poor countries. Kenya, Uganda, Tanzania and Rwanda, for example, decided to stop importing used clothing from 2019 to protect their domestic textile industry. The United States threatened to withdraw tariff preferences, and three of the four countries backed down. Only Rwanda remained tough.

That was not to remain an isolated incident. Geneva's South Center research facility, which is backed by 51 developing countries, warned as early as 2018 that the new US policy opens the door to arbitrary trade restrictions if African countries promote their industries. This shows that Africa also suffers because strong nations have far-reaching opportunities to assert their interests in international trade—and often mercilessly exploit this, for example in negotiations on bilateral agreements.

For a long time, however, the EU was no exception in this regard. On the one hand Brussels urged the developing countries to open their markets—and on the other hand maintained high agricultural subsidies for European producers (see Key Statement 3). This not only worsens the export opportunities for African farmers, it even leads to our highly subsidized food products flooding the markets of the neighboring continent. The German government now doubts whether the far-reaching trade liberalization with simultaneous distortion of competition through EU subsidies was in the interests of African partner countries. "Somehow we have said in terms of ideology that free trade is good," said Günter Nooke (CDU party), Personal Representative of the German Chancellor for Africa, in a TV interview last year.

And then it was attempted to present this to the Africans and to convince them of it. While Nooke did not follow the line of those globalization critics who are generally skeptical about free trade, he made it clear that we should give developing countries more freedom to introduce trade restrictions in certain cases— for example, to temporarily protect emerging industries from foreign competition.

CHAPTER 5

Investments, the silk road and mountains of debt

Despite all the challenges, Africa presents enormous opportunities. China has recognized this and is investing hundreds of billions in the Silk Road Initiative, while German businesses are hesitating. However, Chinese interest poses a considerable risk for developing countries.

Africa is a market with billions of people who are as poor as the Chinese were 30 years ago. There is an enormous amount of catching up to do, and some countries have been reporting high growth rates for years. The continent of poverty is therefore also a continent of opportunity.

Yet so far, these opportunities are only available to a select few. According to the *World Investment Report 2019*, the total amount of foreign direct investment in Africa rose by almost 11 percent within a year to US $45.9 billion. However, it had fallen by 21.5 percent from 2017 to 2018. Today, Africa's share of global direct investment is therefore still very low at 3.5 percent.

The German economy in particular is showing restraint. According to the German Federal Ministry for Economic Cooperation and Development (BMZ), only around 1,000 of approximately 300,000 German companies that are interested in exporting have so far invested in Africa.

GAPS IN INFRASTRUCTURE: WHY GERMAN SMES ARE HESITANT TO INVEST IN AFRICA

However, this should change: the German government wants to encourage private investors to get more involved on the continent. In 2018 for example, the Ministry of Economics extended the Hermes export credit guarantees to cover investments in Ethiopia, Côte d'Ivoire, Ghana, Rwanda and Senegal, and received much praise from the business community for this. The move will lead to a "significant increase in investment and trade activity with our neighboring continent," said Stefan Liebing, Chairman of the Afrika-Verein der deutschen Wirtschaft.

In addition, Chancellor Angela Merkel announced further support measures for investments in Africa at the end of 2018. As a first step, the German government set aside $1 billion for a development investment fund. According to *Handelsblatt*, German and African companies will be paid $400 million each, which will be disbursed via the Deutsche Investitions- und Entwicklungsgesellschaft (DEG), a subsidiary of the Kreditanstalt für Wiederaufbau (KfW). Another 200 million is earmarked for additional investment guarantees and currency hedging. The fund, which was launched in 2019, will be supplemented by an "AfricaGrowFonds" from the KfW, which will finance African start-ups. It remains to be seen whether German companies will be convinced across the board. So far, at any rate, there is no sign of them really taking an interest in Africa. The legal uncertainty and the fear of corrupt officials are too daunting for many. However, the biggest obstacle is probably the poor infrastructure. Business owners report unanimously that many places are lacking the roads, rail networks and communications networks necessary to establish flourishing local branches.

CHINA HAS LONG SINCE ARRIVED – AND IS BUILDING ROADS, PORTS AND MORE
Chinese companies have fewer concerns about this, especially because Beijing is demanding and promoting expansion into

Africa with great determination. According to the *Handelsblatt*, there are already around 10,000 companies from China active on the continent. The Handsblatt Research Institute has calculated that Chinese direct investments in sub-Saharan Africa since 2005 have totaled $306 billion. Another $200 billion have flowed to North Africa and the Middle East.

China has thus become not only Africa's leading trading partner, but also its main donor. As the Brookings Institute reported a couple of months ago with reference to the Africa Attractiveness Report 2019 from the auditing and consulting firm EY, Chinese direct investments totaled more than $72 billion between 2014 and 2018 alone. As a comparison, France and the USA invested less than half of this amount, and Germany invested just a tenth.

The Chinese investment drive in Africa is part of the Belt and Road Initiative. This is a gigantic infrastructure program in which China, together with national governments, is driving forward projects in more than 60 countries located between East Asia and Europe. New highways, railroads, ports and airports are to strengthen trade between Eurasia and Africa and contribute to the emergence of a common economic area.

1.3 TRILLION FOR THE NEW SILK ROAD

The participating countries represent more than 60 percent of the world population and about one third of the global economy. In Germany there is talk of a "new Silk Road," a reference to the historical network of trade routes used for transporting silk from East Asia to Europe. According to estimates, China will invest around $1.3 trillion in the initiative by 2027 (see Key Statement 1).

Africa is increasingly in focus. President Xi Jinping announced at the China-Africa summit in 2018 that his country intended to invest a further $60 billion on the continent in the following three years. He also assured the African heads of government that China is their partner: projects would be tailored more closely to the development strategies of their countries and "more goods would be bought from Africa." Finally, Jinping announced emergency aid for crisis regions and 50 new agricultural aid projects.

The Chinese are currently particularly active in East Africa. Djibouti, the small but strategically located country on the Gulf of Aden, is to become a logistics center on Africa's east coast and a main hub of the new Silk Road. To achieve this, China is not only investing in larger ports, but also their better connection to the rail network. For example, two state-owned Chinese companies completed the construction of an electrified railroad line between Djibouti and Addis Ababa in Ethiopia in 2016. China is not only investing heavily in Djibouti, it has also set up its first naval base outside of its own borders there in order to secure its military position. China has also initiated numerous projects in other countries, including Kenya and Tanzania.

Table 10: The new Silk Road
Selected Belt and Road projects in Africa

Project	Country
Railroad line Mombasa	Nairobi (Kenya)
Railroad line Addis Abeba	Djibouti (Ethiopia/Djibouti)
Industrial park and freeway	(Dire Dawa, Ethiopia)
Economic zone and port	(Bagamoyo, Tanzania)
Economic zone Congo-Brazzaville	(Republic of Congo)

Critics, however, are increasingly skeptical about China's large-scale involvement in Africa. They criticize the fact that Chinese companies often bring their own workers and hardly cooperate with local suppliers. This prevents a transfer of know-how to Africa.

In addition, China is now the largest creditor in many countries, for example in Djibouti, which has accumulated foreign debts amounting to 90 percent of its gross domestic product. In Kenya, the loans borrowed from China since 2000 now amount to $9.8 billion and as such amount to 72 percent of the country's bilateral debt according to the IMF. Other countries have also borrowed billions from Chinese creditors.

Figure 11: On China's drip-feed?
Total Chinese loans from 2000 to 2017 (in $ billion)

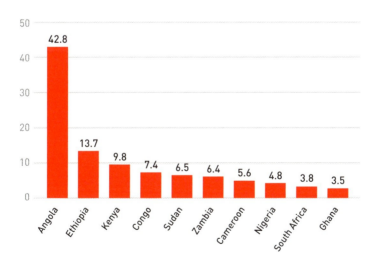

Source: Johns Hopkins University, Interactive Database (accessed 2019)

The total volume of Chinese loans to African states now amounts to almost $150 billion. This year, the *Handelsblatt* reported estimates suggesting that China is the creditor for 17 to 25 percent of "all African public debt." According to the report, debt repayments will be due in many cases from 2020 onward.

"CHINA FIRST": COUNTRIES IN THE DEBT TRAP

The IMF has recently warned against high borrowing from China. The Kiel Institute for the World Economy pointed out in 2019 that developing countries' debts to China are much higher than assumed. Moreover, loan agreements often contained disadvantageous clauses.

There is no question that the interest in Africa is part of an aggressive, long-term industrial policy that Head of State Xi Jinping is using to pursue a clear goal—China is to become the world's leading economic and political power once again. At the same time as the new Silk Road, Jinping has launched other initiatives on a gigantic scale, including Made in China 2025 and a funding program for artificial intelligence. Here, China wants to make the most of its autocratic advantage and profit from the countless amount of data it collects on its own citizens.

Beijing wants to "restore the greatness and dignity of Chinese civilization and overcome the humiliation that the country had to experience for around a hundred years following its violent defeat by the West in the First Opium War from 1839 to 1842," says Theo Summer, former editor-in-chief of the *Zeit* and author of the book *China First. Die Welt auf dem Weg ins chinesische Jahrhundert* (China First. The world on its way into the Chinese century.) Xi Jinping is pursuing the goal of making China "the most powerful military power," "the largest and leading scientific power, an innovation superpower, an infrastructure superpower, the leader in the fight against climate change, the world cultural power and the world power in football."

The central criterion for all these decisions is therefore whether they pave China's road to the top, also with regard to infrastructure investments and loans in Africa. The concerns of the so-called partner states are at best secondary. This creates a dependency that many Africans view with concern. Many ask themselves whether China is deliberately luring countries into a dependent relationship. There is even talk of the "diplomacy of the debt trap."

Although Chinese government representatives assert their good intentions like a mantra, Beijing's determination gives cause for concern time and time again. Sri Lanka is an example of where being in debt to the emerging nuclear power could lead; after the government there was unable to repay loans, it had to give large parts of a port and an adjacent area, 60 square kilometers in size, to China for 99 years.

RUSSIA IS ALSO PUSHING ITS WAY INTO AFRICA

China is not the only nation that is targeting Africa: Russia too has been increasingly pushing its way into the continent of the future for some years now. The first highlight of this program was the Russia-Africa summit in Sochi in October 2019, which was attended by around 40 heads of state and government.

The Kremlin's most important strategic goal is likely to be the development of raw materials and energy resources. Recently, activities in the mining of coltan, cobalt, aluminum, gold and diamonds have been expanded. Russian state-owned companies often play a central role in this.

SECTION II
KEY STATEMENTS

KEY STATEMENT 1

Africa and Europe share a common destiny with enormous potential

Africa's economic growth is in our own interest: we can prevent a mass exodus to the Global North and we have the chance to create a flourishing common market and the world's largest economic area at the same time. With shared values, for mutual prosperity, and against the "America First" and "China First" strategies.

DO WE HAVE TO BUILD NEW WALLS?
The refugee crisis of 2015/2016 has impressively demonstrated the bitter public debates that threaten to break out when droves of people from poor countries start out on their journey towards Europe. Right-wing populists have gained supporters all over the continent, and the German federal government and regional states have spent tens of billions of euros every year, mainly on services such as accommodation, social welfare and integration support.

As a result, European governments have made every effort to limit the number of refugees that reach our borders. Agreements were signed with Turkey and the transit countries in North Africa, which now have tighter controls. However, this has led to many people ending up in refugee camps (or in Libyan prisons, where torture is commonplace according to human rights organizations). Moreover, many refugees die on the dangerous routes through the desert or across the Mediterranean (see Chapter 3). Even today, the concept of "Fortress Europe" has already had consequences that can hardly be tolerated.

If significantly more people set out towards the Global North in the future as a result of the climate crisis, our continent will face an unprecedented endurance test. Unimpeded immigration to Europe would give a further boost to populists, while even greater isolation would result in serious human rights violations. It is doubtful whether we would be capable of meeting this challenge.

> **Lack of prospects, poor living conditions**
> › Mass migration
> › Populism
> › Building walls (in Europe as well?)
> › Are human rights upheld?
> › International conflicts

This is why it is clear to us that only when the people of Africa are better off, that we Europeans can be better off in the long term as well. It is only when poverty and hunger in Africa are defeated that we can live out our European values and maintain the European social model.

Manfred Weber, the European People's Party's top candidate in the European elections at the time, summed it up well at the Ash Wednesday political gatherings in 2019: "Today, Syria is at the center of our attention, but tomorrow it will be Africa," he called out to the audience in Passau. If there is a state of chaos in Africa, he said, Europe will soon be worse off.

WHY WE CANNOT LEAVE THE FIELD OPEN TO CHINA
Europe needs new partnerships in the face of growing protectionist tendencies and intensified competition between geopolitical systems: together with Africa, we can build a prosperous economic area and the world's largest market. This would mean

that the strategies "America First" and "China First" would come to nothing, and the European Economic Model, which is based on reciprocity, would be exported to the Global South.

However, the great powers are still several steps ahead, especially China with its Silk Road Initiative: while Europe is taking half-measures, China is making leaps and bounds, thanks in part to its cleverly designed financial system. The funds for the infrastructure investments are raised through the Chinese "Silk Road Fund" and the Asian Infrastructure Investment Bank (AIIB) based in Beijing. According to a forecast from Morgan Stanley, the investment volume is expected to reach a whopping $1.3 trillion by 2027.

The Chinese are not only securing access to important strategic resources such as cobalt, coltan and lithium. China also has a good chance to extend its sphere of influence right up to Europe's doorstep and to profit from being at the forefront of Africa's economic growth, for example through sales to the emerging new markets and orders placed with Chinese companies.

Contrary to the widespread preconception, China does not only invest where natural resources are plentiful. For example by 2017, China had already spent around $12 billion building railway lines, roads and factories in Ethiopia, a country which is comparatively poor in natural resources. According to a study published this year by the Johns Hopkins University in Washington, this was "more than twice as much as China has invested in oil-rich Sudan and mineral-rich Congo."

"Peking is building an alternative world order," remarked *WirtschaftsWoche* editor-in-chief Beat Balzli in 2018, and issued an urgent warning at the China-Africa summit that had just ended: "Europe is in danger of losing everything in the poker game for global leadership." While nations such as Germany are still only taking half-measures, "China has been thinking big for a long time already," said Balzli.

Beijing is buying "virtually a whole continent". Meanwhile, the West is losing influence. "Even the USA and the old colonial power France have fallen behind China on the list of the most important trading partners."

So it comes as no surprise, Balzli continued, that Chancellor Angela Merkel was greeted in Senegal by the state orchestra playing the Bavarian pop song *Ja, mir san mit'm Radl da* (Yes, we came by bike). Germany comes by bicycle, China comes with the big money: the current "geopolitical relations" couldn't be summed up better, said Balzli. Those in positions of responsibility have to "take drastic countermeasures" immediately.

COMPETITION BETWEEN POLITICAL SYSTEMS: EUROPE VS. USA VS. CHINA

The risks of Chinese expansion have already been identified in Africa. The fact that a number of African countries have fallen into a dangerous dependency due to high debts is probably in keeping with the concept developed in Beijing. We fear that China will take advantage of the situation to force through its own geopolitical interests.

China's expansion in Africa also poses a considerable threat to European companies and to our economic and social model in general. After all, we are in the midst of a competition between political systems that is being fought out more and more ruthlessly. The question remains: will the European social market economy, US digital capitalism or Chinese-style state capitalism dominate the world?

This is forcing us to rethink and to break new ground. The election of Donald Trump as US president made it painfully clear to Europe, and in particular to Germany as an exporting nation, that traditional (trade) partners can no longer be relied upon. Trump aimed to significantly reduce the volume of imports as part of his "America First" strategy. The high German export surplus in particular was a major source of irritation to him. "The Germans are bad," he said as early as 2017 during a meeting with EU leaders, according to the *Spiegel*, and complained, among other things, about the "millions of cars" that German manufacturers sell in the USA. "Terrible. We're going to put a stop to it." A little while later, he followed up on this statement with the first punitive tariffs.

This shows that the "First" strategies present considerable dangers for the European and German economies. And it is by no means only a decline in exports that is at risk, but also aspects such as the loss of a share of the market to powerful IT companies that benefit from concentrated economic and taxation support at home.

In addition, there are fears that European companies will fall behind in the battle for raw materials because they cannot compete with highly subsidized Chinese companies in Africa. This could affect promising industries in particular and even make the transformation of the transport sector more difficult. After all, many of the raw materials used in making batteries for electric cars are sourced in Africa.

HUGE OPPORTUNITIES FOR THE GERMAN ECONOMY

Europe must therefore act with more self-confidence and determination, and in addition to stepping up to its responsibility, also recognize the opportunities that will arise. After all, there is an enormous amount of catching up to do in Africa: in the next ten years, "as much will be built [in Africa] as has been built in Europe in the last 100 years," says German Federal Minister of Economic Cooperation and Development Gerd Müller. This means that the continent presents great development opportunities for European companies, especially as some countries are already making rapid progress.

One of the rays of hope is Ethiopia: in a country that was once considered one of the poorest of the poor, Prime Minister Abiy Ahmed is pushing ahead with reforms. He has made peace with Eritrea and persuaded rebels to give up their weapons. He was awarded the Nobel Peace Prize for these courageous steps, and above all, they have laid the foundations for a remarkable economic boom. His country's economy has grown by more than 7 percent in each of the last few years, sometimes even by double-digit figures. Munich's former mayor Christian Ude (SPD party), who heads the board of trustees of the Menschen für Menschen foundation, Karlheinz Böhm's Ethiopian aid organization, even called it a "fairy tale" in 2019.

Some political decision-makers have recognized that Europe must not leave the African playing field open to the other great powers. But now words need to be turned into deeds. And an important step in competing against US digital capitalism and Chinese state capitalism must be to seek out allies who share our values, and to build new partnerships on an equal footing especially in Africa. In this way, we can:

➤ Reduce our dependence on erratic and aggressive superpowers,
➤ Develop new markets and build a prosperous economic area,
➤ Secure access to important raw materials, and last but not least,
➤ Strengthen the European Economic Model in order to shape global standards based on the social market economy and thus ensure fair conditions for our companies.

Political reforms, technological advancements and better approaches in providing development aid are among the forces driving forward positive progress. The "Marshall Plan with Africa" presented by Minister Müller and in particular the "reform partnerships" are paving the way by linking support to reforms (see Section III – the Agenda). In this way, they are helping to ensure that the framework conditions gradually improve for companies. This also increases the interest of foreign investors to create jobs and train employees in Africa.

We therefore welcome the fact that since spring 2019, the EU has been discussing a strategy to counteract China's aspirations to become a major global power. In this context, it is encouraging that the new Commission has already emphasized Africa's importance on several occasions. It sent an important and appropriate signal when Ursula von der Leyen made her first trip abroad as EU Commission President to Africa, where she called for closer cooperation. In doing so, the CDU politician showed that she is in agreement with the French president: as early as 2019, Emmanuel Macron had made a fiery speech appealing for a strong EU and demanding that we turn our attention to Africa and forge "a pact for the future" with the continent. According to Macron, it was necessary to recognize the "common destiny".

Thus, there are already signs of a paradigm shift in European-African policy. So far, however, this is mostly just rhetoric, and in the meantime, the Chinese are investing heavily. If we really mean business, we have to respond to the Chinese Silk Road Initiative with something substantial. There is one point of attack that we can put to good use in this context: skepticism about China is currently growing among African governments, chiefly because there is growing recognition across the board that developing countries have little to oppose the "America First" and "China First" policies by themselves.

If we really want to stand out and establish genuine partnerships, we must no longer view the continent as our poor neighbors, but rather as a region with huge potential: Africa has what it takes to achieve economic growth similar to that of China over the last 30 years. And we Europeans can provide the decisive impetus for this, in our own enlightened self-interest.

KEY STATEMENT 2

Unregulated capitalism has failed across the board in Africa

For decades, the international community has urged Africa to embrace free and largely unregulated markets. Yet, contrary to the predictions of supporters of the trickle-down theory, the poor have not benefited from the growth. This has exacerbated inequality, and at the same time fueled conflicts that have wiped out progress.

If classical economic theory were to be applied, Africa should be much further in its fight against poverty and hunger. Following the colonial period, many countries initially experimented with socialist systems, but the wind changed direction in the 1980s, with more and more governments opting for the free market.

Finally, in 1990, 40 African countries adopted the Washington Consensus, an IMF plan to restructure their economies according to market economy principles. Economic policy at the time was focused on deregulation, privatization, reducing subsidies and a more liberal trade policy. The IMF and African governments hoped that this would not only stimulate growth, but also significantly reduce poverty, and with it the blatant inequality of income and wealth.

In other words, the market economy should enable people to prosper and ensure the emergence of a middle class. After the colonial era, where wealth was in the hands of just a few, and the era of socialism, where poverty was felt by many, society should now be moving in the direction of creating "prosperity for all", in keeping with the ideas of the liberal prophets.

However, this has not worked; the Washington Consensus has failed miserably in Africa. The World Bank clearly confirmed this once again with its report on *Accelerating Poverty Reduction in Africa* from 2019, in which experts concluded that the benefits of economic growth have not reached the poor.

STIGLITZ VS. WASHINGTON CONSENSUS

The renowned US economist and winner of the Nobel Prize for Economics, Joseph Stiglitz, put the reasons for this in a nutshell in his book *Making Globalization Work*. The Washington Consensus was based on assumptions such as full competition, however such assumptions are "an idealization of reality and of little relevance to developing countries."

For this reason, the withdrawal of the state certainly did not automatically lead to private companies stepping into the breach, as the IMF big shots had hoped. The former chief economist of the World Bank referred to the example of the public-sector marketing boards for agricultural products in West Africa. Following the abolition of these boards, a few well-to-do farmers who had means of transport rose to become local monopolists. Meanwhile, the situation for the rest of the farmers rapidly deteriorated.

Stiglitz added that the advocates of the Washington Consensus had jumped to the conclusion that economic growth automatically benefits all sectors of the population. They had assumed that increasing the wealth of those with economic success would also benefit the poor through their increase in consumer spending and willingness to invest *(trickle-down theory)*. However, in developing countries in particular, growth has exacerbated social inequality, leading to political instability and heightening conflicts. Initial progress has thus been negated across the board.

A DANGEROUS GAP BETWEEN LOW EARNERS AND THE PRIVILEGED

Indeed, the gap between the rich and the poor in Africa is enormous. According to the United Nations, sub-Saharan Africa is "the region with the highest inequality in the world." The Inequality Adjusted Human Development Index (IHDI), which the United Nations publishes every year as a ranking list, supports this finding.

The IHDI measures not only the level of education, health and wealth, but also whether large sections of the population or only small groups benefit from progress. Many African states are at the bottom of the current ranking list, with inequality particularly high in Sierra Leone, Niger, Chad, South Sudan and the Central African Republic. Even comparatively stable countries like Gabon and Mozambique show high disparities:

Table 11: Inequality slows down development
The last 20 places on the Inequality Adjusted Human Development Index

Position	Country	Position	Country
132	Benin	142	Burkina Faso
133	DR Congo	143	Mali
134	Côte d'Ivoire	144	Burundi
135	Jemen	145	Guinea-Bissau
136	Djibouti	146	Comoros
136	Guinea	147	Sierra Leone
138	Haiti	148	Niger
139	Liberia	149	Chad
140	Mozambique	150	South Sudan
141	Gambia	151	Central African Rep.

Source: IHDI (2019), UN

One look at the distribution of wealth confirms the problematic situation. According to the current *Global Wealth Databook* of Crédit Suisse, a maximum of one percent of the population in 20 African countries have the equivalent of more than $10,000 at their disposal. The ratios are particularly low in Malawi (0.1 percent), the Comoros (0.2 percent), Madagascar, Guinea-Bissau, Burundi and Ethiopia (0.3 percent each). By way of comparison, the ratio in Germany is almost 67 percent.

The discrepancies in wages are also enormous, as the so-called Gini coefficient "Wages" reveals. Many African countries have values that are far above the average. The higher the value, the greater the pay gap between low earners and the privileged:

Figure 12: Poor countries, large gaps
Gini coefficient "Wages"

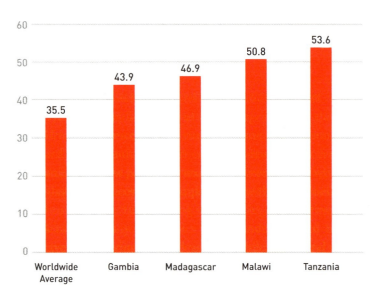

Based on data from OECD, statistics agencies, etc.

In our view, these figures provide compelling evidence that the free market alone will not solve the problems, and the rules of the game we have had up to now for direct market forces in Africa are not nearly enough to win the battle against poverty. Rather, it is necessary to make a break with the Washington Consensus for once and for all, and to establish social market economies with viable state institutions.

KEY STATEMENT 3

Neither "free" nor "fair" trade can defeat poverty

While Europe is urging developing countries to lower their trade barriers, we ourselves are not so keen on practicing what we preach when it comes to market liberalization. The high EU agricultural subsidies in particular are weakening the opportunities for African exports. We must therefore put the interests of the poor at the center of our trade policy, especially since fair trade initiatives are often only a drop in the ocean.

The Nobel Prize winner Joseph Stiglitz and his co-author Andrew Charlton strongly criticized the global free trade system in 2006 in their book *Fair Trade for All: How Trade Can Promote Development*. The liberalization of the previous decades had brought little, especially in the case of African countries. The authors noted that it has sometimes had a negative impact on the poor in particular. Developing countries around the world have suffered from their closer ties to the world market and in some cases experienced "liberal shocks" when more efficient suppliers from abroad suddenly take sections of the market away from domestic companies, even in the agricultural sector.

Furthermore, according to the authors, the industrialized countries shielded their domestic markets with indirect trade barriers. In fact, there is much to suggest that these restrictions cost the developing countries much more than they receive in development aid from the industrialized countries. It is therefore important to lower indirect trade barriers and help developing countries to reduce the "adjustment costs" of trade liberalization.

However, little has changed since then. Although the industrialized countries have repeatedly promised a fair world trade system, only a few isolated acts have followed. And these were then often offset by other measures.

AGRICULTURAL SUBSIDIES REMAIN HIGH

The EU's *Everything but Arms* initiative granted 34 poor African countries largely free access to the European domestic market as early as 20 years ago:

Table 12: Countries that can supply "Everything but Arms" to the EU
African countries that benefit from the Everything but Arms program

#	Country	#	Country	#	Country
1	Angola	13	Comoros	25	Senegal
2	Equatorial Guinea	14	Lesotho	26	Sierra Leone
3	Ethiopia	15	Liberia	27	Somalia
4	Benin	16	Madagascar	28	South Sudan
5	Burkina Faso	17	Malawi	29	Sudan
6	Burundi	18	Mali	30	Tanzania
7	Djibouti	19	Mauritania	31	Togo
8	DR Congo	20	Mozambique	32	Chad
9	Eritrea	21	Niger	33	Uganda
10	Gambia	22	Rwanda	34	Central African Rep.
11	Guinea	23	Zambia		
12	Guinea-Bissau	24	Sao Tomé		

Source: EU Commission (2019)

While the EU has on the one hand opened up its internal market, on the other it has stubbornly maintained its lavish agricultural subsidies for European producers. This distortion of normal trade competition conditions reduces the opportunities for many African farmers dramatically, and even leads to highly subsidized European food products flooding the continent's markets.

Despite continual appeals from African governments, little is likely to change. The European Commission has announced plans to distribute a whopping €365 billion in agricultural subsidies between 2021 and 2027 (of which around €41 billion will go to Germany), mostly in the form of direct payments to farmers. Up to the editorial deadline for this book, it did not look as if anyone was putting up any fundamental resistance to the Commission's plans. The only likely change seemed to be a measured shift of the funds in favor of smaller family farms.

Occasionally, special national subsidies are added to the payments from Brussels for the agricultural sector as well. For example, the German grand coalition decided in early 2020 to make €1 billion available to farmers for investment. After the hot summer of 2018, the federal and state governments had already scraped together funding for drought aid to the tune of €340 million. Many experts criticized this, including Reinhold von Eben-Worlée, president of the association Die Familienunternehmer, which represents family-run businesses. "Risk and liability go hand in hand. It is one of the basic principles of the social market economy," he said. However, this does not seem to apply to agriculture. "It is not the farmers who bear the risk, but the taxpayers."

We are convinced that putting up resistance to noticeably reducing agricultural subsidies makes it difficult to make real advances in reducing poverty, and it is also short-sighted. If we succeed in pushing forward progress in Africa and increasing wages and purchasing power, this will also be positive for European producers. To put it bluntly: if wages in Africa rise, we will no longer need agricultural subsidies anyway.

HOW FREE TRADE AGREEMENTS HARM AFRICAN FARMERS

Although industrialized countries are not so concerned about having free markets themselves, some of them are still pushing for far-reaching liberalization in developing countries in Africa. In recent years, the EU has signed several *Economic Partnership Agreements* (EPAs) with partners, including the Economic Community of West African States (ECOWAS) and the South African Development Community (SADC), to which the countries of the respective region have become members.

Although the German Federal Ministry of Economics points out that in signing EPAs, African countries get "100 percent free access to the European market," while in return they would have to open their markets "only for an average of 80 percent of tariff lines or trade volume." The remaining 20 percent, which is often mainly agricultural products, would remain "permanently protected from European imports."

However, this share is too low, especially against the background of the unaltered high EU agricultural subsidies. In the interest of their farmers and agricultural entrepreneurs, we believe that African countries should be allowed to impose import duties on a larger scale. Farmers in Ghana suffer considerably from the fact that Italian producers export subsidized tomatoes to the West African country. The German government now also doubts that the above-mentioned agreements were all made in the interest of African partner countries (see Chapter 4).

TRADE POLICY: MINIMIZING POVERTY, NOT MAXIMIZING TRADE!

The bottom line is that since the Everything but Arms Agreement in 2001, the EU has too often pushed through its own short-term interests in trade policy. We need a paradigm shift. In the future, the highest political goal should no longer be to maximize trade, but rather to minimize poverty. In specific terms, this means that the EU should reduce its agricultural subsidies and at the same time offer free access to the internal market and deepened trade partnerships to those developing countries that are determined to fight poverty and push ahead with social reform (see The Agenda).

> **BY THE WAY: FAIR TRADE AND ADDING VALUE**
>
> We should not rely on the numerous fair trade initiatives being enough to make real progress. On the one hand, they often fail to have sufficient impact: consumers in the industrialized countries pay a little more for "fairly" traded food such as coffee, cocoa or mangoes, but a large part of the total price paid usually still goes to the middlemen, refiners, food companies and supermarkets in the Global North, and not to the farmers in Africa. The higher prices they receive for their fair trade products are often only a mere drop in the ocean. On the other hand, according to Senegalese economist Ndongo Samba Sylla, the poorest do not benefit from the principle anyway. They would have problems forming cooperatives and having their products certified "because it is too expensive."
>
> Ndongo Samba Sylla criticizes that predominantly "unprocessed products" are sold under the fair trade banner. He is not aware of "a single example where a country has been able to develop through the sale of raw agricultural products." That is why it is urgently necessary that more value is added in the developing countries themselves. This has been happening more often in recent times, but still far too rarely. We therefore warn against too much reliance on fair trade approaches. The voluntary nature of these schemes will not come close to establishing effective standards for truly fair trade.

And what about legal obligations? In their book *Die 1-Dollar-Revolution: Globaler Mindestlohn gegen Ausbeutung und Armut* (The 1 Dollar Revolution: Global Minimum Wage against Exploitation and Poverty), Georgios Zervas and Peter Spiegel propose an EU regulation that defines high standards. In order to obtain approval for sale on the internal market, manufacturers should have to "have their products certified as complying with ecological and social standards—including the minimum wage."

One disadvantage of this approach is that such a certification would be too complex and expensive for many small farmers and medium-sized businesses in Africa, just like the fair trade certificates. We do not believe it is ideal to impose strict EU requirements on African suppliers; in the worst case, strict standards for products and their manufacturers could build up the market power of large suppliers. We therefore need concepts and ideas that extend beyond this.

KEY STATEMENT 4

Africa needs the social market economy

To defeat poverty, we need to focus on the social market economy and the European Economic Model. The countries of Africa are a long way off from this goal, and there are almost no robust social security systems or fair minimum wages in place. This leads to a fundamental market failure: many workers have no alternative to taking on undignified work. This must change.

The need for economic policy reform in Africa is high. Many countries lack an effective, politically determined framework for channeling market forces and making modest corrections. Even in countries where there is no civil war, the authorities often lack the assertiveness to guarantee legal certainty for entrepreneurs.

One of the greatest problems in this regard is corruption. After all, neither fair competition nor a powerful medium-sized economy can develop in places where there is always someone waiting for their palm to be greased, be they civil servants, politicians or the ruling elite.

The problem of the lack of a regulatory framework, referred to as "ordo" by German economists in the sense of ordoliberalism, has long been known, and it is being tackled with growing determination. Accordingly, the Marshall Plan with Africa, spearheaded by Minister Müller (CSU party), and especially the reform partnerships envisage supporting African states in building stable state structures and in the fight against corruption.

THE MARKET FAILURE CONCERNING UNSKILLED WORKERS
Even if African states succeed in establishing stable structures and an ordoliberal market economy, this is not enough to

win the fight against poverty. Standards and rules that ensure fair competition do indeed promote investment and growth. However, higher growth rates do not automatically benefit the poor, as the failure of the Washington Consensus, whose champions advocated the trickle-down theory, impressively demonstrated. It is thus clear that markets that are regulated according to ordoliberal principles alone usually fail in the fight against poverty. And this is a particularly high danger in Africa, where unskilled workers face fierce competition. They can be easily replaced by people looking for a second job, older workers and in many places, even by children. This leads to an oversupply of labor which does not result in a fair price for the work performed. In many countries in the region, workers receive the equivalent of just €1 a day. That is just enough to survive, but not enough to live on.

The oversupply of labor particularly affects the agricultural sector, which employs the largest number of people in Africa. According to an analysis by the European Parliamentary Research Service in 2016, 60 percent of jobs in sub-Saharan Africa are "linked to agriculture." Due to widespread migration to major cities, however, there is also an oversupply of labor in many cities, without the situation of workers in rural areas getting any better.

THE LACK OF SOCIAL SECURITY LEADS TO POWERLESSNESS AND MANCHESTER CAPITALISM

It is a cutthroat fight for jobs, so to speak, which leads us into a vicious cycle: the supposed breadwinners earn too little to be able to provide for their families, which is why children and family members of retirement age often have to help out. This in turn increases the supply of labor, and thus the pressure on wages.

The consequences of this can be seen in statistics from the International Labour Organization: according to the *Global*

Wage Report 2018/2019, the average real wage in Africa fell by three percent within one year in 2017 (see Figure 13), mainly due to sharp economic declines in the populous countries of Egypt and Nigeria, which both had high inflation rates. However, the decline in real wages also reflects the oversupply of labor: companies do not have to compensate for inflation-related losses by increasing nominal wages.

Even if these two countries were to be taken out of the equation, real wages on the continent would only have risen by 1.3 percent. By comparison, the global average was 1.8 percent. Moreover, Egypt and Nigeria were not the only countries to have sharp declines in wages; it is just that the developments in these two countries had a particularly strong impact on the overall African average. The situation has also been particularly dire in Tanzania, Angola, Burundi, Uganda and Kenya in recent years. Real wages in these countries have fallen significantly since 2008, on average between 9.5 and 1.6 percent per year.

Figure 13: Higher wages? No way
Change in real wages in Africa (in percent)

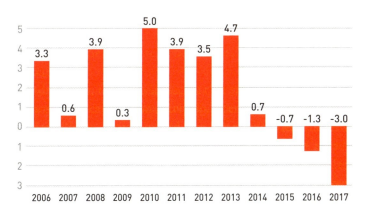

Source: Global Wage Report 2018/2019 (2019), ILO

The figures are an impressive illustration of how powerless African workers are. Their economies are a long way from being social market economies and are often reminiscent of the "Manchester capitalism" that shaped not only Britain but also other European countries until the 20th century.

While we have largely overcome the once widespread exploitation in Europe, and child labor no longer exists in the EU, these practices are still part of everyday life in many African countries, whether it is on West African cocoa plantations or mining for raw materials in the Congo Basin. Millions of Africans have to put up with catastrophic working conditions and appalling pay to ensure that they and their families can survive.

How can change really come about? How can political leaders break the vicious cycle and finally get fair wages and a decent standard of living for those who really need it?

LUDWIG ERHARD AND THE SOCIAL MARKET ECONOMY

Another element is needed, in addition to the *ordo*, to defeat poverty and hunger: an active social policy that the state uses to correct market failures affecting the poor. For as long as there is no social safety net in Africa, millions of people will continue to be forced to offer their labor for a pittance. To put it in other words, Africa needs a social market economy. We are convinced that this is possible and also attractive to businesses. For it is the only economic system that can create "prosperity for all" (instead of "poverty for all" under socialism, or "wealth for just a few" under unbridled capitalism.)

The term "social market economy" was coined by Alfred Müller-Armack, who worked as a high-ranking civil servant for the Federal Minister of Economics Ludwig Erhardt (CDU party), the father of the German *Wirtschaftswunder* (economic miracle). Müller-Armack viewed the concept as a "third way" between a pure market economy and state economic control.

The aim, the economist argued, was "to combine the principle of freedom on the market with that of social equality." The state should therefore not limit itself to establishing an *ordo*, but should also pursue social policies and those aimed at preventing economic fluctuation. Central elements of the concept are the social partnership (for example through co-determination in the workplace), aid money for those in need and a high-capacity social insurance system.

BISMARCK—FATHER OF THE SOCIAL MARKET ECONOMY?

Social security has a longer tradition in Germany than in other countries. As early as 1881, Kaiser Wilhelm I promised "those in need of assistance greater security and abundance of the assistance to which they are entitled." Thus, no worker should have to rely solely on family or church if he or she could no longer work due to illness, accident or old age.

However, the establishment of a social insurance system was not an expression of pure philanthropy: Due to a severe crisis, the social peace was acutely endangered at the time. The anger and despair of laid-off workers erupted in protests, giving a boost to the trade unions as well as to the Socialist Workers' Party of Germany (SAP), which became the SPD in 1890.

That is why Imperial Chancellor Otto von Bismarck urged social legislation in order to remedy the situation. He was particularly concerned with binding workers more closely to the state. Probably the most important initiative in this context was a statutory health insurance scheme, which was launched in 1883. It was not until six years later that pension insurance followed. This was much more controversial – also because it was not financed solely by employers and employees, but received subsidies from the budget.

It would be presumptuous to call Bismarck the father of the social market economy: For the Imperial Chancellor, security and stability interests clearly prevailed. For him, protecting workers was a means to an end—in other words, it was a strategic move and not an expression of economic principles.

Nevertheless, his calculations were largely successful. In this way, Bismarck showed that social security is crucial for peaceful and stable societies. This can certainly be seen as a merit and an expression of his foresight.

Catholic social doctrine, one of whose protagonists was Wilhelm Emmanuel von Ketteler, played an important role in the discussion about social insurance in the second half of the 19th century. The bishop of Mainz advocated mitigating the negative consequences of the liberal economic order and "letting the workers have a share, as far as possible, in what is good in the system, in its blessings." At the same time, it was clear to von Ketteler that socialism was not an alternative—and unlike other church dignitaries, he did not want a return to a society of estates, albeit a reformed one.

The Christian Democrat Ludwig Erhardt, together with Alfred Müller-Armack, drew on both Christian social doctrine and Bismarck's social reforms when he established a "social market economy" after World War II. By setting this course, the two have made a decisive contribution to the fact that broad sections of the population in Germany have benefited from the *Wirtschaftswunder*. As a result, the concept has found supporters beyond Germany's borders, especially in Europe. The EU demanded a "competitive social market economy" in the Lisbon Treaty of 2007. French President Macron even proposed strengthening the social market economy in 2019: "A basic social security system must be introduced in Europe, the place where social security was invented. This should be available to all workers, from east to west, north to south, guaranteeing them equal pay for the same job and a Europe-wide minimum wage should be introduced, adapted to each country and renegotiated jointly every year."

This shows that the social market economy forms part of the EU's sense of identity. We should therefore speak of the *European Economic Model* at the international level. The frequently used term "Rhine capitalism" has long been outdated because it only refers to the countries that border the Rhine.

BY THE WAY: JOHN NASH AND THE FAMILY-RUN BUSINESSES

Many family-run businesses embody the philosophy of the social market economy in a very special way. Unlike followers of the shareholder value doctrine and financial investors who want to maximize profits as quickly as possible and often only look to the next financial quarter, they think in terms of generations, and therefore have a keen sense of how important the common good and social peace are for the area where the business is located and thus for the long-term well-being of their company.

For them, the *business of business is not only business*: responsible, sustainable entrepreneurship is part of their DNA. In contrast, what incentive do hired managers of listed companies, whose contracts expire in a few years, have for thinking in the long term?

Incidentally, it is also supported by game theory that personal (economic) interests and the common good go hand in hand, and by none other than John Nash, mathematician and winner of the Nobel Prize for Economics, who died in 2015.

You may remember the Oscar-winning film *A Beautiful Mind*, starring Russell Crowe, which traces Nash's life. In one scene the young math student is sitting in a bar with his fellow students when a group of girls walk in. The young men find one of the girls particularly attractive, and one man suggests that each of them should try their luck on their own ("Every man for himself, gentlemen!").

He quotes the forefather of modern economics, Adam Smith, as his main authority: "In competition, individual ambition benefits the common good." After a brief moment's reflection, Nash argues against this: If they all crowd around the girl, he argues, "we all get in each other's way, and none of us actually gets her."

In addition, Nash warns, this way you also lose your chance with the other girls, because nobody likes to be second choice. He therefore suggests flirting with the other girls from the very beginning. "Then we won't get in each other's way, and we won't upset the other girls. That's the only way we're going to win." From this, Nash concludes that Adam Smith's guiding principle is "incomplete" and needs to be revised. The best result is achieved "when everyone in the group does what is best for themselves—and for the whole group."

In other words: A maximum level of self-interest does not necessarily lead to the best result. It is much more important to keep the common good in mind, even when competing against others.

Another winner of the Nobel Prize for Economics took a completely different view: the monetarist Milton Friedman believed that entrepreneurs should concentrate on making profit. His seminal essay in the *New York Times Magazine* in 1970 was entitled *The Social Responsibility of Business is to Increase its Profits*. Friedman thus provided the theoretical framework for deregulation, which was implemented from the early 1980s onwards in the United States under Ronald Reagan and in

Great Britain under Margaret Thatcher. In the decades before, Anglo-Saxon economic policymakers had moved closer to the European approach; John Maynard Keynes, a British economist, had even put forward the most influential alternative to laissez-faire capitalism. In his *General Theory of Employment, Interest and Money*, published in 1936, he drew conclusions from the Great Depression and advocated a more active state that controls the economy and channels market forces.

While Friedman's legacy continues to shape the US economy, in Europe the "third way" between unbridled capitalism and state control of the economy has become almost universally accepted. Although Friedman still had numerous followers on the Old Continent after the turn of the millennium, the financial crisis of 2008/2009 and most recently the Covid-19 crisis have further strengthened Keynesian tendencies. Fewer and fewer economists and politicians advocate a "lean" state.

AGENDA 2063 – THE EUROPEAN ECONOMIC MODEL FOR AFRICA?
Many leaders in Africa have also recognized the potential of the social market economy. Accordingly, states such as Algeria, Botswana, Namibia and Cape Verde are trying to create a more close-knit social network. The African Union (AU) has even declared this to be one of its main priorities: social security systems are a central component of Agenda 2063, which the AU drafted in 2013 and adopted two years later. These systems are intended to promote sustainable and inclusive growth and thus eradicate poverty.

In addition, the AU's Agenda 2063 is designed to ensure the rule of law, peace and stability and promote political integration. It is therefore fair to say that Africa is oriented towards the EU as a model.

Two of the projects that the AU is pushing ahead with as part of its agenda are establishing a free trade zone and a high-speed train that connects all commercial centers and capitals. A joint central bank and a pan-African digital network are also planned. While progress has already been made in some areas (such as trade), many projects have stalled due to lack of funding.

Africa has made remarkable progress, but still has a long way to go, said Alassane Ouattara, President of the Côte d'Ivoire, at an EU summit in February this year. Meanwhile, the African Development Bank was pressing for a "faster implementation" of the agenda and criticized that African investors all too often invest their own money outside the continent.

There is still a long way to go, not only in terms of joint projects, but also in terms of reforms at the national level. This especially applies to social security systems: Africa has the lowest social standards in the whole world, writes the International Labour Organization in its *Social Protection Report* 2017-2019. According to ILO calculations, on average less than 18 percent of the inhabitants of African states have any form of insurance. This means no African state is effectively correcting this market failure with regard to unskilled workers.

This has to change. The introduction of effective social security systems is a decisive step on the road from unbridled capitalism to a social market economy because they change the balance of power in favor of unskilled labor and thus correct the market failure described above.

In this way, the two core principles of a society based on solidarity, one that would not leave anyone behind and enable all citizens to live in dignity, would be fulfilled:

➤ People who work can provide for their families.
➤ People who lose their jobs do not have to go hungry.

We are convinced that a social market economy would also reduce social tension, increase stability and unleash further forces for growth. For if the gap between the rich and the poor becomes too wide, the privileged also suffer. They suffer because the lack of purchasing power inhibits the development of their companies and employers. They suffer because they can only enjoy the advantages of their prosperity in isolated, gated hideaways. They suffer because they have to fear that the resentment of society's "losers" will eventually explode. And because it has been shown that socially heterogeneous economies are more susceptible to exogenous shocks and economic crises due to a lack of stable consumer and domestic demand. Thus, rampant inequality is not only an ethical problem, but also a threat to the prosperity of society as a whole.

Let me make this clear: We are convinced proponents of the principle of merit rather than leveling down. But this is not just an expression of solidarity, it is also in the interest of the "winners" to fight against high levels of inequality.

THE POLITICAL WILL IS LACKING IN MANY PLACES

Unfortunately, this message has not yet reached many privileged people and political decision-makers. At any rate, some governments are at best halfhearted in their efforts to combat inequality. The fact that no African country has yet managed to establish a social market economy is not only due to the difficult framework conditions, but also due to a lack of political will.

Nigeria, for example, Africa's most populous country, is among those that do little to combat inequality (although sufficient financial resources are theoretically available to set up a solidarity-based system due to the country's rich oil supplies). The emergency aid and development organization Oxfam analyzed 157 countries for its *Commitment to Reducing*

Inequality Index in 2018 comparing tax systems, workers' rights and social security contributions. The Nigerian government received the worst possible report and came in last place, mainly because of its low social spending. Although the president claimed he wanted to tackle inequality, the benefits for those in need remained "shamefully low," Oxfam criticized.

This has dramatic consequences: despite comparable per capita incomes, 10 percent of children are reported to die before they reach the age of five. Other governments in Africa also fared badly, with Madagascar, Sierra Leone and Chad only a few places ahead of Nigeria:

Table 13: Fighting excessive inequality?

The ten countries with the worst social policies according to Oxfam

Position	Country	Position	Country
148	Bangladesh	153	Sierra Leone
149	Singapore	154	Chad
150	Laos	155	Haiti
151	Madagascar	156	Uzbekistan
152	Bhutan	157	Nigeria

Source: Commitment to Reducing Inequality Index (2018), Oxfam

Please note that we are not embracing all of Oxfam's reasoning here. It seems to us that there is an assumption lurking behind the analysis by the critics of globalization that one simply has to take from the rich and give to the poor in order to provide "justice". Putting aside the questionable concept of justice on which such chains of thought are based, we would like to emphasize that the "rich" are most often medium-sized entrepreneurs who create jobs. We only have a chance at achieving a broad economic boom and winning against poverty if they are economically successful.

Therefore, we should not cheat money from the "rich", but rather oblige them to apply principles of moderate solidarity, and use instruments that benefit everyone in the medium and long term. In other words, the motto should not be "the poor against the rich", and a debate based on jealousy will not get us anywhere at all. Instead, the aim must be to create win-win situations for rich and poor alike.

KEY STATEMENT 5

Minimum wages and insurance for the unemployed play a key role

A decisive step on the way to the European Economic Model is social security benefits for people who lose their jobs. This would improve the negotiating position of workers, make exploitation more difficult and help establish a minimum wage that is a reality and doesn't just exist on paper. The good news is that even poor countries can establish robust social systems.

Adequate wages and a decent job; some people might find this aspiration presumptuous or even naive when viewed against the background of the harsh reality in Africa. But all great changes begin with new ideas, bold targets and taking small steps.

A social safety net for the unemployed seems to us to be of utmost importance. This not only guarantees support for people in times of need, but also changes the balance of power in the labor market; if workers have at least a temporary alternative to taking undignified jobs, this strengthens their negotiating position. This in turn can help to ensure that the legally required minimum wages are actually paid. After all, hardly anyone would be willing to work permanently for less.

Skeptics of the market economy should note: both rich and poor benefit equally from an unemployment benefit system that is cleverly designed. After all, we are not talking here about a classic top-down wealth redistribution. So it is not a matter of taking from the rich to give to the poor or even going as far as to level out the differences in income and wealth.

On the contrary: a functioning unemployment system is an expression of the principle of reciprocity and above all, it is not a zero-sum game. It raises the bottom of the income pyramid to a higher level because it not only boosts consumption but also the willingness to educate and invest. This is because people who are protected from the negative consequences of crises and emergencies are more likely to spend their savings on ensuring a better future. In this way, unemployment benefits unleash new forces for economic growth. This also benefits those who make a special contribution to the development of a social security system through paying taxes and financial contributions.

MINIMUM WAGES ARE NOT POSSIBLE WITHOUT PUTTING SOCIAL SECURITY IN PLACE

In our opinion, simply increasing the statutory minimum wage, as some experts propose, is not enough. The lowest minimum wage levels, which according to a study in many regions of Africa are between US $100 and $200 per month (converted into local purchasing power, see Figure 14), often exist only on paper. According to the ILO's *Social Protection Report*, existing regulations are often circumvented in Africa because nobody monitors their compliance. As long as these power structures in the labor market do not change, companies will continue to find ways and means to circumvent them.

Moreover, effective minimum wage levels only really benefit those who have work. A further problem is that minimum wages do not automatically go hand in hand with better working conditions. A gradual increase in the minimum wage must therefore be accompanied by other measures. These include a functioning unemployment benefit system and more effective checks and controls.

As a result of the disadvantages of isolated minimum wages described above, we are also skeptical about a global minimum

Figure 14: Often existent only on paper, sadly
Monthly minimum wages in US dollars (converted into local purchasing power)

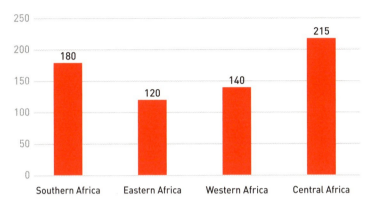

Source: Minimum Wages in Sub-Saharan Africa (2015), IZA Institute of Labor Economics

wage level of US $1 per hour, as proposed by Georgios Zervas and Peter Spiegel in their book *Die 1-Dollar-Revolution: Globaler Mindestlohn gegen Ausbeutung und Armut* (The 1 Dollar Revolution: Global Minimum Wage against Exploitation and Poverty). For without any additional measures, this would again only exist on paper. In the last chapter of their book, Zervas and Spiegel do indeed additionally recommend "an effective system of unemployment and social security" in developing countries. Their concept, however, envisages that all states in the world pay 1 percent of their GDP into a *Global Goal Fund* administered by the United Nations. We consider this to be unrealistic because it would require too many different countries with completely different interests to agree on a common line. We are also convinced that developing countries should set up their own social security systems. In our view, being at the mercy of the international community is not a desirable solution. Africa needs help to help itself.

AFRICAN STATES CAN HAVE WELFARE SYSTEMS

Those who claim that a social safety net is unrealistic in Africa, referring to empty state coffers and weak institutions, are making it too easy for themselves. In many places, political leaders could very well afford to support the unemployed, old and the sick if they wanted to, and if they began to build up a more effective financial administration to reduce tax losses. Some countries like Ghana have recently made great progress in this area.

Experts are therefore convinced that even poor countries can afford robust social systems. This would require about "3 to 5 percent of their gross domestic product," said the senior UN economist Khalid Malik in a report published by *Deutsche Welle* as early as 2014. "This is definitely possible." And the profit is enormous, "because the investment leads to more prosperity."

Markus Loewe from the German Development Institute (Deutsches Institut für Entwicklungspolitik [DIE]): "African states can have welfare systems," he wrote in a guest article for the *Zeit* newspaper in 2010. Seven years later, the economist and co-author Christoph Strupat put it in a nutshell: international comparisons showed "that even poor countries can finance basic social security systems." "Much can be achieved," even "with very small amounts."

Loewe also emphasized "the central role that social security plays for economic and political development in developing countries." It not only protects against extreme poverty and strengthens domestic stability, it also increases the willingness to invest, in entrepreneurial activities for example. He pointed out that countries with "effective basic social security systems" are better able to cope with economic slumps such as the global economic and financial crisis of 2008/2009.

Incidentally, a review of the German *Wirtschaftswunder* underscores the fact that not only rich countries can introduce social systems: when the then federal government introduced nationwide social insurance including unemployment benefits at the end of the 1940s and beginning of the 1950s, the state coffers were also empty. Nevertheless, it laid the essential foundations of the social market economy, and thus created an important prerequisite for widespread prosperity.

FROM VIETNAM TO CHILE: SUCCESS IN THE FIGHT AGAINST POVERTY

It is true that we cannot present any scientific proof of the positive effects of unemployment benefits that has been gathered in a methodologically rigorous way. After all, no matter which country you look at, different factors always overlap each other, and complex interactions must always be taken into account. In addition, the various systems differ considerably.

However, we have analyzed how former developing countries have developed after they introduced social security for the unemployed. Moreover, we found strong indications that the instrument makes a decisive contribution to reducing poverty rates. This releases further driving forces for growth and makes economies more crisis-resistant. Fears that social security systems overburden developing countries and are even counterproductive because they restrict the competitiveness of the economy are therefore unfounded.

Of course, a look at Latin America and Asia is particularly revealing: many countries on both continents began to create more comprehensive social security systems as early as the 1990s, including Brazil, Chile, China, Thailand and Vietnam. China, for example, added elements of the social market economy to its state capitalism by gradually introducing and expanding social security insurance in the 1990s. Admittedly there are significant regional differences, and especially in rural areas, many people still have poor insurance coverage. But the reforms have contributed to a significant reduction in poverty: more than half of the people who have escaped poverty worldwide in the past 30 years live in China.

In the Asia-Pacific region, people are now much better protected from losing their jobs because of social reforms. According to the ILO, an average of 22.5 percent of the unemployed receive benefits, which is almost four times higher than in Africa. In China, 18.8 percent of the unemployed now receive state assistance; in Thailand this is 43.2 percent, and in Vietnam as much as 45 percent. The situation in Latin America is worse, but still significantly better than in Africa. On average, 12 percent of people who lose their jobs receive unemployment benefits, with the rate in Chile being particularly high at 45 percent.

What is the actual economic impact of these important social reforms? A closer look at Vietnam, Thailand and Chile reveals that poverty rates have always declined significantly, while the per capita GDP has risen sharply:

Table 14: Vietnam
GDP after the introduction of a robust unemployment insurance system in 2010

	2010	2011	2012	2013	2014	2015	2016	2017
GDP per capita (in US $)	1,310	1,515	1,723	1,871	2,012	2,065	2,171	2,343
Poverty rate (in %)[1]	4.2	n/a	2.8	n/a	2.6	n/a	2	n/a
Poverty rate (in %)[2]	n/a	n/a	17.2	n/a	13.5	n/a	9.8	n/a

Table 15: Thailand
GDP after the introduction of a robust unemployment insurance system in 2004

	2004	2006	2008	2010	2012	2014	2016	2017
GDP per capita (in US $)	2,660	3,369	4,379	5,075	5,860	5,954	5,979	6,594
Poverty rate (in %)[1]	0.8	0.7	0.1	0.1	0.1	0	0	0
Poverty rate (in %)[2]	26.8	21.9	20.4	16.4	12.6	10.5	8.6	n/a

Table 16: Chile
GDP after the introduction of a robust unemployment insurance system in 2002

	2000	2003	2006	2009	2011	2013	2015	2017
GDP per capita (in US $)	5,101	4,788	9,485	10,243	14,706	15,941	13,737	15,346
Poverty rate (in %)[1]	4.4	4.2	2.4	2.6	1.6	0.9	1.3	0.7
Poverty rate (in %)[2]	36	35.4	29.6	25.3	22.2	14.4	11.7	8.6

[1] According to the World Bank definition (data is not available for all years)
[2] According to national standards (data is not available for all years, significantly higher thresholds)
Source: World Bank, national authorities, own research

As mentioned above, other factors have always contributed to this development, including market-economy reforms, economic surges, demographic dividends and new trade agreements. And we know the difference between causality and correlation. But in view of the astonishing parallels, we believe that this isn't a matter of pure coincidence. The figures, and common sense, suggest that a cleverly designed unemployment benefit reduces poverty rates and unleashes the potential for growth. Thus, they reinforce the fact that entrepreneurs need not fear social reforms.

WAGE INCREASES? RATHER A LITTLE INFLATION THAN A LOT OF POVERTY

However, the introduction or expansion of social security systems can pose major challenges for companies in the short term. After all, they often have to withhold a kind of solidarity levy on wages and then increase it, for example, when official minimum wages become a reality.

For economists with a monetarist orientation, this is a horror scenario. If companies had to raise prices because of higher wages, they argue, this would worsen their competitiveness and destroy jobs. In addition, there is the danger of inflation, which eats up nominal wage increases and has other negative consequences, from misallocations to the devaluation of pension schemes.

This risk cannot be dismissed outright, but to put it bluntly: a little inflation is better than a lot of poverty.

In addition, the risk can be minimized if unemployment benefits and wages are raised gradually so that prices do not rise too quickly and become too high. The good news in this context is that the higher costs do not usually translate 1:1 into a surge in inflation, because the average workload of companies increases. This is because social benefits and higher wages strengthen domestic demand and willingness to invest. We have already referred to Henry Ford's fitting remark about how important it is that his workers can also afford a car. There is a quote from Robert Bosch that perhaps sums up this connection even more aptly: "I don't pay good wages because I have a lot of money. I have a lot of money because I pay good wages."

DIGITIZATION PUTS AN END TO THE LOW-WAGE STRATEGY

Underlying the skepticism about rising wages is often the idea that Africa, like once China, must become the outsourcing backyard of the industrialized countries and attract foreign companies with low personnel costs. However, anyone who believes that African countries could increase their competitiveness through wage undercutting is not taking digitization into consideration. Many companies in the industrialized countries have been having other ideas for a while; more and more businesses are investing in connected and automated production facilities at home, where intelligent robots and machines do most of the work, and often at an even lower cost (apart from the initial investment) than the workers in the Far East.

"Digitization is leading some countries to cut back on their offshoring activities and bring back some of their production from abroad," Professor Enzo Weber from the Institute for Employment Research told the *WirtschaftsWoche* recently. Digitization has therefore "so far had predominantly negative effects" for emerging markets.

The Covid-19 crisis has further strengthened the trend towards deglobalization and the shortening of supply chains. There is a growing danger that companies from industrialized countries will be held accountable for poor working conditions at suppliers in emerging and developing countries. This is illustrated, for example, by the lawsuit filed by four Pakistanis who demanded compensation from the German textile discounter Kik for the death of their relatives in a factory fire. Not forgetting the ongoing debate about the supply chain law which is not yet concluded and could lead to strict legal requirements, regardless of any actual shortcomings.

It is therefore not surprising that labor cost advantages often take a back seat when choosing business locations abroad. From an African perspective, this is also an argument against relying exclusively on low-wage strategies in attracting international businesses. On the contrary, it would be short-sighted if states were to hastily put their faith in attracting international corporations by offering low wage levels.

EMERGING MARKETS: GROWTH IN EXPORTS DESPITE HIGHER WAGES

A closer look at export statistics confirms the fact that wage increases need not unduly burden the competitiveness of an economy. Take Vietnam for example, where both the average wage and the minimum wage have risen significantly since the late 1990s. Nevertheless, exports have increased. In Thailand and Chile too, exports have been rising along with wages for a long time:

Figure 15: Vietnam

Development of wages and exports (indexed values)

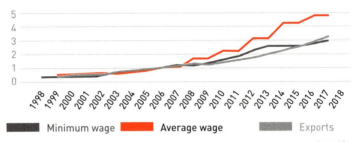

Source: World Bank, Vietnam Institute for Economic and Policy Research (VEPR), own research

Figure 16: Thailand

Development of wages and exports (indexed values)

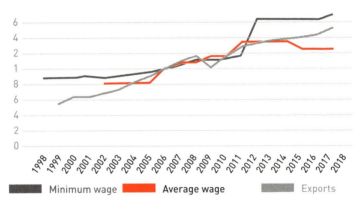

Source: World Bank, Thailand Development Research Institute, Bank of Thailand, national authorities

A comparison of minimum wages and GDP per capita shows a similar picture: per capita economic output has risen more strongly in Vietnam and Thailand than the minimum wage in each country, and a similar trend was observed in Chile. So these

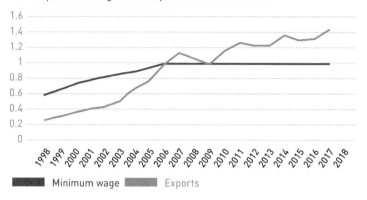

Figure 17: Chile
Development of wages and exports (indexed values)

Source: ILO, World Bank, own research

figures also suggest that social reforms are not an obstacle to growth—on the contrary.

WHAT MAKES A GOOD UNEMPLOYMENT BENEFIT
However, the introduction of unemployment benefits does not automatically unleash economic growth by any means. A look back at German history shows this too. The first attempt failed: when the Reichsanstalt für Arbeitsvermittlung und Arbeitslosenversicherung (Imperial Institute for Employment and Unemployment Insurance) was founded in 1927, it was already too late. A short time later, the Great Depression struck, which is why the predecessor of the Bundesarbeitsagentur (Federal Employment Agency) was chronically underfinanced and was unable to have any impact. Contrary to what many believe, Chancellor Otto von Bismarck did indeed introduce statutory health, accident and pension insurance in the 1880s, but not unemployment benefit. This did not exist until 1918, and until the Reich assumed responsibility for it in 1927, it was the responsibility of the municipalities, which often found themselves overwhelmed with this task.

So what does an effective unemployment benefit system look like? How much should the initial contribution be? Should it be a tax-financed basic social security benefit system, similar to the German Hartz IV (unemployment benefit paid after the first 12-18 months of unemployment), or a classic unemployment insurance based on contributions from employees and employers? Or a combination of both? And which contract terms and sanctions make sense? Specific concepts cannot be developed on the drawing board, but only in the country itself. After all, the answers to the questions mentioned above and many more, depend on the specific framework conditions, and these differ profoundly in the various African countries.

We therefore cannot propose "one size fits all" solutions. Especially because this practice, which sometimes turns into a know-it-all and patronizing attitude, has led to the failure of many a well-intended development cooperation project. One thing can be said however: it will not be sufficient to introduce or expand a contribution-based unemployment insurance scheme in most countries. After all, according to the ILO, only just under 15 percent of the workforce in Africa are classic employees. Most of them work as day laborers who are officially self-employed or not registered as workers at all.

Figure 18: Continent of day laborers

Only a small amount of workers in Africa are classic workers (share in %)

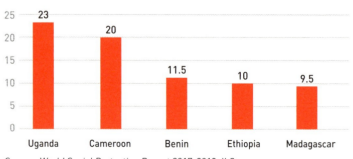

Source: World Social Protection Report 2017-2019, ILO

Classic unemployment insurance does not help these workers if they become unemployed, and this is also the main drawback of most existing systems: they apply predominantly only to workers who were previously in fixed employment.

BASIC SECURITY BENEFITS ACCORDING TO THE PRINCIPLE "SUPPORT AND CHALLENGE"

Thus it is quite clear: as a general rule, we (also) need a kind of conditional basic security benefit system for people who have not paid into a social security fund anywhere. By this however, we do not mean an "unconditional basic income" as is currently being discussed in industrialized countries. Instead, we advocate the principle of "support and challenge" and recommend that the payment of basic security benefits be linked to clear criteria.

A possible model could be, to some extent, the *Bolsa Familia* program that was introduced in Brazil in 2003. Payments to the poor are linked to numerous conditions. Pregnant women, for example, have to attend preventative medical checkups and classes on topics such as breastfeeding and healthy eating. In addition, families have to send their children to school and ensure that they attend at least 85 percent of the lessons.

It also seems important to us that people who are able to work should actually look for a job. However, this leads to a tricky question: How strict do the criteria have to be for people to have an alternative to undignified work on the one hand, yet an incentive is not created for people to do nothing at the expense of the general public on the other? Resolving this issue is anything but trivial. But here, too, the same holds true that only those in positions of responsibility in Africa can find the right balance. That is why we Europeans must not define the exact models when we support and promote the development of social security systems. Instead, we must give partner states scope to use tailor-made solutions, and observe whether these work or not.

CASH TRANSFERS: A GOOD BASIS FOR THE NEXT STEP
It is also important to be open to other instruments. One interesting model is the so-called *Social Cash Transfer Program*, which is supported by the German Development Ministry in Malawi. The payments are targeted at the most needy; recently over 63,000 households with around 310,000 people benefited. The transfer payments are linked to certain criteria such as income, household assets and the number of children.

Experience was gained in setting up a social security agency in the course of the project, especially in regard to identifying eligible beneficiaries, the payment procedure and complaint management. At the same time, the Malawian Court of Audit was strengthened to ensure the program was monitored effectively according to the BMZ.

The project in Malawi is an example that shows that a lot can be achieved with a small amount of money in development aid. The BMZ points out the fact that external evaluations have shown that the program has significantly improved the living conditions of a large number of people. Families that receive the social cash transfers eat more regularly. Their children go to school longer and are healthier, and there are fewer teenage pregnancies. The funding not only alleviates the situation of those with the greatest hardship, but also improves their prospects so they are able to move forward under their own steam—helping people to help themselves with the best of intentions. This should be an incentive to expand cash transfer systems step by step to make them comprehensive social security systems.

In addition to cash transfers, Malawi has launched other initiatives within the framework of the Malawian *National Social Support Program* (MNSSP), including public work programs for the unemployed and microcredits for start-ups and the self-employed. The country has also launched the *Economic Empowerment Pilot Project,* again with German support. It provides one-off payments to small entrepreneurs and to the founders of local cooperatives so that people can save together and loans can be granted to the members of the cooperatives. The results were promising, especially when small entrepreneurs were given training as well, for then the number of people who used these payments for productive investments increased.

The successes in Malawi prove two things: In many places, it has been recognized that social security systems are the decisive tool in the fight against poverty and hunger. Secondly, there has been considerable progress in development aid. Based on many years of experience, funds are increasingly being used for specific purposes and experts are monitoring the effects very closely in order to readjust the programs if necessary or to try out new approaches. This shows, for example, in the detailed evaluations of the Malawi project.

So the time has come to shift up a gear. Thanks to the experience and skills of development economists and local leaders, promising new approaches can be turned into comprehensive state social programs, which should initially focus on robust unemployment benefits.

IMPORTANT: FEWER DAY LABORERS, MORE EMPLOYEES

In addition to setting up a basic social security system, it is important to move as many people as possible from false self-employment and working on the black market into the official labor market and thus under the scope of a classic unemployment insurance. This should become a central task of the financial and labor authorities, which many African states are currently establishing and expanding, partly with German assistance as part of the Marshall Plan with Africa.

It is necessary to provide positive incentives in addition to checks and controls. And taking a look to the south of the continent shows that there are powerful instruments available: South

Africa's *Broad-Based Black Economic Empowerment Program* (B-BBEE) has created strong incentives for companies to hire, train, and support employees with a dark skin color and for them even to become shareholders. A *scorecard* is used as part of the program to assess how a company performs in each area in detail. Those with too few points will not receive any contracts from the state; in addition, many customers pay attention to the B-BBEE score.

We do not want to enter into discussions of whether and to what extent the program discriminates against "whites" at this point, and certainly do not advise applying the model directly to other countries. However, the central idea of making government procurement dependent on compliance with certain standards has the potential to encourage companies to officially hire more people. In addition, governments can offer further benefits to companies with a high proportion of formal employees. These include, for example, easier access to development loans.

KEY STATEMENT 6

Fair wages and social reforms lower birth rates, and trigger an "upward spiral"

If it is possible to increase the average income of the poor through fair wages and social benefits, an "upward spiral" is triggered, for when per capita income rises, the birth rate falls, until at some point the population stops growing. This would give Africa a "demographic dividend," just as once was the case in the Asian powerhouses.

Rates have considerable disadvantages, a fall in birth rates offers tremendous opportunities for individual women and society as a whole. For example, the proportion of women who work is growing, which, according to the Berlin Institute for Population and Development, can trigger a "jump in national income." More-over, in the medium term, youth unemployment will fall because few young people will gradually enter the labor market. Experts speak of a demographic dividend in this context. However, the income of the poor must rise for birth rates to fall and for an upward spiral to emerge. "The number of children born always falls when people's living conditions improve," write the researchers from the Berlin Institute in their recent study *Africa's Demographic Trailblazers*.

To illustrate this connection, we have selected three emerging markets in which population growth has come to a standstill. The figures from the World Bank and the national statistics offices each show impressively that the per capita gross domestic product has risen sharply in the same period:

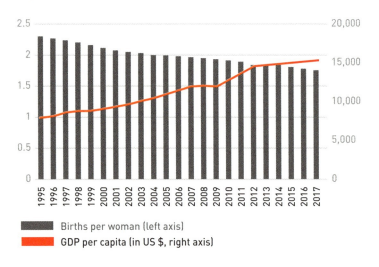

Figure 19: Chile

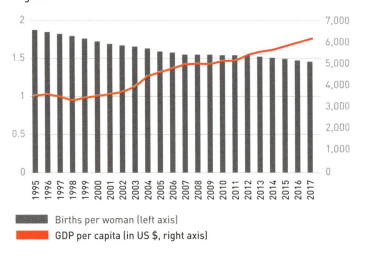

Figure 20: Thailand

Figure 21: Vietnam

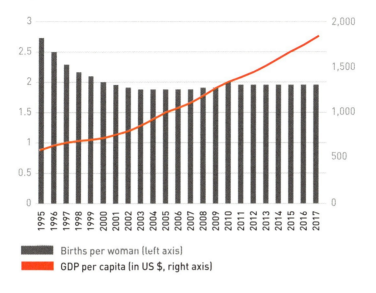

Births per woman (left axis)
GDP per capita (in US $, right axis)

SOCIAL BENEFITS, LOWER BIRTH RATES

Scientific studies suggest that the introduction of robust social security systems has fueled this development. In their statistical analysis *Fertility and Social Security* from 2015, economists from the USA and the United Kingdom came to the conclusion that an increase in state social security benefits of 10 percent of GDP in the USA and Europe would be accompanied by a reduction in the birth rate of between 0.7 and 1.6 children per woman.

Admittedly, the analysis focuses on state pension systems, as those who can rely on receiving a pension can have fewer children to be secure in old age. Unemployment benefits can also increase planning security, and as we have already mentioned, they have a secondary effect which is often underestimated: they improve the negotiating position of employees and thus help to establish minimum wages. In doing so, they promote an effect that the Berlin Institute considers crucial to reducing birth rates in Africa. It is urgently necessary to create "formal and more productive" jobs. Here again, we must stress that jobs alone are not enough; people must also be officially employed and paid a decent wage.

THE CRITICAL THRESHOLD: TWO CHILDREN FOR EACH WOMAN
How much prosperity is needed to trigger an upward spiral? Here, a look at countries that have had a "democratic dividend" in recent decades can provide some revealing clues. According to the Berlin Institute, this group includes "the Asian powerhouses of Taiwan, South Korea, Malaysia, Thailand and Indonesia." In many other emerging and developing countries too, the birth rate is approaching the critical threshold of two children per woman, under which the population stops growing. The birth rate has already fallen below the threshold in many places (see Table 17, pp. 146/147).

The picture in Africa is still different. Even the seven countries that the Berlin Institute classifies as "Africa's demographic trailblazers" in its study have far higher birth rates (see Table 18, pp. 148/149).

There are obvious differences: it is difficult to predict what level of GDP per capita is required for the birth rate to drop to the decisive value of two children per woman because of cultural differences, not to mention conversion problems between different currencies. Poor Nepal, for example, is already approaching this value with an economic output of $2,702 per capita, while Kenya and Senegal are only just below the birth rate of four children per woman despite higher prosperity.

This is confirmed by experts who assume that birth rates in many African countries will not fall as sharply as on other continents as per capita incomes rise. Nevertheless, the correlation is also clear in Africa. If per capita income increases, birth rates fall, until at some point the population stops growing. And higher social benefits can massively accelerate this development.

THE FIRST TARGET: 300 DOLLARS PER MONTH

In our opinion, the first target in the poorest countries should be a per capita income in the order of about $300 per month. Statistics show that the magic birth rate of two children per woman will then be reached or is within reach in many countries, and population growth will come to a standstill.

Let us take Ethiopia as an example: with a per capita GDP of around $1,000, Ethiopia had a birth rate of five children per woman; at just under $2,000, it was four. If this development continues, the magic threshold of two children per woman should be achieved at $4,000. A first step in the right direction would be a minimum wage of $1 an hour, accompanied by the robust unemployment benefit we are proposing and in real life, not just on paper! Depending on the working hours, this would amount to $200 to $300 per month and would significantly raise the average income level in many places.

Table 17: When it's time

At what GDP per capita* does population growth come to a standstill because the birth rate drops to around two children per woman?

	Bangladesh		Brazil		Chile		Costa Rica		Jamaica	
	Birth rate	GDP p. capita	Birth rate	GDP p. capita	Birth rate	GDP p. capita	Birth rate	GDP p. capita	Birth rate	GDP p. capita
2000	3.17	1,301	2.30	9,011	2.11	9,603	2.37	7,828	2.58	6,
2001	3.07	1,372	2.23	9,215	2.07	10,019	2.29	8,138	2.53	6,
2002	2.97	1,420	2.16	9,513	2.05	10,373	2.22	8,395	2.48	6,
2003	2.88	1,491	2.10	9,688	**2.02**	**10,876**	2.16	8,791	2.44	6,
2004	2.78	1,586	**2.03**	**10,399**	2.00	11,843	2.11	9,287	2.40	7
2005	2.69	1,718	1.98	10,949	1.98	12,775	2.07	9,815	2.36	7
2006	2.60	1,864	1.93	11,602	1.96	15,787	**2.03**	**10,695**	2.33	7
2007	2.52	2,024	1.88	12,501	1.95	16,981	2.01	11,711	2.29	8
2008	2.45	2,163	1.85	13,260	1.93	16,548	1.98	12,327	2.25	8
2009	2.38	2,264	1.82	13,212	1.90	16,214	1.95	12,139	2.21	7
2010	2.33	2,393	1.81	14,242	1.88	18,236	1.92	12,734	2.17	7
2011	2.28	2,571	1.79	14,973	1.86	20,438	1.89	13,397	2.14	8
2012	2.24	2,758	1.78	15,408	1.83	21,620	1.87	14,144	2.10	8
2013	2.20	2,941	1.77	16,002	1.82	22,579	1.84	14,555	2.07	8
2014	2.17	3,142	1.75	16,242	1.80	22,978	1.82	15,187	2.05	8
2015	2.13	3,346	1.74	15,699	1.79	22,960	1.80	15,741	**2.03**	8
2016	2.10	3,584	1.73	15,222	1.77	23,228	1.78	16,420	2.01	8
2017	**2.08**	**3,877**	1.71	15,553	1.77	24,747	1.77	17,110	1.99	

* GDP per capita with the application of purchasing power parity (in current international dollars)

Colombia		Libanon		Nepal		Sri Lanka		Vietnam	
Birth rate	GDP p. capita	Birth rate	GDP p. capita	Birth rate	GDP p. capita	Birth rate	GDP p. capita	Birth rate	GDP p. capita
39	6,539	2.23	9,993	4.03	1,220.1	2.24	4,392	**2.01**	**2,030**
35	6,703	2.13	10,220	3.88	1,285.1	2.25	4,392	1.95	2,182
31	6,879	**2.04**	**10,235**	3.72	1,284.8	2.26	4,600	1.92	2,332
27	7,191	1.94	10,256	3.58	1,341.2	2.27	4,930	1.90	2,518
24	7,678	1.84	10,733	3.43	1,422.1	2.28	5,298	1.89	2,757
20	8,191	1.75	11,030	3.29	1,499.4	2.28	5,765	1.89	3,032
16	8,901	1.68	11,361	3.15	1,578.9	2.28	6,350	1.90	3,312
12	9,646	1.63	12,662	3.01	1,658.7	2.27	6,913	1.91	3,609
08	10,036	1.60	14,020	2.87	1,776.8	2.26	7,418	1.92	3,851
04	**10,118**	1.60	15,279	2.74	1,852.9	2.23	7,689	1.94	4,050
01	10,570	1.61	16,115	2.61	1,945.3	2.20	8,355	1.95	4,318
8	11,464	1.64	15,694	2.49	2,031.1	2.17	9,193	1.95	4,633
5	12,016	1.67	15,345	2.38	2,143.7	2.14	10,171	1.96	4,914
2	12,661	1.70	14,936	2.29	2,244.2	2.11	10,618	1.96	5,211
0	13,384	1.71	14,612	2.22	2,394.6	2.08	11,250	1.96	5,563
7	13,801	1.72	14,176	2.16	2,471.6	2.06	11,833	1.96	5,932
5	14,101	1.72	14,204	2.12	2,485.0	2.05	12,357	1.95	6,303
3	14,503	1.71	14,513	**2.08**	**2,702.4**	**2.03**	**12,863**	1.95	6,790

Source: World Bank (https://data.worldbank.org, accessed 2020), own research

Table 18: Africa's trailblazers
How GDP per capita* and birth rates are developing in successful African countries

	Ethiopia		Botswana		Ghana	
	Birth rate	GDP p. capita	Birth rate	GDP p. capita	Birth rate	GDP p. capita
2000	6.52	490	3.39	8,076	4.83	1,790
2001	6.38	527	3.29	8,155	4.75	1,857
2002	6.22	528	3.19	8,659	4.68	1,920
2003	6.04	512	3.11	9,116	4.61	2,008
2004	5.87	581	3.04	9,488	4.55	2,123
2005	5.69	652	2.99	10,094	4.49	2,260
2006	5.52	725	2.95	11,104	4.44	2,415
2007	5.36	807	2.92	12,148	4.39	2,520
2008	5.20	888	2.90	12,944	4.35	2,733
2009	5.06	948	2.89	11,841	4.31	2,814
2010	4.92	1,052	2.88	12,786	4.27	2,997
2011	4.80	1,163	2.88	13,596	4.23	3,404
2012	4.68	1,254	2.86	14,211	4.19	3,702
2013	4.56	1,375	2.84	15,805	4.15	3,948
2014	4.44	1,505	2.81	16,462	4.10	4,045
2015	4.32	1,637	2.77	16,055	4.04	4,083
2016	4.20	1,736	2.73	16,622	3.98	4,176
2017	4.08	1,903	2.68	17,024	3.93	4,502

* GDP per capita with the application of purchasing power parity (in current international dollars)

Kenya		Morocco		Senegal		Tunisia	
Birth rate	GDP p. capita	Birth rate	GDP p. capita	Birth rate	GDP p. capita	Birth rate	GDP p. capita
5.18	1,690	2.78	3,553	5.47	1,899	2.14	6,002
5.11	1,745	2.72	3,853	5.39	1,981	2.09	6,315
5.04	1,734	2.68	3,986	5.31	1,974	2.05	6,445
4.98	1,771	2.64	4,257	5.25	2,093	2.02	6,831
4.91	1,861	2.61	4,530	5.20	2,217	2.00	7,398
4.84	1,980	2.59	4,773	5.16	2,354	1.99	7,836
4.76	2,114	2.57	5,231	5.13	2,420	2.00	8,422
4.68	2,256	2.56	5,495	5.11	2,538	2.02	9,135
4.58	2,243	2.56	5,865	5.10	2,619	2.06	9,607
4.48	2,271	2.57	6,085	5.08	2,620	2.10	9,866
4.37	2,425	2.58	6,311	5.06	2,669	2.14	10,223
4.27	2,557	2.58	6,688	5.04	2,684	2.18	10,121
4.17	2,652	2.58	6,922	5.00	2,791	2.21	10,604
4.07	2,782	2.57	7,255	4.96	2,834	2.23	10,971
3.99	2,909	2.56	7,480	4.90	2,989	2.23	11,377
3.92	3,029	2.53	7,792	4.84	3,121	2.22	11,498
3.85	3,160	2.49	7,858	4.77	3,257	2.20	11,619
3.79	3,292	2.45	8,225	4.70	3,458	2.18	11,936

Source: World Bank (https://data.worldbank.org), Africa's Demographic Trailblazers: How falling fertility rates accelerate development (2019), Berlin Institute for Population and Development, own research

KEY STATEMENT 7

Socio-ecological market economy: The world is ready for "prosperity for all"

A strong economic boom in Africa could massively aggravate the climate crisis due to the increase in energy consumption. However, this conflict of objectives can be overcome thanks to new green technology. Prosperity for all is possible without destroying the very foundations of our existence. Africa must consistently focus on green tech and renewable energy to achieve this, with our support. The Covid-19 economic stimulus packages offer a unique opportunity to do so.

There is no question that time is running out in the fight against global warming. The new EU Commission President Ursula von der Leyen now wants to set the right course with her *Green Deal* and mobilize €1 trillion for climate-friendly projects via the European Investment Bank (EIB). However, there are justified doubts as to whether our ecological footprint will be substantially smaller in the foreseeable future because most industrialized countries have made only very limited progress so far. What's more, if we now succeed together to overcome poverty in Africa with the help of the *European Economic Model* and release forces that drive growth, this could accelerate global warming even further. This raises the question of whether our planet can afford prosperity for all. Or will success in the fight against poverty inevitably lead to additional greenhouse emissions? That would undermine these successes just as much as the efforts of the industrialized countries to finally save CO_2 effectively.

We will return to the question in a moment; first, however, we must take note of two things: Firstly, us drivers, frequent fliers and energy wasters from industrialized countries have so far benefited from the fact that many Africans are unwillingly protecting the climate because they can afford neither a car nor an electricity connection, not to mention vacation flights. Minister Müller noted in this context that "the richest 10 percent of the world cause 50 percent of all CO_2 emissions."

Secondly, the people who suffer the most from our way of life and our hesitation to fight against the climate crisis in many places are the people in poor countries, i.e. those who cause the lowest emissions. They are losing their livelihoods due to climate change, which they have played little part in creating. According to the German federal government, around 20 million people are already affected in the Sahel zone which borders on the Sahara in the south.

1,000 COAL-FIRED POWER STATIONS FOR AFRICA?

Let's get back to the question of the ecological consequences of "prosperity for all": the dangers of the desired economic boom cannot be denied. Currently, 600 million Africans are not connected to the electricity grid. "If every African household gets a coal-powered electricity connection in the future, 1,000 new coal-fired power plants would have to be built," Minister Müller warned in an interview in 2018, adding, "We can only persuade Africans to give up coal if we support them in building climate-friendly, future-proof technologies."

The good news, however, is that we could resolve the supposed conflict between poverty reduction and climate protection, or between social and ecological goals, because the earth is able to sustain "prosperity for all" thanks to environmentally and climate-friendly technologies, especially in the field of renewable energy, and with an eye on green hydrogen.

In June 2020, the International Energy Agency (EIA) presented a *Sustainable Recovery Plan*, which its experts had developed together with the IMF. The clear message is that if governments set the right course now, they can lay the foundations for sustainable, climate-friendly growth. The Covid-19 economic stimulus packages therefore contain the "unique opportunity" worldwide to kill two birds with one stone: to boost the economy and at the same time, restructure it. The experts emphasize that the costs of clean technologies are much lower today than after the financial crisis.

Developing countries in particular should benefit from the required investments in renewable energy, low-emission transportation, energy-efficient buildings and climate innovations. The *Sustainable Recovery Plan* is intended to accelerate economic growth by around 1.3 percentage points per year, supply 420 million people with "clean cooking solutions" and connect a further 270 million people to the energy grid.

HUGE OPPORTUNITY FOR THE "SUNNY CONTINENT"

The promotion of solar power is rightly already a central component of the German government's Marshall Plan with Africa. "The solar continent of Africa has the opportunity to massively expand its energy supply on the basis of renewable energy without a detour to environmentally harmful technology—directly future-proof, sustainable and cost-effective," a BMZ paper states.

This is true, and underlines the fact that, as in the fight against poverty, Africa and Europe have identical interests in renewable energy. Africa can make its economy fit for the future and take a shortcut to a secured and sustainable energy supply. In addition, renewable energy has a great export potential, especially in the form of green hydrogen.

The German Federal Government is therefore justified in focusing on Africa in particular in its new hydrogen strategy.

It is indeed possible that social and ecological progress can be mutually supportive. In this context, it is worth taking a look at the environmental Kuznets curve, an environmental and economic curve that shows how increasing prosperity benefits nature. In simple terms, the message is that those who have enough to eat are more concerned about the environment and the climate. If developing countries succeed in becoming emerging economies, nature and climate protection will therefore move higher up the agenda. China, for example, has been pursuing its economic growth for decades without regard for its natural resources. But in recent years, a change in thinking has set in, because the basic needs of many people have been met and the negative consequences of the over-exploitation of nature are becoming increasingly visible. However, the environmental Kuznets curve is controversial because its shape varies greatly from country to country. It is therefore difficult to predict at what income level environmental degradation will start to decline. Critics also dislike that the curve suggests an inevitability.

THE MARSHALL PLAN AS A TOOL TO STOP CLIMATE CHANGE
In order to speed things up in Africa, Germany wants to provide strong support for the development of renewable energy systems in accordance with the Marshall principle of "support and challenge." The German government has announced that it will "raise private capital for the modernization and transformation of the energy sector," "make a concerted effort to share the experience gained from the *Energiewende* (transition to a low-carbon energy supply) for the expansion of renewable energy sources" and "expand incentive systems for the development of decentralized energy solutions in rural areas."

These are not empty promises. [Germany's] reform partner Ghana has drafted a Renewable Energy Law, which is intended to increase the share of renewable energy to more than 10 percent. In return, Ghana will receive not only know-how, but also low-interest loans from Germany. The reform partners Côte d'Ivoire, Senegal and Morocco are also focusing strongly on solar energy. For example, the world's largest solar power plant is being built in Morocco with German support, which will supply electricity to 13 million people. This plant will also help to produce climate-neutral fuels, including methanol from green hydrogen. Africa could thus play an important role in making the transport sector more climate-friendly.

In view of better and cheaper technologies and many years of experience, the German government is counting on being faster and better this time than with previous ambitious energy export projects.

SUSTAINABLE PACKAGING, INNOVATIVE AGRICULTURE
Berlin is already using the Marshall Plan as a tool to advance the fight against climate change. This is right and can be developed further. After all, new technologies have huge potential not only in terms of supplying energy, but also, for example, in the disposal of waste. There are innovative concepts and technologies here too that significantly reduce the volume of waste and the associated logistics, and in this way we can also save resources. We know what we're talking about: the Schoeller Group has many years of experience in this field (see By the way on p. 156).

Anyone who reads up on Africa will quickly find out that there are projects everywhere on the continent whose initiators, be they foundations, development aid organizations or private companies, are testing new ideas and technologies to solve fundamental problems. Often they receive important support from state economic development agencies.

Technical progress will make an important contribution to the fight against hunger and global warming. Fatalism is completely out of place here. On the contrary: despite all of the obstacles, we believe there is a good chance that there will be more and more of these rays of hope that will gradually brighten up the overall picture.

Many countries in Africa have the unique opportunity to skip several stages of development and build a sustainable economy, whether it be based on energy supply, mobility, agriculture or recycling. From garden hoses to sensor-controlled irrigation systems, from wood stoves to solar systems, from vintage trucks to electric vehicles—the possibilities are endless and the potential is enormous.

BY THE WAY: FAIR TRADE AND VALUE CREATION
The Schoeller Group has been intensively involved in sustainable packaging logistics for many years and has made great technological progress in this area. The subsidiary Schoeller Allibert produces durable and reusable plastic packaging such as beverage crates and transport containers. Schoeller Allibert is already active in 50 countries and is the European market leader.

With its Desert Food Foundation, the Schoeller family are also focusing on technological innovations for African agriculture: modern desalination plants can play an important role in dry regions to improve the water supply for people and agriculture.

This is shown by a project that the Desert Food Foundation started in 2015 in Kenya's poorest region on the western shore of Lake Turkana. This lake, which was formerly known as Lake Rudolf, is already severely affected by climate change; due to increasing drought, more and more water is evaporating, which not only leads to siltation, as has already been mentioned, but also to salinization of the lake. This is a catastrophe for the region because climate change is thus not only affecting fishing but also agriculture, which needs the water to irrigate the fields.

The foundation has therefore founded an innovative agricultural business in Nariokotome Anam on around 10,000 square meters of arable land. The centerpiece of the farm is a state-of-the-art reverse osmosis plant that runs on solar energy and desalinizes the lake water. It produces 30,000 liters of fresh water every day.

The pilot farm provides more than ten families with jobs. The employees receive agricultural training. The guiding principle is helping people to help themselves. The farm now supplies the entire village of more than 300 families with drinking water and food (further information further information at: www.desertfood.org).

THE ECOLOGICAL, SOCIAL AND DIGITAL MARKET ECONOMY

In terms of digital transformation, Africa can also skip several stages and directly build a sustainable digital infrastructure. While we have to upgrade outdated networks and face a number of problems in the process, Africa can directly benefit from the latest technology, it can accelerate from zero to a hundred, so to speak. In Nigeria, for example, mobile payment has long been the norm. And in Kenya, M-Pesa was a payment system for cell phones, long before Apple Pay was launched in the USA. It is often easier to start from scratch than to rebuild and remodel.

This digital transformation not only increases productivity, but also promotes innovation and thus unleashes additional forces for growth. For companies, including those from Europe, this is a huge opportunity, especially because the populations of many African countries are young and digitally-savvy. Once the first hurdles have been overcome, many African countries could catch up more quickly than seems conceivable today, with all the associated benefits for people in Africa, Europe and the rest of the world.

And before you all cry out that we are naive: at the beginning of the 1990s, who would have expected that the Asian powerhouses and China would experience such a rapid boom? At that time, everyone was looking to Japan—the Asian mainland was seen by many as a hopeless case. And who would have thought that the former Soviet Republic of Estonia would become a model digital state?

Let us be clear: it is not only necessary but also possible to combat climate change and poverty at the same time, because new technologies can help resolve the conflict of competing objectives. What's more, successes can be mutually beneficial, and happen in the foreseeable future. Europe can provide the decisive impetus for this, within the framework of genuine partnerships and with a paradigm shift in Africa policy.

SO, LET'S GET TO WORK!

SECTION III
THE AGENDA

Europe can demand and support reform – and spark change

Reform-minded countries in Africa need our support: Europe can make a decisive contribution to an economic upswing that also benefits the poor. For this we need an entirely new Africa policy—and we need it now, because the timing is better than ever.

With our Agenda for Africa, we propose to demand and support reforms in line with the social market economy using three powerful tools. Germany and the EU should…

…**promote infrastructure** investment in Africa with the aim of building a European Silk Road. Infrastructure is the foundation on which a country's economy prospers, and its expansion can provide the initial spark for entrepreneurial investment and the economic reconstruction of Africa.

…**agree fair trade deals** that focus, above all, on poverty reduction rather than trade maximization. Europe must no longer relegate Africa to a mere supplier of raw materials.

…**expand development aid** for reform-minded countries and make it more efficient. The German government's paradigm shift, linking assistance to reforms, is positive, but the policy must be consistently pursued. We are therefore advocating for an upgraded Marshall Plan.

With these three tools, Europe can kick-start an investment and economic boom, while promoting sustainable, inclusive growth. We want to do this by linking support in all three areas to social reforms, so that growth finally benefits the poor.

The focus here is on building up basic social security and unemployment benefit systems in order to change the balance of power in the labor market and establish minimum wages that are not just agreed to on paper. As we explained in the previous sections, the incomes of the poor then also rise, leading to falling birth rates and triggering an upward spiral (the "demographic dividend"). A per capita income of around $300 per month is an important threshold in this respect, because after this is achieved the population often stops growing.

The timing is more favorable than ever, because low interest rates offer a once-in-a-lifetime opportunity to mobilize capital for the development of our neighboring continent. The ongoing renegotiation of the EU-Africa Pact could therefore usher in a new era.

What is particularly important to us: our agenda is not mere theory. It has been developed in close consultation with numerous political decision-makers and experts on both continents. It is based on knowledge that has matured in practice, and on instruments and institutions that already exist, but which have not (yet) come close to realizing their full potential.

TOOL 1

Infrastructure financing – Let's build a European Silk Road to Africa!

Infrastructure is the key prerequisite for entrepreneurial commitment, inclusive growth and broad-based prosperity. With an intelligent approach to financing, Europe can mobilize capital for investment and make change happen.

The German government wants to encourage German entrepreneurs to invest in Africa with the help of new incentive schemes. However, the results have so far been negligible and we fear that it will stay that way. Because even where corruption is being successfully combated, there is a major obstacle: poor infrastructure. It is clear that Africa needs an infrastructure offensive as a first step and to spark change.

We propose that Europe mobilize €1 trillion within a decade for infrastructure programs in reform-minded African countries. In our view, this is the most powerful tool with which to export the social market economy to Africa. In light of low interest rates, we have a once-in-a-lifetime opportunity to use European investment capital to fuel African development and usher in an end to poverty. After all, infrastructure policy is also social policy; according to the African Development Bank, there is strong evidence that investment in infrastructure promotes inclusive growth and reduces inequality.

In our view, public investment in roads, railways, communications, energy and water networks must be a central goal. Building up these networks is not only one of the core tasks of the state, but also forms the basis for private entrepreneurial commitment. As anyone who has followed the rise of China will know, it all began with increased state investment in infrastructure.

INFRASTRUCTURE BOOSTS PRODUCTIVITY

Infrastructure is the platform, so to speak, on which a social market economy with rules and standards can flourish. Especially since such investments do more than just improve the economic environment. They can also effectively pave the way for fair wages in two key respects. First, states can demand high social standards of construction companies and other contractors, including fair pay, official employment contracts and good working conditions.

Secondly, better infrastructure increases economic productivity, thereby creating scope for wage increases. Infrastructural deficits in sub-Saharan Africa depress productivity by a whopping 40 percent, costing 2 percent economic growth annually, notes the *Gesellschaft für Internationale Zusammenarbeit* (German Corporation for International Cooperation, GIZ) in a recent project outline called Improving Infrastructure in Africa.

However, in view of their empty coffers, governments in developing countries generally do not have the scope to fund such projects from their own resources. It is estimated that there is an annual funding gap of up to $108 billion on the continent. This corresponds to almost 100 billion. In the industrialized countries on the other hand, there is plenty of capital. In fact, wealthy citizens are on the lookout for safe yet reasonably profitable investment opportunities when interest rates are low. According to a study by the direct bank ING-DiBa, German savers alone are hoarding €253 billion in cash—around €30,000 per citizen. And that amount is likely to have increased due to consumer caution during the Covid-19 crisis. Even higher amounts lie dormant in innumerable savings accounts whose interest rates are now well below inflation.

There are therefore enormous capital reserves that European states and financial institutions can mobilize to provide loans to reform-minded countries in Africa for infrastructure projects, and these loans would come with lower interest rates, longer maturities and generally fairer conditions than those offered by Chinese lenders under the Silk Road Initiative. In many cases, guarantees should be sufficient to enable African countries to finance the projects from their own resources. In this way, Europe can put together financing packages that are more attractive to reform-oriented African governments than offers from the Far East, despite them being tied to reforms.

This is a great opportunity to counter China within the context of the competition between political systems and to launch our own infrastructure offensive based on genuine partnerships. However, to do this we need to stop taking half measures in Africa and start thinking big to outshine the Silk Road Initiative. The fact that the EU Commission in January announced that it would mobilize an additional €2 billion for investment in renewable energy, urban infrastructure and start-ups in Africa and the EU neighborhood could, at any event, be a start.

AFRICA BONDS, SOFT LOANS AND REFORMS

Many political decision-makers share this view. In a guest article for the *Handelsblatt* in August 2020, German Federal Minister of Economic Cooperation and Development Gerd Müller and EPP leader Manfred Weber called for a "European investment and development bank" and an "investment and innovation offensive" in Africa.

The European Bank for Restructuring and Development (EBRD) could play a central role in Africa going forward. In our view, it is perfectly placed to grant infrastructure loans with a duration of at least 20 years to reforming countries, in close coordination with the African Union, the development banks on our neighboring continent and the World Bank. To generate the necessary funds they could, for example, issue Africa Bonds.

Alternatively, development banks such as the EBRD could issue guarantees for bonds issued by African governments. Such securities should be met with significant investor interest thanks to current low interest rates, even with interest rates of 1 or 2 percent. And coupling the loans closely with reforms in Africa would at the same time minimize default risks for development banks (and also the risk for European taxpayers, who de facto own these banks).

In other words, if Europe uses its creditworthiness to raise capital market funds via guarantees, we can make a huge difference with modest resources. The infrastructure program we are proposing would, at most, lead to a manageable additional burden on European budgets, for example in the form of debt-financed capital increases for the development banks.

Little by little, we would see results that would also benefit our economy in the long term: as new sales markets emerge in Africa, as flourishing, fair and free trade leads to growing prosperity on both sides, and as we become more independent of the capricious major powers China and the USA.

THE ESM AS A MODEL

Our concept is based in part on the European Stability Mechanism (ESM), which is refinanced with bonds and designed to help heavily indebted eurozone countries with loans or securities. The ESM has proven that the concept of "cash for reforms" works. Certainly, it is open for debate whether the reform requirements imposed on countries such as Greece during the debt crisis were too strict. But the fact is, those countries that received money from the ESM have performed better economically than the eurozone average in recent years.

Compared to hunger and mass deaths in Africa, the EU's financial and debt crisis that resulted in the creation of the ESM was a modest challenge. For Africa, therefore, an entirely new financial architecture creating new opportunities to support the poorest countries is even more appropriate. In the same way that the EU helped Greece to recover from the debt spiral, it could help kick-start an upward spiral in African countries.

THE STRENGTHS OF THE EBRD

While the new EU Commission President Ursula von der Leyen aims to transform the European Investment Bank (EIB) into a climate bank as part of the Green Deal, the above-mentioned EBRD could take the lead in the economic reconstruction of Africa. Why do we consider the EBRD particularly suitable? The bank, which is based in London, was established in 1991 to assist countries in Eastern Europe and the former Soviet Union in their transition to market economies after the fall of the Iron Curtain. It is owned by the EU, the European Investment Bank (EIB) and 69 countries. Europe is the dominant force: 63 percent of the capital comes from EU member states, compared to just 10 percent from the USA. This creates scope to influence the EBRD.

The bank is currently active in 38 countries on three continents, including Egypt, Tunisia and Morocco in Africa. In these locations it generally provides loans for infrastructure projects and to small and medium-sized enterprises, though it sometimes also participates directly via equity investments. It also advises governments of developing and emerging countries on how to transform their economies to create a more business-friendly environment, for example, through greater legal certainty, more effective administrative structures and protection against unfair competition.

As such, the EBRD has been linking investment in infrastructure to reforms for many years, and this experience means that it is tailor-made for our approach.

The German ambassador to Uganda, Albrecht Conze, has already proposed extending the EBRD's mandate, which currently only covers North Africa, to sub-Saharan Africa. Conze notes that the institute is particularly suitable for infrastructure investments because it has already supported a number of countries in "reforming their banks and financial systems, liberalizing pricing, privatizing state enterprises and creating solid legal frameworks for property and land rights," through advice, training and expert knowledge, "all things, incidentally, that the Chinese do not offer".

So the EBRD provides money and practical support, driving forward reforms. Eric Berglöf, Director of the Institute for International Affairs at the London School of Economics and Political Science and former EBRD Chief Economist, also advocates for a reassessment of his former employer: "Europe needs a robust and agile development bank that can cooperate with, but also keep pace with, the Chinese Silk Road Initiative institutions and the newly strengthened US development agencies," he wrote at the end of 2019 in a guest article for *WirtschaftsWoche*. Particular attention should be paid in this endeavor to "the risks and opportunities in Africa".

Until recently, Berglöf was member of a high-level EU expert group that examined the architecture of European development finance. He concluded that because of the connection between its commitments and political reform, the EBRD is "a genuine development bank with a wide range of activities, close dialogue with national governments and a strong presence on the ground," but it is "weak where development needs are greatest—in fragile states and especially in sub-Saharan Africa".

This needs to change. The EBRD could "divest its EU investments and focus instead on the European neighborhood and sub-Saharan Africa," suggested Berglöf, and pointed out that plans for such a move had already been prepared in 2013. In this way, according to Berglöf, the EBRD could be transformed into the "European Bank for Sustainable Development", which would then work together with institutions such as the World Bank,

African Development Bank and national European development institutions, which work in many regions where the EBRD is yet to have a presence.

The EIB could then take over responsibility for commitments in Europe. Unlike the EBRD, it is entirely owned by the EU and has a less pronounced focus on policy reform in developing countries. EIB advisory services are mainly related to concrete projects; it is safe to assume that the general framework conditions will apply within the European Union. This is another reason why a new division of responsibilities makes sense—the EBRD could focus on Africa and leave EU business to the EIB.

Berglöf's proposal also shows that the crucial structures, banks and funding pools already exist, we just need to combine them more efficiently—finally unlocking the huge potential.

Table 19: Development banks and institutions (selection)

Name	Based	Commitments 2019
European Bank for Reconstruction and Development (EBRD)	London	€10.1bn
European Investment Bank (EIB)	Luxembourg	€63.3bn
European Development Fund (EDF)	Brussels	Approx. €4.4bn[1]
German Investment Corp. (DEG, subsidiary of KfW)	Cologne	€1.85bn
African Development Bank Group (ADBG)	Abidjan	Approx. €2.4bn[2]
World Bank	Washington	Approx. €52.7bn

[1] €30.5bn for the period 2014 to 2020
[2] 2017, converted at exchange rate on 3.9.2020
Source: own research

WHY WE SHOULD NOT DEMONIZE DEBT

There is no doubt that the EBRD and other development banks need to be better capitalized for the above-mentioned engagement in Africa. "To increase its lending capacity, the EBRD would need additional capital," says Berglöf. "As only EU shareholders would be likely to contribute, their voting rights would increase." This would facilitate EU influence over the strategy, while retaining a multilateral approach.

Given low interest rates, it would make most sense for the EU or its member states to finance the capital increases with debt. The trick is that capital increases allow banks to grant a significantly larger volume of loans or guarantees, depending on their individual statutes. In this way, Europe could unlock the potential of the capital markets, and with comparatively little effort enable large loans for reform-minded African states. This could even be possible without accruing fresh debt, because financial guarantees are not included as part of the debt calculation under current accounting standards.

In any case, we see no reason to be too concerned about possible new borrowing. In view of historically low interest rates it is pertinent to ask: when, if not now? It should also be remembered that Europe has considerable room to maneuver in this respect; we could take on another $10 trillion before reaching US debt levels.

In any case, increasing numbers of economists warn against demonizing debt. Former IMF chief economist Oliver Blanchard, for instance, has a mantra: "You can use public debt—if you use it properly." And Nobel laureate Paul Krugman, a long-time advocate of Deficit Spending, says only "idiots" still believe that government deficits are a major problem. In fact, the prolonged period of low interest rates makes high debt levels less daunting, because they do not restrict governments' scope for action in the same way as previously (at least in the industrialized countries). Debt also creates wealth, if governments use it to finance roads, utility networks, bridges and other infrastructure projects. Even if it sounds paradoxical, African countries can, to put it crudely, become richer by borrowing from Europe. The prerequisite for this is, of course, that we offer them fair conditions.

On the other hand, if these countries remain reliant on China and are forced to accept less favorable conditions, the risks are high. It is true that sub-Saharan Africa's debt ratios average 60 percent of gross domestic product and are therefore below the level of most industrialized countries. But given low tax revenues, this is no license for carefree borrowing, especially from China. That is why Europe is sought-after as a fair, long-term lender or guarantor, which seeks sustainable partnerships for the common good. We are able to mobilize capital at low interest rates, and we can and should pass on these advantages to reform-minded countries—for our mutual benefit.

THE EUROPEAN CENTRAL BANK AND POVERTY

In this context, we advocate that the ECB be obliged to pay closer attention to global social imbalances, because it could then invest in Africa Bonds if deemed economically sensible by those in charge. We are certainly aware that this risks politicizing the central bank, which could have disastrous long-term consequences, for example in the form of inflation resulting from excessive increases in money supply. At the same time, however, we are convinced that the problem is manageable as long as we only modify objectives and are careful not to compromise the bank's independence.

Moreover, in view of the unimaginable suffering in Africa, we should avoid blindly clinging to economic dogmas. Especially because under former President Mario Draghi, the ECB has managed to debunk some supposed economic truths. For example, despite the doomsayers, its long-held policy of low interest rates caused neither inflation nor a crash. In our view, this is reason enough to question monetarist beliefs and sound out new ways; the possibilities are potentially even greater than we thought.

Discussions are already under way as part of the EU's Green Deal as to whether the ECB should buy green bonds, which the EIB issues to finance climate projects, on a large scale. The Green Deal aims to make Europe climate-neutral by 2050, mainly through investments in renewable energies, eco-efficient buildings and environmentally friendly mobility. The mechanism is similar to our financing concept for the economic reconstruction of Africa. Here, too, the aim is to use the potential of the capital markets to finance important and meaningful investments. The extent to which the ECB, as a major force in the capital market, could effectively support this without forfeiting its independence is worthy of discussion.

BY THE WAY: SECURITY ZONE IN LIBYA, CIVIL WARS IN "SAHELISTAN"

Africa Bonds could also be used to help tackle the refugee crisis. Specifically, this could involve the establishment (in cooperation with the AU) of a security and free trade area in North Africa. One possible location could be the failed state of Libya—though of course only on the basis of a UN mandate and with the consent of relevant local political forces. Within this zone, the EU and AU could jointly invest in port facilities, transport routes, housing, schools, hospitals and more, attracting European companies in the medium-term with tax and customs privileges. This would pave the way for the security zone to become, in the longer term, a vibrant economic and free trade area with high social and economic standards.

There is no doubt that numerous hurdles must be overcome to achieve this goal. But that should not prevent us from discussing it and exploring possibilities, because we would potentially be solving several problems at once: we could eradicate smuggling, protect people from the 'Mediterranean death trap' and arrange for regulated migration to Europe. Those migrants not entitled to asylum could possibly even stay in the security zone and find decent, fairly paid work. We are convinced that the whole region would benefit from such an approach.

It is also clear that a military presence is essential for the stability of any security zone. The EU should therefore be ready to support African partners in this respect, underscoring yet again the need for a European army and a common EU foreign policy worthy of the name. In this context, we should be prepared to support reform-minded African countries, if asked, with military deployments to guarantee security and keep terrorists in check. A European army would be an advantageous fourth tool with which to secure reforms in line with the social market economy.

TOOL 2

Development aid – Why we need an upgraded Marshall Plan

To ensure the poor also benefit widely, we must integrate development cooperation more closely with social reform and infrastructure investments.

It would certainly be wrong to accuse industrialized nations of ignoring Africa after the end of colonial rule. Americans and Europeans, in particular, have spent considerable sums on development aid in recent decades; estimates suggest that up to $2 trillion have flowed into Africa. And the money keeps flowing. According to OECD data (Development Aid at a Glance), industrialized countries and institutions such as the World Bank pay out more than $50 billion every year. But criticism of the present system of development aid has become louder in recent years, especially as statistics show that hundreds of millions of Africans continue to suffer from poverty and hunger.

WHAT HAS CONVENTIONAL DEVELOPMENT AID ACHIEVED?
In an interview with *Handelsblatt* in October 2018, drugstore entrepreneur Dirk Rossmann, who has been active in Africa for many years, criticized that the industrialized countries had "invested many billions in assistance, and achieved almost nothing". In a background report on the subject shortly afterwards, editors of the same newspaper postulated: "The countries that have received the most aid are the worst off today."

We think this criticism is too sweeping—some initiatives and organizations have done great work and can be proud of their achievements. But the bottom line is that the relationship between the cost and return of development aid is far from healthy.

Moreover, development concepts are often underpinned by a patronizing attitude, namely a one-dimensional view of Africa as a continent of wars, crises and disasters; a hopeless case, where donor nations are trying to prevent a worst-case scenario. But Africa is also a continent of opportunities. Several countries are in the process of making tremendous progress, and are necessary and exciting partners for the industrialized nations. These governments need positive impetus rather than handouts.

This is why more and more politicians and economic experts in Africa are calling for a rethink. According to Ghanaian President Nana Akufo-Addo, development aid in its traditional form does not help, and in fact even does harm, because it creates dependencies and slows down initiatives for reform. Kenyan economist James Shikwati blames development aid for destroying incentives to do good business, thereby driving Africa further into dependence. Shikwati, director of the Kenya-based Inter Region Economic Network (IREN), also complains that payments from abroad help consolidate power structures from which few benefit. To put it bluntly, development aid primarily benefits autocrats and oligarchs. It props up the outdated systems that secure their privileges, while at the same time rewarding a lack of enthusiasm for reform.

Moreover, experts suspect that a significant proportion of aid flows directly into the pockets of heads of government, ministers and high-ranking officials. The management consultant Prinz Asfa-Wossen Asserate estimates that around €600 billion that were due to flow into development projects instead trickled off into other channels. "They landed in Swiss accounts or were put into real estate in France, London or elsewhere," he noted in a guest article for the *Frankfurter Allgemeine Zeitung* in 2017.

While this figure represents a rough estimate, recent studies support the suspicion that corrupt elites are syphoning off large sums. For example, a team of economists conducting research on behalf of the World Bank discovered that in the quarters in which financial aid is disbursed to poor countries, deposits in offshore accounts held by private individuals from those countries increased by an average of 3.4 percent. The logical conclusion is that of every $100 paid out in development aid, an average of $7.50 ends up in tax havens.

TURNING AWAY FROM THE BLANKET APPROACH

This is why it is high time for a paradigm shift. The website of the German Federal Ministry for Economic Cooperation and Development (BMZ) states that Germany is moving "away from a blanket approach towards targeted support for reform-minded countries". This is the driving principle behind its reform partnerships and the G20 Compact with Africa—an initiative developed under the German G20 presidency and launched in 2017 to intensify cooperation with reforming countries and accelerate progress in this regard. The main objective is to bring about more legal certainty and improve conditions for investors, and in this way promote entrepreneurial commitment.

At the same time, policymakers hope that the policy will increase the will to reform, potentially even triggering a race to reform. But what does "targeted support" look like? Germany and the other donor countries send money and experts to assist in the establishment of anti-corruption and antitrust authorities, tax offices and audit courts. They also promote, among other things, the development of dual training systems, effective security architecture and renewable energy.

To this end, the international development community expects comprehensive reforms. Just like with Gerhard Schröder's Agenda 2010 [when the then-chancellor reformed the German welfare system], the principle is "demand and support". Those developing African countries that take decisive action to strengthen the rule of law and democracy and to fight corruption will receive more support. To this end, Germany is reducing, for the time being, the number of countries with which it cooperates intensively on development from 85 to 55.

In contrast to the 1990 Washington Consensus, the reforms demanded this time around are not primarily linked to privatization and deregulation. On the contrary, they envisage a stronger role in the market for politics and public institutions. In essence, it is about establishing a functioning public administration and an environment that encourages private investment.

Given the need to finance "functional public administration", the attitude of the international development community in tax matters has changed; here too, pressure is increasing. Ultimately, it is no longer possible to sell the idea that the tax-to-GDP ratio in the poorest African countries—below 17 percent according to the BMZ, compared to the OECD average of 35 percent—is serviceable. Estimates suggest that African countries miss out on around $100 billion a year in tax revenues, which could be used to invest in infrastructure, develop social security systems and for administration.

Let it be understood, this is not about tax increases that discourage investors and entrepreneurs. It is about the consistent enforcement of existing tax laws and, in particular, depriving the privileged of the opportunity to evade them (which increases inequality).

So far, 12 African states have committed to meeting the demands of the G20 Compact with Africa, including Egypt, Burkina Faso, Rwanda and Togo, as well as Germany's reform partners. The World Bank alone will provide $5.4 billion for these countries if they actually implement the reforms.

Germany has already concluded six formal reform partnerships based on the G20 Compact. In 2017, Cote d'Ivoire, Ghana and Tunisia were the first countries to sign up. Three additional reform partners—Morocco, Senegal and Ethiopia—were added at the Africa Summit in Berlin in November 2019. In total, they will receive an additional €1.8 billion from Germany in 2019 alone.

Table 20: Compact with Germany
How Germany helps its reform partners

Country	Grant[1]	Main focus
Ethiopia	€269.0m	Economic development
Cote d'Ivoire	€216.9m	Renewable energies
Ghana	€233.2m	Renewable energies
Morocco	€571.0m	Banking/finance
Senegal	€108.0m	Economic development
Tunisia	€338.4m	Banking/finance

[1] in addition to existing commitments, also in form of low-interest loans
Source: BMZ (2020)

Take Ghana, a country praised as an "anchor of political stability for West Africa," by German Federal Minister of Economic Cooperation and Development Gerd Müller at the German-African economic summit in Accra in 2019. "There are courts of auditors, there is increasing legal certainty," he said. Tax revenues have quadrupled since 2010. Even Africa's former poorhouse, Ethiopia, has become a source of hope. Prime Minister Abiy Ahmed has made peace with arch-enemy Eritrea, released political prisoners and appointed opposition members to key positions. Moreover, women's rights are high on the agenda, and women make up half of his cabinet.

Ethiopia's prime minister was praised in 2019 by International Crisis Group, an independent non-governmental organization based in Brussels, which noted that nobody expected Abiy to push ahead with such radical reforms in such a short time. According to observers, these reforms are already paying off economically. The German government now wants to continue to fuel these developments.

What is clear is that Germany will closely monitor whether its reform partners keep their promises. The partnerships involve a detailed monitoring process. For example, a final installment of funding for Tunisia was withheld until the country had hired 40 new employees for its anti-corruption agency as pledged.

ADDITIONAL REFORM-MINDED COUNTRIES: FROM ALGERIA TO TOGO
What are the continent's other reform-orientated countries? In addition to countries involved in the Compact with Africa, those considered to be making progress include Algeria, Botswana, Mauritius, Namibia and South Africa. This is evident in, among other sources, the *Transformation Index* produced by the Bertelsmann Foundation, which analyzes political reforms in 131 emerging and developing countries. Country experts examine 17 criteria, including the stability of democratic institutions, monetary and fiscal stability, and market and competition regimes.

Table 21: Selected reform-minded African countries
Current ranking among 131 developing and transition countries

Rank	Country	Score[1]	Rank	Country	Score[1]
13. (...)	Mauritius	8.25	37. (...)	Namibia	6.50
16. (...)	Botswana	7.89	41. (...)	Botswana	6.43
26. (...)	South Africa	6.96	50. (...)	Benin	6.18
32 (...)	Ghana	6.75			

[1] Scale from 1 to 10
Source: Transformation Index (2019), Bertelsmann Foundation

Development Minister Müller singled out Rwanda and Togo for particular praise. According to the World Bank's *Doing Business Report*, they are among the ten most reform-minded countries in the world. Progress in digitization is particularly impressive. Among other things, exporters of agricultural products in Rwanda can now create their "certificates of origin" digitally. Meanwhile, Togo has digitalized its cadastral system and introduced an online system for corporate income tax returns.

We have observed developments in Togo with particular interest. After all, one of the two authors, Martin Schoeller, acts as honorary consul for the former French colony. The positive developments in the country are no more evident than in its economic growth, which has reached between 4.4 and 6.5 percent annually over the past decade.

Nevertheless, Ghana's neighbor is still one of the poorest countries in the world. Almost half of its inhabitants live below the poverty line, resulting in alarmingly high levels of infant mortality and child labor. The process of democratization is also not yet complete.

BY THE WAY: DO REFORM PARTNERS NEED TO BE FLAWLESS DEMOCRACIES?

Is Togo a good candidate for a reform partnership with Germany? We think that, in view of the country's business-friendly reforms, the German government should seriously consider the idea. However, Minister Müller has made it clear that he expects political reforms first, including the holding of local elections.

Indeed, Togo is no flawless democracy right now. President Faure Gnassingbé is the son of former dictator Gnassingbé Eyadéma, who died in 2005, and the non-governmental organization Freedom House rates the country as only "partially free".

With 47 out of 100 possible points, Togo lags some way behind Ghana (83) and Tunisia (70), but only just behind Côte d'Ivoire (51), which is already an official German reform partner. And the latest developments have been positive.

The situation in Togo leads inevitably to the delicate question of how democratic our reform partners need to be. For the sake of the hungry, we think Germany, the EU and the G20 should—at least initially—be open to supporting countries other than those with flawless democracies. Even governments with authoritarian tendencies should have a chance to access support as long as they respect human rights, expedite reforms and establish a clear road map for democratization. The bitter truth is that for people who have too little to eat, free elections are not the top priority. And especially in unstable countries, a certain amount of muscle can be necessary to successfully set the course for change. Rwanda's authoritarian president Paul Kagame, for example, has spurred positive economic development that benefits more than just a small elite; indeed, the African Development Bank has just designated the country as undergoing "inclusive growth".

ETHIOPIA— A "DEVELOPMENT DICTATORSHIP"

Or take the example of Ethiopia: The former poorhouse of Africa was a kind of "development dictatorship" for years. The authoritarian government invested "billions in infrastructure" and had "achieved remarkable successes in the education and health sectors," wrote *Der Spiegel* in 2019. Since the turn of the millennium, the poverty rate has therefore been "more than halved" to 27 percent. But, *Spiegel* continued, "freedom and self-determination," was "withheld from the people" by the authoritarian regime, per the credo "growth first, then democracy". Today, democracy is within touching distance; the reform-minded prime minister Abiy Ahmed has announced free elections. This example shows that authoritarian leaders can drive important economic reforms while paving the way for democracy. We therefore argue that countries that are (still) under authoritarian rule should not automatically be excluded from reform partnerships. In view of acute hunger crises, there is no time to wait for perfect democratic conditions in every case. For us Europeans, the fight against poverty and hunger should remain the priority for now, to allow the basic conditions necessary for a life of dignity.

Regardless of the degree of democratic maturity, however, we must demand that potential reform partners meet high standards with regards to the rule of law. This involves agreeing to the jurisdiction of international arbitration, the conclusion of investment protection agreements and the admission of Interpol. International development cooperation is just not possible without these standards.

We are well aware that this approach nevertheless risks empowering leaders who afterwards transpire to be unscrupulous autocrats. It would not be the first time. This makes it all the more important to closely monitor reform processes.

WHY THE MARSHALL PLAN MUST BE EXPANDED

To summarize, the reform partnerships and the G20 Compact initiative are taking us in the right direction. Germany and the G20 states are no longing relying on a blanket approach to disburse funding, but are providing targeted support to help build stable political and economic structures—as long as recipient governments show a genuine reforming zeal.

So far, however, the main concern has been to strengthen the rule of law and ensure fair competition. The social aspect has only played a subordinate role. In our view, this is a serious mistake. Because the danger is that the poor and hungry will fail to benefit from higher investment and growth rates.

Just like after the Washington Consensus, we may end up waiting in vain for the trickle-down effect that libertarian economists are so fond of predicting. Moreover, growth impulses fizzle out if inequality and instability remain high. The people that need it most urgently are excluded from the benefits.

We therefore strongly advocate expanding the list of demands to include a social component. The Marshall Plan with Africa already states that reform-minded countries should strive for "compliance with international environmental and social standards," increase "investments in social security" and develop "comprehensive social security systems". But in comparison with other requirements, there is a lack of concrete specifications. It remains unclear what exactly constitute "comprehensive security systems" and "international social standards". Moreover, social policy has played at best a subordinate and in some cases no role at all in negotiations with reform-oriented countries.

We therefore propose an upgraded Marshall Plan that makes the establishment or expansion of functioning social security systems a key condition for additional, stronger support. One concrete demand must be the introduction of robust unemployment benefits, because they alter the balance of power on the labor market and increase the likelihood that statutory minimum wages will actually be paid. It is therefore a crucial step towards inclusive growth and a social market economy.

TOP UP THE BUDGET FOR DEVELOPMENT AID

In addition, we believe that the current BMZ budget of €11 billion needs to be substantially increased. "I don't understand why, when everyone is talking about the causes of mass migration, the finance minister is looking to save money on development cooperation of all things," criticized Minister Müller in a newspaper interview in 2018. This is "setting the wrong priorities"; Germany can and must "achieve much more". The EU is also doing too little; it intends to increase funding for Africa from just €5 billion to €6 billion annually. "That's not even close to enough, and is a tenth of what we spend on agricultural subsidies," says Minister Müller. He is right.

Let's not forget that development aid, just like the infrastructure program we propose, can be an investment in the future. And it pays off. As well as opening up new markets and trade partnerships in a prospering Africa that will strengthen Europe in the competition between systems, it also brings about savings in other areas. After all, the German federal government alone is estimated to spend tens of billions each year on housing, training and integrating refugees. Added to this are expenditures by the municipalities, not to mention the significant payments to transit countries such as Libya, Niger and Turkey, and the costs of border security and "migration management", for which the EU has set aside a whopping €35 billion until 2027.

Imagine how much more effective it would be to spend at least some of these sums in Africa to improve the prospects of the population locally. For example, by connecting them to the electricity grid, improving transport infrastructure or through social security systems.

Besides Germany, the EU also needs to do more. It is therefore right to Europeanize the Marshall Plan. In 2018, the French and German governments published a position paper calling for the EU's external aid to "increasingly be used as a catalyst" to "achieve a leverage effect tailored to the economy of each beneficiary country". If this is meant seriously, the European budget for development cooperation must be substantially increased. We should also have the courage to break new ground. As such, we propose that development aid be provided partly in the form of interest payments or guarantees for infrastructure loans (see Tool 1). Assuming that reform-minded African countries receive these at a rate of 1 percent, we could finance a credit volume of €1 trillion, with €10 billion per year in interest. This would allow us to combine our first and second tools, and use development aid to promote not only social reforms but also infrastructure investments.

TOOL 3

Trade – Let's put an end to "Europe First" for good

Change through trade is not inevitable. To make the European Economic Model the common denominator for intercontinental cooperation, we must link international treaties to social standards, and offer fair deals to reform-minded countries, rather than simply treating them as mere suppliers of raw materials.

In 2018 Jean-Claude Juncker, the then-president of the European Commission, proposed a far-reaching EU-Africa free trade agreement and a "partnership of equals," which would promote investment and help create 10 million jobs over the following five years.

We were admittedly skeptical—and remain so. Thanks to the Everything But Arms agreement, companies from most African countries can already export duty-free to Europe. So far, however, this purported free trade has been of little use to them, mostly because of the consistently high EU agricultural subsidies and other indirect trade barriers.

And let's be honest, even if the remaining customs duties and quotas were abolished, many African entrepreneurs would still be unable to deliver their goods to Europe. Take Mauritania, for example; fishermen there are generally not in a position to comply with all the hygiene regulations necessary to supply their catch to European wholesale markets.

As such, there is a danger that additional or expanded Juncker-style free trade agreements could even be a retrograde step. Especially if, in return, African countries are required to open their markets equally wide, as the EU has mostly demanded in previous agreements. That is "Europe First" in true Trump style.

In our view, we need to reboot our trade policy. Instead of an obsessive focus on trade maximization, as traditionally propagated by the World Trade Organization (WTO), we should declare poverty minimization the top priority in trade relations with developing countries. We must at long last focus our attention on the losers of globalization and work resolutely to ensure that world trade benefits not only individual countries or social classes, but as many people as possible.

This would represent a revival of the spirit of the 2001 World Trade Conference in Doha, which explicitly declared "poverty reduction" as its goal. All people should benefit from the "improvements in opportunities and increased prosperity" that world trade brings, it was stated back then. Unfortunately, that pioneering spirit dissipated swiftly afterwards.

FIRST: REDUCE EU AGRICULTURAL SUBSIDIES

An important first step would be to reduce EU agricultural subsidies. "Over the next seven years, the EU wants to support its farmers with 400 billion euros," criticized Minister Müller in an interview with *Handelsblatt* in 2018. "How can we expect African farmers to be competitive?" Müller's ministry notes on its website that, although Africa could in theory feed itself, the continent spends $35 billion a year on food imports.

African heads of state and government are therefore arguing vehemently for a reduction in EU agricultural subsidies—including during the renegotiation of the EU's Cotonou Agreement with 79 countries in sub-Saharan Africa, the Caribbean and the Pacific. Because if subsidies for farmers and agribusinesses reduce, food from the EU will become more expensive; in turn, this will increase sales potential and export opportunities for African farmers. Whether the developing countries will be successful in asserting their demands remains to be seen, even though in theory they have a stronger hand to play than in the last round of negotiations, because the EU is more interested than ever in curbing migration to Europe. To achieve this, however, agriculture in Africa, in particular, must offer better employment prospects.

SECOND: INTENSIFIED PARTNERSHIPS WITH REFORM COUNTRIES
Europe can no longer simply point to duty-free access for the 34 poorest African countries and rest, self-satisfied, on its laurels. Even without customs duties, there are multiple obstacles complicating the situation for African suppliers. These include high product standards, too little protection against highly subsidized competitors from industrialized countries (the "reciprocity principle") and tariff systems that make value creation in Africa itself unattractive (and thus de facto relegate Africa to a mere supplier of raw materials). This means that exporters of finished products often have to pay high duties. For roasted or soluble coffee, for example, German customs demands a tax of up to 4.78 per kilogram, while raw coffee beans remain tariff-free. The German government is already considering suspending the coffee duty for fair trade products to make processing and value creation in Africa more attractive.

We also advocate offering deeper trade partnerships to those developing countries that are determined to fight poverty and establish or expand social systems. In this way, we can link international treaties to basic social standards, and make the European Economic Model, based on reciprocity, the common system.

Indirect trade barriers must be a central focus of this. For example, the EU should provide exporters with targeted support to meet hygiene, product and other EU standards. Possible measures include sending export consultants abroad or offering targeted financial assistance. We should also be prepared to discuss exceptions.

In addition, we must allow our partner countries the opportunity to protect their own producers from foreign competition, including through import duties or quotas. In recent economic agreements, the EU has compelled potential partners to largely dispense with such instruments. We consider this unreasonable and appeal to those responsible to reverse these decisions. If we are serious about poverty reduction, we must give reform-minded developing countries more leeway, including to introduce unilateral trade restrictions.

In addition, all tax, customs and product regulations that make local value creation unattractive—such as the aforementioned the German coffee duty—must be closely examined. As long as we relegate Africa to a role as supplier of raw materials, and value creation continues to take place primarily in the global North, we are impeding decisive progress in the fight against hunger and poverty.

As well as new bilateral agreements with reform-minded states, a trading community including the EU and selected African countries would also be conceivable; in other words, a single agreement with several countries that would be a first step towards a common African-European economic area. In addition to social standards, we need further abiding common rules, for example with regard to environmental protection and technical standards.

Those that stubbornly resist reform, however, should be denied more leeway, and even have to reckon with the possible reintroduction of trade barriers for their own exporters. These could, for example, include customs duties that have been suspended under economic agreements.

BILATERALISM OR MULTILATERALISM?

We are aware that a transition to bilateralism poses a threat to developing countries, because stronger parties may use the opportunity to exploit their relative power. However, realistically, this is also the case with the multilateral WTO approach. After all, the industrialized countries have manifestly failed to follow up on the promises made at the Doha Conference. Moreover, developed countries have—de jure and de facto—greater leverage when it comes to trade disputes in the multilateral context. This is also the result of weaknesses in the WTO dispute resolution system.

Our approach of holding political decision-makers to account by linking trade facilitation to social reforms seems fairer than merely encouraging companies in developing countries to comply with higher social standards. The planned Supply Chain Act, under which large German companies will be required to check whether suppliers abroad are involved in human rights violations, is a good example. The changes are certainly welcome, because they will increase the onus on companies, but they may also have negative consequences. Because if German importers start demanding detailed documentation and certification this will put many small businesses in developing countries, for whom such a process is too expensive or complicated, at a disadvantage. The legislature should therefore avoid setting the requirements too high. At the same time, it is necessary to push all the more resolutely for local political reforms to guarantee human rights. If a partner country has the correct legal framework and is enforcing the rule of law, the relevant problems can be tackled more effectively and, above all, on a broader front.

Nobel Prize winner Joseph Stiglitz called for trade agreements to be tied to social reforms as early as 2006. If "social imbalances" in trading partners mean that companies in these countries are able to use their economic clout to skimp on wages and labor costs, trade is an important "conduit" to stimulate reforms.

The EU has already taken the first steps to link trade partnerships to certain statutory social standards. "We make sure that our partners ratify the conventions of the International Labour Organization, which, for example, prohibit child labor," said the then EU trade commissioner Cecilia Malmström in 2018 in an interview with *Zeit*.

It is now critical that we continue along this path and link the removal of trade barriers with the introduction or expansion of social security systems. This would make trade, alongside financing infrastructure projects and reorienting development aid, the third powerful tool with which to export the social market economy to Africa.

BY THE WAY: TEST LABORATORY TOGO
Sanctions and investment restrictions, which we will mention briefly, are additional tools with which to export the social market economy. The EU could make life more difficult for companies, oligarchs and politicians from countries that refuse to reform. We have a richly stocked arsenal at our disposal for this purpose; from entry bans and port closures for yachts belonging to profiteers of human rights violations and even investment restrictions. One effective instrument would also be an obligation to prove the origins of funds earmarked for investment in Europe.

It is clear that Europe has multiple instruments at its disposal, and depending on the country, we can use all of them or just a couple. Every country needs a tailored solution.

We are currently trying to win over political leaders in Germany and the Republic of Togo for a pilot project. Martin Schoeller knows political decision-makers in Togo, where he serves as honorary consul, as well as their German counterparts—above all, Johannes Singhammer, a long-serving member of the Bundestag, who now works as a special advisor to the German Development Ministry. A trial run is therefore possible; at the very least a limited one.

Togo is better suited to our approach than almost any other country. As part of its National Development Plan 2018-2022 (NDP), the government is already expanding social security systems, while at the same time pressing ahead with investments in infrastructure. Flagship projects include the construction of a modern deep-sea port in the capital Lomé, where very large ships will be able to dock. This should boost exports of strategic products such as coffee and cocoa.

Togo also wants to expand road, rail and digital networks under the NDP, which the Tony Blair Institute for Global Change actively helped develop. Economic growth is expected to increase from around five to more than seven percent annually as a result of these measures. The government also wants to reduce the proportion of the population in absolute poverty and lower inequality.

Those is charge have recognized that investment in infrastructure is a critical step towards initiating development, especially if accompanied by social reforms. However, Togo is dependent on support to raise the €6-7 billion funding necessary for the NDP (the volume corresponds to about €1,000 per inhabitant). To date, the money from international partners has trickled in rather slowly. The World Bank released $150 million

($87.5 million as a grant, the rest as a loan with a 38-year duration) at the end of 2019, and a little later. the French Development Agency (AFD) pledged €40.7 million. Other institutions have also participated.

This is good news, but not good enough. Responsible persons in Togo report protracted negotiations and exacting demands, especially from European investors. The Chinese, it is said, are much less complicated but also offer less favorable terms.

We believe that Togo's reform efforts deserve more determined support. Development banks should therefore make more money or guarantees available for infrastructure financing, for example through the proposed Africa Bonds, as part of a pilot project linking support to reforms. We also believe Togo has the potential to join the ranks of our reform partners, who receive increased amounts of development aid. And last but not least, we should consider an intensified trade partnership, in line with the three tools laid out in our agenda.

OUTLOOK

The new EU-Africa Pact is the opportunity of the century

The renegotiation of the so-called Cotonou Agreement offers the perfect opportunity to chart a decisive new path in European-African cooperation. We must make use of it.

A number of important steps have been taken in development policy in recent years. First and foremost, the reform partnerships under German Federal Minister of Economic Cooperation and Development Gerd Müller's Marshall Plan with Africa, mentioned above, which link support to reforms. This paradigm shift promotes change and will make reform-oriented states more attractive to investors and entrepreneurs, thereby creating wealth and jobs.

However, that is not enough. If the new Africa policy is to develop real teeth and create millions of jobs, it must be a common European project. Above all, it must address the two other key instruments of development cooperation, trade and infrastructure financing, which have so far been neglected and left to the Chinese. These coming months offer a huge opportunity. The EU is currently negotiating with 79 African, Caribbean and Pacific (ACP) states on the Cotonou follow-up agreement, which is due to be concluded before the end of the German EU presidency (i.e. by the end of 2020). As things stand, the aim is to conclude three individual agreements with the African, Caribbean and Pacific regions.

The 2000 pact covers six core areas: Human development, human rights/good governance, business/trade, environment/

climate, migration/mobility, and peace/security. Yet, as promising as the agreement sounds, it has made little difference so far.

In January 2020, Minister Müller insisted that the new agreement must be a "Jahrhundertvertrag" (once in a century contract). The EU can no longer view Africa simply as a market for its subsidized and cheap agricultural products. The renegotiation has the potential to usher in a new era. With the right priorities and formulations, those responsible could pave the way for a decisive new start in EU-Africa policy and a common economic area within just a few weeks.

WHAT COUNTS NOW

The agreement can act as a framework for the accelerated development of infrastructure coupled with social and ecological reforms that pave the way for broad prosperity. In other words, it could be the initial spark and ideal basis for reform partnerships through which European funds are mobilized, infrastructure programs launched and social security systems expanded. But what does the agreement need to include in order to achieve these goals? What are the crucial issues? What hurdles must be overcome?

First: We advocate pressing for clear formulations with regards to social security in discussions regarding principals, goals, development strategies and forms of cooperation. The subjects of welfare systems and wages must be central to the treaty. Therefore, we propose, among other things, a new preamble that emphasizes the importance of this aspect in the common fight against poverty. This would be the basis for linking development aid more closely to social reforms and making the social market economy a common model.

Second: We must include the topic of "support for infrastructure financing" in the treaty. In addition, during the course of negotiations, we should also make clear our intention to extend the African mandate of development banks such as the European Bank for Reconstruction and Development (as the basis for an infrastructure initiative).

Third: To ensure that these institutions are able to play the central role that we envision for them to mobilize capital for infrastructure loans, the agreement should enable new forms of development aid. Particularly important, in our view, is the chance to offer aid in the form of interest payments or guarantees for infrastructure loans (to countries that meet the reform criteria).

Fourth: We think it is particularly important to formulate, clearly and unambiguously, the goal of removing indirect trade barriers and promoting value creation locally. This would lay the ground for new bilateral trade agreements, in which the EU allows developing countries greater scope of action. At the same time, it can create incentives for European companies to relocate labor-intensive activities from Asia to Africa. This would reduce their dependence on the Far East and, especially in light of the experience of the Covid-19 crisis, increase the resilience of the supply chain.

Fifth: In the course of the negotiations we should make concessions that go beyond the text of the treaty. For example, we need to substantially enlarge the European Development Fund, which had €30.5 billion at its disposal between 2014 and 2020. Among other things, this could take the form of interest rate guarantees for infrastructure loans, which would ordinarily not result in any additional burden on European households. It is also important to ensure that EU agricultural policy does not counteract the goals of the agreement.

Sixth: One problem with the current agreement is that it also includes countries in the Caribbean and Pacific, which have, to some extent, independent needs and interests. The

EU should therefore conclude separate agreements as planned with these regions, so that it can concentrate exclusively on Africa with the Cotonou Agreement.

The German EU Presidency offers both Müller and Chancellor Angela Merkel, whose terms in office are drawing to a close, an excellent opportunity to build an effective legacy. The federal government seems willing, with Merkel's Personal Representative for Africa Günter Nooke already calling for far-reaching changes. The new agreement should "not just be an extension of the old one," said Nooke in 2019, "it is time for an EU-Africa pact of equals".

Moreover, the conditions are favorable for the final negotiations in several respects:

➤ There are politicians in decisive positions on the European side who have recognized that it is high time for a new start (besides Merkel, this includes Emmanuel Macron).
➤ The actors on the African side, such as the Togolese foreign minister and lead negotiator Robert Dussey, can point to considerable reform efforts and successes.
➤ Low interest rates are opening up new opportunities in development finance, especially with regard to infrastructure.
➤ The Covid-19 crisis has increased awareness that the major challenges of our time can only be solved collectively, and that social welfare systems are not simply an expression of solidarity, but a prerequisite for social and economic stability.

Until now, we were missing an overarching concept to refine and develop the many ideas and approaches, and tie the loose ends together. Our agenda fills this gap, and could be brought to life with the new Cotonou Agreement.

To ensure that it sparks an African economic miracle, as a first step we propose supplementing the preamble in some places (see excerpt, amendments in bold) and, as a second step, to specify the goal of a European-African economic zone (this proposal was submitted to the German Federal Ministry for Economic Cooperation and Development in September).

POST-COTONOU AGREEMENT / AFRICA-EU

HAVING REGARD TO the Treaty establishing the European Community, on the one hand, and the Georgetown Agreement establishing the Group of African States... on the other;

AFFIRMING their commitment to work together towards the achievement of the objectives of **urgent** eradication of poverty **and thereby, also flight from poverty**, sustainable development and the gradual integration of **the African** countries into the world economy;

ASSERTING their resolve to make, through their cooperation, a significant contribution to the economic, social and cultural development of the **African** states and to the greater well-being of their population, helping them face the challenges of globalization and strengthening the **Africa**–EU Partnership in the effort to give the process of globalization a stronger social dimension;

REAFFIRMING their willingness to revitalize their special relationship and to implement a comprehensive and integrated approach for a strengthened partnership based on political dialogue, development cooperation, economic, **financial** and trade relations, and **support in the financing of infrastructure projects**;

ACKNOWLEDGING that a political environment guaranteeing peace, security and stability, **social security systems**, respect for human rights, democratic principles and the rule of law, and good governance is part and parcel of long-term development; acknowledging that responsibility for establishing such an environment rests primarily with the countries concerned;

ACKNOWLEDGING that sound and sustainable economic policies **within the framework of the social market economy** are prerequisites for development, **and that robust social security systems are essential for growth that benefits all sections of the population**;

CONSIDERING that the development goals and principles agreed at the United Nations Conferences, **in particular the commitment to eradicate hunger (Zero Hunger Challenge)** and the target set by the OECD Development Assistance Committee to reduce by half the proportion of people living in extreme poverty, **are a responsibility and obligation at the same time**, and that they **must** guide cooperation between **African** states and the EU within this Agreement, **especially having fallen far short of the original target of halving extreme poverty by 2015...**

ANXIOUS to respect basic labor rights, taking account of the principles laid down in the relevant conventions of the International Labour Organization, **as well as to ensure that minimum wages rise continuously, in turn significantly reducing population growth within 15 years due to the negative correlation between income and birth rate;**

European-African Economic Zone:

1. Economic objective:
The EU and AU intend to develop a joint economic zone that will promote ESG standards and the 17 UN sustainable development goals (SDGs), in order to achieve prosperity for the population and facilitate the exchange of products, services, know-how and financing between the two unions—Europe and Africa.

2. Infrastructure:
The EU is interested in contributing to infrastructure projects and financing on a country-by-country basis, with coordination and consultation with the AU dependent on a binding agreement on certain core standards that should also ease cross-border projects and cooperation. (Most of the SDGs will automatically be achieved when the minimum wage level abolishes extreme poverty.)

Guiding principles for infrastructure cooperation projects EU-AU:

1. Qualified European infrastructure companies to be selected through a public tender (based on regional infrastructure planning) shall cooperate with qualified African counter-parties, if existing in the country.

2. At least **80% of the workforce** should be local and employed via contracts including defined social welfare benefits such as health insurance, unemployment insurance and **minimum wages** (to be negotiated and revised periodically).

3. Up to 20% of the workforce (Europeans) must be capable of **transferring know-how and training**. A professional training program in parallel to the execution of the works, to transfer know-how to the regional workforce, is mandatory.

4. **Transparency:** Contracts, construction documentation and project management and control shall be, for example, blockchain-based, and accompanied by teams from both sides; international auditors and international arbitration shall apply and be enforceable.

5. **Financing via loans shall be in euros** at low interest with durations of up to 30 years and longer, non-amortizing for the first 15 years. (Comment: While Chinese loans may cost 6%, European loans will have a 6% amortization, but only after 15 years. In this time a strengthening of the African banking system can also be achieved.)

Appendix

Executive summary: An overview of our key statements and recommendations

1. The world's largest economic area: Europe and Africa share a common destiny with enormous potential.

What is good for Africa is also good for Europe in the long run; *the more people that are better off there, the better off we will all be in the long term.* Together we can prevent a mass exodus to the Global North, and more importantly build a flourishing economic area that creates widespread prosperity and shapes the global rules of play.

So instead of looking to the South in pity, we have to make one thing very clear: Africa is a market with billions of people who are as poor as the Chinese were 30 years ago. This development backlog holds enormous potential for our economy: it is likely that more will be constructed in Africa in the coming decades than was built in Europe in the last 100 years. This is another reason why reform-minded nations in Africa deserve to be seen as equals, not as merely the recipients of charity.

2. Competition between political systems: we must not leave the field open for China

China has seen the continent's vast potential and is making great strides with its new Silk Road Initiative, while Europe is still faltering. In view of the intensified competition between political systems, this is not only an economic but also a geostrategic risk. In the era of "China First" and "America First", we need new partnerships to strengthen the European economic and social model.

That is why we are proposing an infrastructure offensive linking Europe, Africa and India. A "Spice Route 2.0" can become the initial catalyst for growth in the African economy—and the timing is more favorable than ever in view of the low interest rates.

3. Unregulated capitalism has failed across the board in Africa—the social market economy is the winner of the systems.
Africa has been focusing on free markets for decades, spurred on by the international community. But contrary to the prophecies of proponents of the "trickle down" theory, the poor have hardly benefited from the economic growth. Instead, inequality has deepened in many places, accompanied by political instability.

In the medium term, this has led to significantly lower growth rates than economic theory would have us believe. Merely attracting investors and stimulating short-term economic growth is therefore not sufficient: we have to ensure that everyone benefits, especially with regard to the poor.

So-called consumers have to be able to consume, on both humanitarian and economic grounds.

4. Neither "free" nor "fair" trade have led to any noticeable improvements in Africa
Just like the unregulated market, barrier-free trade has done little to improve the situation. Most developing countries in Africa and the majority of their inhabitants are among the losers of trade liberalisation. One of the reasons for this is that Europe is hanging on to lavish *agricultural subsidies*. And fair trade initiatives? They do help, but are often *only a drop in the ocean*. This is mainly because a large proportion of the value created by these schemes is usually kept in Europe. Africa continues to be merely the supplier of raw materials. The

bottom line is that keeping such schemes on a voluntary basis is not enough to establish effective standards for genuine fair trade. What is needed is a change of course in industrial and trade policy as a whole, one that opens up greater opportunities for African products.

5. The social market economy is a huge opportunity for Africa
Those who want to defeat poverty and famine must resolutely pursue the social market economy or the "European Economic Model". However the countries of Africa are a long way from achieving this, and robust social security systems are few and far between.

This leaves us with a fundamental market failure: unskilled workers in particular have no alternative to taking on undignified jobs due to an oversupply of labour. If the price does not create a balance between supply and demand, the state must intervene, and follow these two basic principles: Those who work must be able to feed their family. *And those who become unemployed must not go hungry.*

6. Minimum wages and safeguards for the unemployed play a key role
A vital step towards the European Economic Model is the introduction of *social security (net?)* for people when they lose their jobs. This would provide many with an, alternative to underpaid work, at least temporarily. In turn, this would strengthen the bargaining position of unskilled workers in particular.

Moreover, such safeguards, in combination with social regulations linked to government contracts and incentives for the adoption of official employment contracts, could help to establish a real *minimum wage*. In Africa, the minimum wage often only exists on paper.

7. Social reforms and fair wages lead to falling birth rates, and trigger an upward spiral

One of the core messages of this book is that social benefits and higher wages are crucial to halting population growth. Statistics show that higher per capita incomes lead to lower birth rates: in many cases, the population stops growing once 300 US dollars a month is achieved, giving states a "demographic dividend".

So we are not talking about a wealth redistribution in the sense of "take from the rich and give to the poor". Social benefits unleash forces of economic growth and *raise the bottom of the income pyramid*. They are not a zero-sum game, but win-win for workers and businesses alike.

8. Sustainability: the world is ready for "prosperity for all".

Can we expect the earth to cope with an economic upturn in Africa, or would it increase the speed of climate change? Thanks to technological progress and the circular economy, we can increase prosperity without harming the environment and climate. Protecting the climate and boosting the economy are not mutually exclusive; we can fight poverty and global warming at the same time, and tap into the potential of the sunny continent.

To achieve this, Europe must also demand and promote renewable energy and other clean technologies. Germany is well positioned to exert a positive influence here because it is just as well-known as being the country of the "Energiewende" (transition to a low-carbon energy supply) as it is for its social market economy.

9. Europe has three powerful tools at its disposal to demand and promote reform, and to export the social market economy to Africa.

The concept of "cash for reform" that Europe has used to overcome the government-debt crisis has huge potential for the development of Africa. That is why we want to support countries that are pushing for reforms to introduce a social market economy in three ways:

➤ **Finance:** We propose that Europe should mobilise one trillion euros over ten years through their development banks for infrastructure programmes in transition countries. The focus should be on the development of transport, communication, energy and water infrastructure, as these form the foundations for private business activity. They will provide a stimulus for economic growth that will turn agricultural countries into mature industrial and social states in the medium term. Low interest rates offer a great opportunity to develop Africa with capital from Europe. In this way, Europe can overtake the Chinese Silk Road initiative.

➤ **Development aid:** We advocate extending the Marshall Plan to Africa and making the establishment of effective social security systems a condition for more intensive development cooperation ("Marshall Plan Plus"). To achieve this, the budget of the German Federal Ministry for Economic Cooperation and Development and the European Development Fund must be significantly increased and the programmes must be more closely linked to investments. Europe should therefore also offer development aid in the form of interest payments and/or interest guarantees. In this way, we can leverage development aid—at best by a factor of 100 (at one percent interest). This allows for more clout without having to raise taxes. Development ministries and institutions, such as the GIZ, can oversee the awarding of contracts for investment in infrastructure and coordinate the monitoring of reform progress.

➤ **Trade:** We are calling for a paradigm shift in trade policy. The primary political objective in trade relations with developing countries should no longer be how best to maximise trade, but rather how best to reduce poverty. To put it more specifically, this means the EU should reduce its agricultural subsidies and offer transition countries stronger trade partnerships, in the form of fair trade agreements that add more value to the supply chain in Africa. That would be real fair trade!

10. Cotonou: The new EU-Africa agreement is the chance of the century

The EU can set a clear course for our agenda in the new EU-Africa agreement, which is currently being negotiated. We therefore call on the EU Commission and the German government, which took on the EU Council presidency in July, to see the "Cotonou follow-up agreement" as the chance of the century: we should make generous offers to our African negotiating partners, but at the same time make it clear that we expect increased reforms designed to create broad-based prosperity.

Specifically, this means that the issues of *social reforms, fair trade and the financing of infrastructure* must be placed at the heart of the agreement.

> **At a glance**
> 1,000 billion Infrastructure Program by 2030
> 1. Financing of infrastructure through African Infrastructure Bonds (long-term, 30+ years) issued by the European Development Banks; up to $100 bn per year
> 2. Pass on with a moderate margin of <3 % and long-term duration of > 30 years
> 3. Combine infrastructure investments with economic clusters, higher wages and social standards
> 4. Assure standards and transparency through joint control systems
> 5. Slow population growth automatically when wages reach €1 per hour instead of €1 per day, approx. by 2030

Our answers to biases and sweeping judgments

When we talk about Africa with people, sometimes we encounter raised eyebrows or even a pitiful smile. There is no doubt—some of our dialogue partners consider the idea that we can defeat poverty and hunger to be naive, presumptuous, or even both.

Time and again, for example, people say that Africa is "just different", that development aid is a "bottomless pit" and that a European-style social security system is "utopian". Here are our answers to typical biases and sweeping judgments:"

IS AFRICA "DIFFERENT?"

Yes—just like every other continent. But when dialogue partners argue this way, they often mean something else: what they really want to say is that Africa is just a hopeless case. Despite the huge challenges, we are nevertheless convinced that fatalism is out of place. Who would have thought that the Asian states would experience such an unprecedented upswing, as we have been able to see for decades? And who would have believed in a German economic miracle in the post-war period?

One thing is certain: In some African countries, the road is particularly long—mainly because of long-standing civil wars and the climate crisis. But at the same time, there are encouraging developments in many places, for example in Germany's reform partners such as Ghana and Senegal. And in Ethiopia, the new head of government and Nobel Peace Prize winner Abiy Ahmed is pushing ahead with impressive reforms that are driving economic success. This impressively demonstrates that what is supposedly impossible is indeed possible. Let's tackle further "hopeless cases"!

ARE AFRICANS DIFFERENT?

Sometimes a racist undertone can be detected in these sweeping judgments. Even if no one says so openly, some people still seem to cultivate the prejudice that Africans tend to have an aversion to work. Some racist stereotypes persist even in the 21st century.

If someone is convinced of this, it is no wonder that they would dismiss a decline in population growth and an economic miracle in Africa as utopian. At this point, we would say: anyone who has seen with their own eyes how people live and work in Togo, Kenya or elsewhere is immune to such prejudices.

IS DEVELOPMENT AID A "BOTTOMLESS PIT"?
There is no question that the developments of the last decades are devastating. Since the end of colonial times, it is estimated that up to two trillion dollars have flowed into Africa. And much of this has literally trickled away without any lasting effect. Because civil wars have thwarted tentative progress. Because oligarchs and corrupt civil servants have been lining their own pockets. And last but not least, because many concepts did not specifically aim to improve structures.

But Minister of Economic Cooperation and Development Gerd Müller (CSU party) has consistently addressed the core problem in his Marshall Plan with Africa and especially in the reform partnerships: development aid is now more closely tied to reforms. This creates the right incentives—and will ensure that in the future aid will primarily flow to where it falls on fertile ground.

Moreover, government and private development aid workers have learned from past mistakes. Instead of handing out charity, projects are increasingly focused on improving structures and helping people to help themselves. For example, aid workers are training farmers, coaching small entrepreneurs, building schools and implementing solar plants. This creates a ripple effect even beyond aid projects. The claim that development aid is of little use is therefore a lame excuse.

OR WILL THE NEXT WAR RUIN EVERYTHING YET AGAIN?
Of course, we cannot rule this out. But who would have thought after the Second World War that Europe would become a largely peaceful continent? And that is precisely what Africans want to achieve. That is why they formed the African Union (AU) back in 2002, to which all the countries of the continent belong.

The core element of the AU is the African Peace and Security Architecture (APSA), in which the EU is the most important partner. The APSA includes its own peacekeeping missions to support countries in their fight against militias and terrorist organizations. For example, more than 20,000 African soldiers are stationed in Somalia, mostly from Kenya, Ethiopia, Uganda and Burundi. And compared to previous interventions by the West, they have achieved a certain degree of success.

We are confident that closer cooperation and joint peace missions have the potential to make Africa a more peaceful continent. For this, however, the continent needs more European support—not only in terms of the economy, but also the military.

IS OUR AID EVEN NECESSARY?
One argument that we also hear is based as much on skepticism about development aid as on neoliberal confidence in the trickle-down model. Where development aid is necessary, it is sometimes said to be useless. And where it does help, it is unnecessary. Such countries are capable of boosting economic growth and eradicating poverty on their own.

Some proponents of this school of thought combine this with a demand that we focus fully on disaster relief following crop failures, floods, or droughts.

Our perspective: We must not play off disaster aid against development aid. Of course, the former has priority because human lives are acutely threatened. Therefore, the German government and the international community should always be in a position to help in the short term, both financially as well as with advice and action.

But we are convinced that medium and long-term development cooperation is just as necessary. Even beyond acute catastrophes, millions of people are suffering—especially in Africa. And we firmly disagree that development aid is "useless". If we do it right, we can achieve a lot with little money and give poor countries a decisive boost. Waiting to see whether they will eventually be able to do it on their own is not an option for us.

DOES DEVELOPMENT AID LEAD TO DEPENDENCY?
This is a legitimate question. In the past, development aid has indeed helped keep ailing and corrupt systems alive—cementing the status quo, often to the benefit of the ruling elite.

But these times are coming to an end. Government and private development aid workers have long since stopped handing out money according to a blanket principle; instead they use it directly on the ground to help people help themselves. In this way, they build up expertise and infrastructure—as a crucial basis for further progress under their own steam, completely independent of development aid.

ARE DEMANDS ON AFRICAN REFORM PARTNERS A FORM OF NEOCOLONIALISM?
Those who not only support, but also challenge, exert a certain pressure. And of course, those responsible in Africa could misunderstand this as paternalism. We do not accept this objection. By drafting the Marshall Plan with Africa, Minister Müller has made our aim clear: partnerships based on an equal footing and on the common goal of eradicating poverty (and thus preventing a mass exodus).

Our impression is that this aspiration has also shaped the tone of the bilateral talks so far; a colonial attitude seems to be alien to the German negotiators. But there is still a fine balance: on the one hand, we must formulate clear expectations and closely monitor whether reforms are implemented; and on the other hand, we must leave room for African solutions.

This will inevitably trigger debates that we should conduct with vigilance. After all, it would not be the first time that the reforming zeal of heads of state and government suddenly faltered, for whatever reason. If we cave in as soon as our demands are discredited as neocolonial presumptuousness, no one will be served—least of all those who are most at stake: the poor and the hungry.

ARE EFFECTIVE SOCIAL SECURITY SYSTEMS FEASIBLE IN POOR COUNTRIES?

It is undoubtedly a great challenge to establish robust social security systems. The biggest problems include empty state coffers, a low rate of formal employment and the lack of administrative structures. But we are convinced that these hurdles can be overcome if the political will is present.

Development economists tirelessly emphasize that even poor countries can afford effective social systems. To do so, they often have to build up better administration of taxes in order to increase government revenues and, at the same time, create incentives for official employment. This is difficult, but it is not rocket science. And many African countries have long since begun to take steps.

In addition, many governments have gained substantial experience with cash transfer programs in recent years in terms of identifying beneficiaries and organizing payments. In many places, therefore, there is already a solid basis in place to facilitate the next stage. The goal of effective social security is thus no more ambitious than it was in post-war Germany.

DON'T WE NEED TO STIMULATE GROWTH AND INCREASE TAX REVENUES FIRST?

Again and again, we hear that the time is not yet ripe or that African countries must first create the right conditions. We often hear: Let's attract private investors, ensure more growth, and build up an efficient financial administration first. But when exactly is the time right for social reforms?

We fear that we won't get anywhere with a checklist mentality. And the poor have no time to wait for the first items on the list to be checked off–especially since they cannot hope for a trickle-down effect. After all, investments and growth alone generally have nothing to offer them.

That is why we need to address several challenges simultaneously and coordinate specific measures. Then progress in the individual areas can fuel each other, because social security systems unleash forces for growth.

DON'T WE HAVE TO TAKE CARE OF "OUR" POOR FIRST—AND WHAT DOES AFRICA HAVE TO DO WITH US?

Another argument against development aid and infrastructure financing is: We also have too many poor and homeless people at home—and should help them instead of spending money in other countries. Here is an urgent appeal: Let's not play the poor of this world off against each other. Of course, we should also close gaps in the social net in this country to enable everyone to live in dignity (without, of course, turning the net into a hammock).

But one thing is clear: In sub-Saharan Africa in particular, the hardship is incomparably greater than in this country, and it is much more difficult for people to escape poverty through their own efforts. Moreover, we are convinced that solidarity must not stop at borders.

Those who do not support development cooperation for ethical reasons should at least do so out of pure egoism—and more resolutely than ever. Because climate change is hitting

Africa hard; and at the same time, globalization and digitization are ensuring that poor people all over the world know how well we are doing [in the Global North}. If Africa remains poor, several millions of people will flee to European countries, triggering serious social conflicts. At worst, this could bring nationalists to power and endanger our prosperity and peace based on European cooperation.

We are firmly convinced that the concept of "fortress Europe" cannot be sustained in the long term; it should be clear to everyone: If Africa does not fare better, we will soon fare worse.

Bibliography and references

CHAPTER 1

Beegle, Kathleen u.a.: Accelerating Poverty Reduction in Africa, Washington, DC: World Bank (https://openknowledge.worldbank.org/handle/10986/32354)

UN-Generalversammlung: Sustainable Development Goals, in: Resolution 69/315. Entwurf des Ergebnisdokuments des Gipfeltreffens der Vereinten Nationen zur Verabschiedung der Post-2015-Entwicklungsagenda, 1.9.2015 (https://www.un.org/depts/german/ gv-69/band3/ar69315.pdf)

Food and Agriculture Organization of the United Nations: State of Food Security and Nutrition. Safeguarding against economic slowdowns and downturns, Rom: FAO 2019 (http://www.fao.org/3/ca5162en/ca5162en.pdf)

Food and Agriculture Organization of the United Nations: Africa. Regional Overview of Food Security and Nutrition 2019, Accra: FAO 2020 (http://www.fao.org/3/ca7343en/CA7343EN.pdf)

Grebme, Klaus von u.a.: Welthunger-Index. Wie der Klimawandel den Hunger verschärft, Dublin u.a.: Welthungerhilfe 2019 (https://www.welthungerhilfe.de/aktuelles/publikation/detail/ welthunger-index-2019/)

International Labour Organization: World Social Protection Report 2017-19, Genf: ILO 2017 (https://www.ilo.org/wcmsp5/groups/public/--- dgreports/---dcomm/---publ/documents/publication/wcms_604882.pdf)

CHAPTER 2

Abela, Guy J. u.a.: Climate, conflict and forced migration, in: Global En-vironmental Change 54 (2019), p. 239-249 (https://pure.iiasa.ac.at/id/eprint/15684/1/1-s2.0-S0959378018301596-main.pdf)

Food and Agriculture Organization of the United Nations: Global Report on Food Crises, Rom: FAO 2018/2019 (http://www.fsincop.net/ fileadmin/user_upload/fsin/docs/global_report/2018/GRFC_2018_ Full_report_EN_Low_resolution.pdf und https://www.fsinplatform. org/sites/default/files/resources/files/GRFC_2019-Full_Report.pdf)

University of Notre Dame: Notre Dame Global Adaption Index, Notre Dame 2018 (https://gain.nd.edu/our-work/country-index/)

International Organization for Migration of the United Nations: Missing Migrants Project, Genf: IOM 2014-2020 (https://missingmigrants.iom.int/ report-missing)

Bundesamt für Migration und Flüchtlinge: Asylgeschäftsstatistik, Nürnberg: BAMF 2019/2020 (https://www.bamf.de/DE/Themen/Statistik/ Asylzahlen/AsylGesStatistik/asylgeschaeftsstatistik-node.html)

Goldin, Ian u.a.: Migration and the Economy. Economic Realities, Social Impacts & Political Choices, Oxford 2018 (https://www.oxfordmartin. ox.ac.uk/downloads/reports/2018_OMS_ Citi_Migration_GPS.pdf)

Chami, Ralph u.a.: Are Remittances Good for Labor Markets?, IMF 2018 (https://www.imf.org/en/Publications/WP/Issues/2018/05/09/ Are-Remittances-Good-for-Labor-Markets-in-LICs-MICs-and-Fragile-States-45839)

CHAPTER 3

Bardt, Hubertus: Afrikas divergierende wirtschaftliche Potentiale, Köln: IW 2017 (https://www.iwkoeln.de/fileadmin/publikationen/ 2017/357305/IW-Trends_2017-03-03_Bardt.pdf)

United Nations: World Population Prospects, New York: UN 2019 (https://population.un.org/wpp/Publications/Files/WPP2019_ Highlights.pdf)

Angenendt, Steffen u.a.: Bevölkerungswachstum, Fertilität und Kinderwunsch, Berlin: SWP 2014 (https://www.swp-berlin.org/fileadmin/ contents/products/studien/2014_S20_adt_pop.pdf)

Cilliers, Jakkie: Fertility, growth and the future of aid in sub-Saharan Africa, Brüssel: ISS 2017 (https://issafrica.s3.amazonaws.com/site/ uploads/aitwr-6-2.pdf)

Addati, Laura u.a.: Maternity and paternity at work. Law and practice across the world, Genf: ILO 2014 (http://www.ilo.org/wcmsp5/groups/public/---dgreports/---dcomm/documents/publication/wcms_242617.pdf)

CHAPTER 4

African Development Bank Group: African Economic Outlook 2020, Abidjan: ADBG 2020 (https://www.afdb.org/en/documents/ african-economic-outlook-2020)

African Development Bank Group: African Development Bank Outlook 2018, Abidjan: ADBG 2018 (https://www.afdb.org/en/documents/annual-report-2018)

CHAPTER 5

United Nations: World Investment Report 2019, New York: UN 2019 (https://unctad.org/en/PublicationsLibrary/wir2019_en.pdf)

Bundesministerium für Wirtschaft und Energie: Pro! Afrika - Perspektiven fördern, Chancen nutzen, Wirtschaft stärken, Berlin: BWE 2017 (https://www.bmwi.de/Redaktion/DE/Downloads/S-T/ strategiepapier-pro-afrika.pdf?__blob=publicationFile&v=22)

Morgan Stanley: Inside China's Plan to create a modern Silk Road, New York 2018 (https://www.morganstanley.com/ideas/china-belt-and-road)

Africa Attractiveness Report 2019, Johannesburg: EY 2019

Trebesch, Christoph u.a.: Chinas Overseas Lending, Kiel: ifw 2019 (https://www.ifw-kiel.de/fileadmin/Dateiverwaltung/IfW-Publications/Christoph_Trebesch/KWP_2132.pdf)

SECTION II: THE KEY STATEMENTS

Sommer, Theo: China First. Die Welt auf dem Weg ins chinesische Jahrhundert, München: C. H. Beck 2019

Stiglitz, Joseph: Making Globalization Work, New York: Norton 2006

Stiglitz, Joseph u.a.: Fair Trade For All. How Trade Can Promote Development., Oxford: Oxford University Press 2005

Spiegel, Peter u.a.: Die 1-Dollar-Revolution: Globaler Mindestlohn gegen Ausbeutung und Armut, München: Piper 2016

Global Wage Report 2018/2019, Genf: International Labour Organization 2019 (https://www.ilo.org/global/publications/ books/WCMS_650553/lang--en/index.htm)

Macron, Emmanuel: Für einen Neubeginn in Europa, Paris 2019 (https://www.elysee.fr/emmanuel-macron/2019/03/04/fur-einen-neubeginn-in-europa.de)

Global Wealth Databook 2018, Zürich: Crédit Suisse 2018 (https://www.credit-suisse.com/about-us/de/research-berichte/studien-publikationen.html)

The Commitment to Reducing Inequality Index, Nairobi: Oxfam 2018 (https://www.oxfamamerica.org/explore/research-publications/the-commitment-to-reducing-inequality-index-2018/)

Loewe, Markus u.a.: Keine Stabilität ohne soziale Sicherheit, Bonn: Deutsches Institut für Entwicklungspolitik 2017 (https://www.die-gdi.de/die-aktuelle-kolumne/article/keine-stabilitaet-ohne-soziale-sicherheit/)

Kriegesmann, Karina: Das brasilianische Transferprogramm „Bolsa Familia", Berlin: Konrad-Adenauer-Stiftung 2011 (https://www.kas.de/de/web/sopla/publikationen/einzeltitel/-/content/das-brasilianische-transferprogramm-bolsa-familia-)

Fallstudie Malawi: Grundsicherung. Ein Netz für sehr arme Menschen aufspannen, Berlin/Bonn: Bundesministerium für wirtschaftliche Entwicklung und Zusammenarbeit 2016 (http://www.bmz.de/de/themen/2030_agenda/historie/MDGs_2015/unser_beitrag/malawi_soziale_sicherung/index.html)

Kaps, Alisa u.a.: Afrikas demografische Vorreiter – Wie sinkende Kinderzahlen Entwicklung beschleunigen , Berlin: Berlin-Institut für Bevölkerung und Entwicklung 2019, (https://www.berlin-institut.org/publikationen/studien/afrikas-demografische-vorreiter.html)

Boldrin, Michele u.a.: Fertility and Social Security, Cambridge: JODE - Journal of Demographic Economics, Cambridge University Press 2015 (https://www.cambridge.org/core/journals/journal-of-demographic-economics/article/fertility-and-social-security/4FA674742794B-C43650452A21CBD1C0D)

SECTION III: THE AGENDA

Müller, Gerd / Weber, Manfred: Europa muss ein Signal setzen, Handelsblatt vom 17.8.2020

Conze, Albrecht: Es ist Zeit für die EBRD: Wie Europa auf Chinas Dominanz in Afrika reagieren kann, Kampala 2019 (https://www.united-europe.eu/de/2019/07/es-ist-zeit-fuer-die-ebrd-wie-europa-auf-chinas-dominanz-in-afrika-reagieren-kann/)

Berglöf, Eric: Es ist Zeit für eine schlagkräftige europäische Entwicklungsbank, WirtschaftsWoche vom 13.12.2019

Development Aid at a Glance – Statistics by Region – 2. Africa, Paris: OECD 2019 (http://www.oecd.org/dac/financing-sustainable-development/development-finance-standards/official-development-assistance.htm)

Juel, Jørgen u.a.: Elite Capture of Foreign Aid - Evidence from Offshore Bank Accounts, Washington: World Bank Group 2020 (https://documents.worldbank.org/en/publication/documents-reports/documentdetail/493201582052636710/elite-capture-of-foreign-aid-evidence-from-offshore-bank-accounts)

Afrika und Europa: Neue Partnerschaft für Entwicklung, Frieden und Zukunft – Eckpunkte für einen Marshallplan mit Afrika, Berlin/Bonn: Bundesministerium für wirtschaftliche Entwicklung und Zusammenarbeit 2017 (http://www.bmz.de/de/laender_regionen/marshallplan_mit_afrika/)

The G-20 Compact with Africa – A Joint AfDB, IMF and WBG Report, Abidjan / Washington: International Monetary Fund u.a. 2017 (https://www.compactwithafrica.org/content/compactwithafrica/home/documents.html)

Transformation Index, Gütersloh: Bertelsmann Stiftung 2019 (https://www.bti-project.org/de/home.html?&cb=00000)

Doing Business 2019, Washington: World Bank 2018 (https://www.doingbusiness.org/en/reports/global-reports/doing-business-2019)

„In eine gemeinsame Zukunft investieren: Die Wirtschaftspartnerschaft zwischen Afrika und der EU im Post-Cotonou-Rahmen", German-French paper, Berlin/Paris 2018

FURTHER SOURCES:

Statistisches Bundesamt, Deutsche Welle, Handelsblatt, Neue Züricher Zeitung, Süddeutsche, WirtschaftsWoche, Die Zeit, Menschen für Menschen – Karlheinz Böhms Äthiopienhilfe, SOS Kinderdörfer

The authors

MARTIN SCHOELLER, 64, is co-founder and managing partner of the Schoeller Group in Pullach (around 4,000 employees, 1 billion euros in group sales) and until recently was regional chairman of the association Die Familienunternehmer (the family entrepreneurs) in Bavaria. He has been involved with Africa for many years, among other things as the initiator of the Desert Food Foundation and as Honorary Consul of the Republic of Togo. In this function, he is in close contact with political decision-makers on site and in Germany in order to develop aid concepts. (schoeller.org and desertfood.org).

DANIEL SCHOENWITZ, 43, is a business journalist, columnist and publicist in Düsseldorf. After studying economics, he graduated from Georg von Holtzbrinck Schule für Wirtschaftsjournalisten (school for business journalists) and worked for six years as an editor for *WirtschaftsWoche*. Since 2010, the economics graduate has been writing as a freelance author for media such as *Die Zeit, Manager Magazin, WirtschaftsWoche* and *GermanBoard-News*. (www.danielschoenwitz.de; Twitter: @dschoenwitz).

Weitere verschollene oder unbekannte Essays,
Handschriften oder Reden von Stefan Zweig

Zweigs Romane sind seit Jahrzehnten Millionenbestseller. Dass der
als Essayist nicht minder bedeutsam, um nicht zu sagen: brillant,
nd zumeist wenig Beachtung. Eine neue Buchreihe entreißt nun
Arbeiten dem Dunkel des Vergessens. Was dabei zu Tage kommt,
drucksvoll, hochinteressant, ja: sensationell. Dies auch bezüglich der
lität!

n besonderes Verdienst ist es, dass Klaus Gräbner in jahrelanger pe-
Recherche weitverstreute unveröffentlichte, verschollene oder verges-
exte von Stefan Zweig zusammengetragen und transkribiert hat. Die
sind mit viel Sorgfalt zu einzelnen Themen (sei es Zeitgeschichte,
elle oder tagespolitische Themen, die deutschsprachige Literatur
die übersetzte) zusammengefasst, sodass jedes dieser hochwertig
teten Bücher ein schillerndes, zuweilen durch Faksimiles und/oder
lungen bereichertes Gesamtkunstwerk ist.

tranScript
*Literaturwissenschaftliche
Sonderreihe+*

№ 1 Stefan Zweig: »Erst wenn die Nacht fällt«
Politische Essays und Reden 1932 – 1942
UNBEKANNTE TEXTE

№ 2 Stefan Zweig: »Nur die Lebendigen schaffen die Welt«
Politische, kulturelle, soziohistorische
Betrachtungen und Essays 1911 – 1940
VERGESSENE TEXTE

№ 3 Stefan Zweig: STERNBILDER
Sammlung verschollener Essays über deutschsprachige Klassiker
on Bettina von Arnim über Friedrich Schiller bis Karl Marx

№ 4 Stefan Zweig: ZEITLOSE
Sammlung verschollener Essays über fremdsprachige Klassiker
Von Aischylos über William Shakespeare bis Paul Verlaine

VOR DEM STURM

Stefan Zweig

VOR DEM STURM
Europa zwischen 1900 und 1914
Aus dem Nachlass

Herausgeber: Klaus Gräbner

Kommentiert von
Laura Rösner (EDITION ROESNER)

Stefan Zweig

N° 5
tranScript
*Literaturwissenschaftliche
Sonderreihe*

EDITION ROESNER
artesLiteratur

Titelbild: © EDITION ROESNER

Gefördert durch das

BUNDESKANZLERAMT ÖSTERREICH
KUNST

und das Land Niederösterreich

KULTUR
NIEDERÖSTERREICH

Erste Auflage
© 2018 by EDITION ROESNER
Krems an der Donau
Datenverarbeitung:
Light Server Systems/Jürgen Dorn
Druck: Theiss GmbH, Österreich
Alle Rechte vorbehalten
ISBN 978-3-903059-70-2

www.edition-roesner.at

Inhalt

7 Europa zur Jahrhundertwende

17 Serbien und der Panslawismus

34 Beginn der Einkreisung der Zentralmächte

46 Von Mürzsteg bis zur türkischen Revolution
(1903 – 1907)

55 Die Annexion
1908

71 Die vollendete Einkreisung Deutschlands
und Österreich-Ungarns
1908 – 1912

81 Tripolis und der Balkankrieg
1912 – 1913

92 Die Balkankriege, die Londoner Konferenz
und Albanien
1913

103 Die Ermordung des Thronfolgers
1914

117 Die Kriegserklärung
1914

141 Nachwort *von Klaus Gräbner*

Europa zur Jahrhundertwende

Friedensglocken läuten das neue Jahrhundert, das letzte des zweiten Jahrtausends ein. In Haag wird mit Kelle und Spaten emsig ein Bau gefördert, der Tempel des Friedens soll dort erstehen für alle Völker Europas, ein hochragendes Denkmal ihrer Brüderlichkeit. Zum zweiten Mal schon haben sich die Gesandten aller Länder dort versammelt, um den Krieg zwischen den Kulturmächten für ewig zu verbannen, zum zweiten Mal, seit jenes merkwürdige Manifest des Zaren am Goethetag des Jahres 1898[1] in die Welt gegangen war, in dem der letzte Autokrat des Kontinents, der Herrscher der gewaltsamsten Nation Europas, die Völker einlud, die unfruchtbaren Rüstungen einzustellen und ihre Ansprüche nicht mehr den Waffen, sondern einzig der moralischen Einigkeit ihrer Führer dem Schiedsspruch der ständigen Haager Konferenz anheimzustellen. Die Worte des Manifestes – das in seltsamer Ironie gerade der russisch-japanische Krieg kaum vier Jahre später[2] in Fetzen riß – sind noch heute und gerade heute bezaubernd in ihrem Klang: „Die Aufrechterhaltung des allgemeinen Friedens und eine mögliche Herabsetzung der übermäßigen Rüstungen […] stellen sich in der gegenwär-

---

[1] *Manifest des Zaren am Goethetag des Jahres 1898:* Vermutl. das „Friedens-Manifest des russischen Zaren Nikolaus II." vom 24. August 1898; es ist nach wie vor nicht bekannt, an wen dies erging oder wer antwortete.

[2] *Russisch-japanischer Krieg:* Am 12. August 1903 wurde der Abzug der russischen Truppen aus der Mandschurei gefordert. Nachdem hier keine Einigung eintrat, beschloss am 4. Februar 1904 eine Konferenz den Angriff; sechs Tage später wurde der Krieg erklärt.

tigen Lage der ganzen Welt als ein Ideal dar, auf das die Bemühungen aller Regierungen gerichtet sein müßten. [...] Im Laufe der letzten zwanzig Jahre hat der Wunsch nach einer allgemeinen Beruhigung in dem Empfinden der zivilisierten Nationen besonders festen Fuß gefaßt, die Erhaltung des Friedens ist als Endziel der internationalen Politik aufgestellt worden. [...] Eine Konferenz würde mit Gottes Hilfe ein günstiges Vorzeichen des kommenden Jahrhunderts sein. Sie würde in einem mächtigen Bündnis die Bestrebungen aller Staaten vereinigen, welche aufrichtig darum bemüht sind, den großen Gedanken des Weltfriedens triumphieren zu lassen über alle Elemente des Unfriedens und der Zwietracht. Sie würde zugleich ihr Zusammengehen besiegeln durch eine solidarische Weihe der Prinzipien des Rechts und der Gerechtigkeit, auf denen die Sicherheit der Staaten und die Wohlfahrt der Völker beruht."

Die Friedensglocken klangen, und gläubig lauschte ihnen Europa zu. Der Weltkrieg, ein mörderischer Zusammenstoß der Großmächte, schien auf unübersehbare Zeiten vermieden. In allen Staaten hatte mit der fortschreitenden Industrialisierung der Sozialismus Stimme und Geltung gewonnen, dessen erster Programmpunkt der Ausgleich nationaler Feindseligkeit war. Der Fortschritt der Zivilisation hatte eine Werterhöhung des einzelnen Menschenlebens mit sich gebracht: Zu kostbar schien selbst in den Millionenmassen jede einzelne Existenz, um leichtfertig politischen Ambitionen geopfert zu werden, zu sehr war der allgemeine Wohlstand Bedürfnis geworden, als daß man ihn ohne Zwang auf das Spiel setzen wollte. Dazu kamen Bindungen mehrfacher Art, die den Frieden zu verbürgen schienen, vor allem die Persönlichkeiten der Monarchen. Die Königin Viktoria hatte das Jubiläum einer sechzigjährigen Regierung zu feiern, Franz Joseph I. das einer halbhundertjährigen Regentschaft, beide gesinnt, durch eine Freundschaft der europäischen Länder die friedliche Entwicklung ihrer eigenen zu erhöhen, der junge Zar hatte unter Wittes[3] Einfluß öffentlich jenes pazifistische Manifest zum Grundstein seiner Politik nach außen hin verkündet und der energische Wille Kaiser Wilhelm II., der mit Unruhe zu Beginn seiner Regierung von Frankreich aus beobachtet worden war, jede Möglichkeit eines bewaffneten Konfliktes niedergetreten. Nirgends war im Anbeginn des Jahrhunderts in den äußeren Zeichen des Weltbildes die Möglichkeit einer Verschattung zu erkennen.

Aber auch der innere Trieb der europäischen Staaten war damals nicht gegeneinander gewandt. Der fortschreitende Industrialismus, der Ferntrieb des Handels hatten es mit sich gebracht, daß der Expansionswille der Nationen nicht so sehr an den engen Grenzen drückte, als er überland in den Kolonien gleichsam eine Verlängerung und Vervielfachung der heimischen Produktionsmöglichkeiten anstrebte. Damit waren die Reibungsflächen der Politik zwar vermehrt, gleichzeitig aber von den Zentren der nationalen Erregung entfernt, der Funke eines Konflikts konnte nicht so leicht überspringen in das Herz der Nationen und dort die Flamme der Volkserregung entfachen. Das Volk bedarf einer gewissen Sinnlichkeit der Konflikte und sieht ungern jenseits des engeren Blickkreises das Ziel seiner Leidenschaft; so konnten die gleichzeitigen Ambitionen der Mächte in Afrika, Asien und den Archipelen niemals jene Unruhe schaffen, die fast immer die notwendige Vorbedingung eines Krieges ist. Die politischen Auseinanderset-

---

[3] *Sergei Juljewitsch Witte:* Russischer Eisenbahn- und Finanzminister; erster Regierungschef Russlands, der mit der Kabinettsbildung beauftragt wurde (1905 – 1906); 1849 – 1915.

zungen zu Beginn des Jahrhunderts waren darum wesentlich diplomatische und als solche eher geneigt, in Verträgen geordnet und beschwichtigt zu werden, als wie die wahrhaft nationalen Konflikte der Vergangenheit in gegenseitige Befeindung und Krieg auszuarten.

Der Friedenswille der europäischen Staaten um die Jahrhundertwende begründete sich überdies durch innere politische Notwendigkeiten. Fast alle Nationen waren damals mit sozialen und innerpolitischen Problemen beschäftigt. Deutschland und Österreich-Ungarn, die Zentralmächte Europas, der Drehpunkt aller möglichen politischen Verschiebungen beharrten fest in sich selbst.

D e u t s c h l a n d ist erstarkt, aber noch immer in Selbstordnung begriffen: Es hat nachzuholen gehabt in den dreißig Jahren seines Bestandes, was in den nachbarlichen [Ländern] seit hunderten Jahren schon Ordnung und Gewohnheit geworden war. Seit zwanzig Jahren erst hatte es eine Handelsflotte, kaum mehr als ein Dezennium seine Kolonien –, und die ungeheure Geschwindigkeit, mit der es sich aus einem im Wesentlichen agrarischen Staatengebilde in den größten Handels- und Industriestaat des Kontinents entwickelt hat, fordert im Gesetzeswesen, in der Verwaltung unablässig Reformen. Spät gekommen, rasch in die erste Reihe der Nationen aufgerückt und doch voll des Willens, ohne Gewalt seine Stellung sich zu erobern, bedarf es einer weisen Ordnung seiner Kräfte, einer zielbewußten Organisation und vor allem des Friedens, den es durch mehrfache Bündnisse für sich bekräftigt weiß. Der Dreibund als Grundlage, eine wohlwollende und schon traditionell gewordene Freundschaft mit Rußland und England ermöglichen ihm, den noch immer lebendigen Revanchegedanken in Frankreich nicht mit dem Schwert niederschlagen zu müssen, sondern sein allmähliches Erlöschen ruhig abzuwarten und die Jahre dieses unbesorgten Abwartens einzig für den Ausbau seiner inneren Einheit und Kraft nutzbar zu machen.

Ö s t e r r e i c h – U n g a r n wiederum, das sich die schwere Aufgabe gestellt hat, die Vielheit seiner Nationen zu ordnen, ohne in diesem Widerstreit der einzelnen Völker jemals gewaltsame Lösungen zu erzwingen, ist eben durch diesen Willen zur friedlichen Auseinandersetzung von durchaus friedlicher Tendenz genötigt. Jede äußere Machterweiterung würde zunächst das innere Gleichgewicht seiner Nationen verrücken und stören: So ist seine Absicht keine expansive, sondern einzig eine pazifikatorische. Das Verhältnis Österreichs zu Ungarn, das eine ständige Aussprache fordert, will mit Liebe und Sorgfalt immer neu befestigt sein. Aber um das höchste Ziel zu erreichen, gleichsam den Sinn Österreich-Ungarns für die Weltgeschichte, die friedliche und dauernde Versöhnung der Slawen und Deutschen im Reiche, um diese unwandelbare Einigung zu einer Tatsache zu gestalten, muß jede äußere Veränderung im Staatsgebilde vorläufig ausgeschlossen sein, weil sie das Erreichte wieder in Frage stellte, die Diskussion wieder in Fluß brächte. Kaiser und König Franz Joseph vertritt mit seiner Persönlichkeit gleichsam in höchster symbolischer Form diesen Willen zum unveränderten friedlichen Bestand; seit fünfzig Jahren Monarch, ist er für alle Völker des Reichs das Unwandelbare geworden, die lauterste Idee des Friedens und der Versöhnung. Die Bündnisse bekunden nach außen deutlich die Gesinnung zum unveränderten Bestand, denn gerade die Nationen, denen Österreich-Ungarns letzte Kriege vor einem Menschalter galten, Deutschland und Italien, sind ihm geeint, die Beziehungen zu den Nachbarmächten ohne jede

Feindlichkeit. Groß und friedlich tritt auch Österreich-Ungarn in das neue Jahrhundert.

Selbst F r a n k r e i c h , das ungebärdig und unversöhnlich seinen Schmerz um Elsaß-Lothringen zu einer lauten Drohung gegen Deutschland und den Frieden Europas umgestaltet hatte, ist merkwürdig versöhnlich gestimmt um jene Jahrhundertwende, denn es macht eine gefährliche moralische und politische Krise durch. Die kleine Affäre eines wegen Spionage verurteilten Offiziers war allmählich zur wichtigsten politischen Entscheidung für das ganze Land geworden. Vergebens hatte man sich bemüht, die lästige Angelegenheit des Kapitän Dreyfuß[4] unter einem Urteil zu verscharren, mit einem zweiten Urteil neuerlich zu begraben und dann mit einer Amnestie zu verschleiern: Der Prozeß ist aber damals längst nicht mehr die Affäre eines Einzelnen, sondern der Kraftmesser für die republikanische und die reaktionäre Partei, deren Widerstreit allmählich zu einem offenen Ringen zwischen Staat und Kirche emporwächst. Die Ministerien stürzen, Skandale unterwühlen das Vertrauen in die Armee und mit diesem Vertrauen auch die Neigung zum Kriege mit Deutschland, umso mehr als die politische Niederlage bei Faschoda[5] gegen England, als die frischere Wunde den alten Schmerz um Elsaß-Lothringen vergessen macht. Die Eroberung eines großen Kolonialreiches, der verdoppelte Reichtum, bindet die Energie an das eigene Land, und so ist selbst die unge-

---

[4] *Alfred Dreyfus*: Jüdischer Offizier im französischen Generalstab; u. a. aufgrund der Dreyfus-Affäre bekannt, welche sich um die ungerechtfertigte Verurteilung wegen Landesverrates drehte (1894 – 1906); 1859 – 1935.

[5] *Faschoda-Krise*: Seit 1905: Kodok; fand 1898 zwischen Großbritannien und Frankreich statt; neben dem Panamaskandal und der Dreyfus-Affäre die dritte Krise für Frankreich.

bärdigste Kriegspartei seit dem Jahre 1870 genötigt, sich dem europäischen Willen nach Frieden zu fügen.

I t a l i e n , als geeintes Reich gleichaltrig mit Deutschland, ist wie dieses mit seiner inneren Konsolidierung beschäftigt. Der unglückliche Krieg gegen Abessinien hat seinen Willen zur kolonialen Ausbreitung merklich gehemmt, aber gleichzeitig die Organisation des Handels und der Finanzen gefördert. Auch seine Ambitionen sind wesentlich wirtschaftliche, und die rasche offenkundige Gesundung nach der schweren Krise stärkt das nationale Bewußtsein gegen die radikalen und revolutionären Tendenzen, die mit der Ermordung des Königs Humbert ihren Höhepunkt überschritten haben. An die beiden Zentralmächte gebunden, kann es seine ganzen Kräfte zur Entfaltung bringen und wird in diesem Bündnis erst wahrhaft zur Großmacht.

Das Wesentliche und Entscheidende aber für die friedliche Stimmung zu jener Jahrhundertwende ist die Tatsache, daß die beiden Staaten, die nicht nur Ausgestaltung ihrer eigenen Volksgrenze, sondern Weltherrschaft, ein Imperium im Sinne Roms anstreben – daß England und Rußland, die beiden einander und eigentlich jedem Staate feindlichen Mächte mit ihren Bestrebungen von Europa abgelenkt sind. Ihre Eroberungsgier hat von dem kleinen Brocken gelassen, um den sie sich jahrzehntelang gezankt, sie sparen die gewaltsame Aufteilung der Türkei und Aufteilung des persischen Erbes für eine andere Stunde: Ihrem Ehrgeiz sind nun ganze Weltteile gerade groß genug.

E n g l a n d vollendet in einem schweren und nicht eben heroischen Kriege die Eroberung des afrikanischen Weltteils. Stück um Stück hatte es, die Rivalität der europäischen Völker schürend und nutzend, an sich gerissen, und seine ungeheure Anstrengung ging während der letzten

Jahrzehnte dahin, die einzelnen abgerissenen Teile in ein Ganzes zu verbinden. Die Kap-Kairo-Bahn, die vom Norden bis zum südlichsten Punkte den ganzen ungeheuren Erdteil Afrika durchmißt, soll einzig durch englisches Gebiet gehen, und die Diplomatie scheut vor keinem Mittel zurück, um dieses gigantische Ziel zu erreichen. Zuerst wurde Ägypten den Türken geraubt wie einst das Kap den Holländern. Ein Versuch, durch zügellose Agitationen gegen die „belgischen Greuel" unter der Maske der Moral den Kongostaat in die Hand zu bekommen, scheitert an der diplomatischen Geschicklichkeit des Königs Leopold[6]; auch das deutsche Kolonialgebiet, das den Weg sperrt, zu rauben, ist die Stunde noch nicht gekommen. So wendet sich England zunächst gegen die Schwächsten, gegen die Burenrepubliken, deren unerwarteter Widerstand es zu äußerster Anstrengung nötigt, anderseits aber sich die ungeteilten Sympathien ganz Europas gewinnt. England steht in seiner *splendid isolation* außerhalb der europäischen Interessensphäre in dieser Stunde der Jahrhundertwende, und die Abwesenheit seiner agitatorischen und eigensüchtigen Interessen ist sofort als eine Entspannung aller Gegensätze fühlbar.

R u ß l a n d wiederum, seines unangenehmsten Konkurrenten um die Weltmacht ledig, lenkt seinen Willen nach Osten. Auch seine Landgier, mächtig am eigenen Wachstum genährt, will ein ganzes ungeheures Reich, die chinesische Welt mit ihren hunderten Millionen, sich unterjochen. Mit brutaler Stoßkraft hat dieses kräftige Volk sich aus dem halbasiatischen Binnenland an die Meere vorge-

---

[6] *Leopold II.*: Gründete den Kongo-Freistaat; Schätzungen über das Kongogräuel liegen bei zehn Millionen Opfern. Hier folgt Zweig bedauerlicherweise der Geschicklichkeit des Königs Leopold.

trieben, an die Ostsee zuerst, wo Peter der Große seine Hauptstadt baute, unter Katharina sodann an das Schwarze Meer. Zum Mittelmeer verwehrte ihnen England den Weg durch die sorgfältig gehütete Dardanellensperre: So drängt die ungeheure Welle ihrer Kraft gegen den Stillen Ozean. In Strömung und Gegenströmung hat sich der russische Machtwille bald gegen Europa, bald gegen Asien, nach Westen oder nach Osten geworfen, und bei jedem Zurückebben war ihnen ein Stück Land zugefallen. Aber der Machthunger ist am eigenen Riesenmaße gigantisch geworden, nicht Landstriche mehr wollen sie, sondern ganze Reiche. Persien, die Mandschurei und China sind ihre nächsten Ziele, darum gebietet ihre Politik ihnen in Europa Zurückhaltung und maskiert mit dem Friedensmanifeste den brutalen Eroberungsdrang. Im Gegensatz zu Österreich-Ungarn ist Rußland keineswegs bemüht, die Vielfalt der Völker in sich harmonisch aufzulösen: Die gleiche rücksichtslose Gewalt, die fremde Länder mit den Waffen an sich zwingt, knechtet auch die sprachliche und politische Freiheit. Jede Unruhe wird, statt nach innen besänftigt, nach außen abgelenkt, das äußere Raummaß ist die Norm der Entwicklung und nicht die innere Ordnung. Nur Ablenkung nimmt daher Rußland seine Gefährlichkeit für den europäischen Frieden, und wenn zu jener Stunde die Last seiner Menschenwucht und die Drohung seiner stets aggressiven Gesinnung geringer auf Europa drückt, so ist der Grund in jener Wendung nach Osten zu suchen. Sobald die Schwerkraft des Kolosses nach dem Stillen Meere sich neigt, können die nachbarlichen Reiche ruhig atmen: Nur die Beschäftigung Rußlands, nicht seine Gesinnung, verbürgt die Ruhe der Welt.

So dürfen die Friedensglocken klingen und in den Herzen widerhallen. Am Balkan brodeln wie immer kleine

Kämpfe, aber Europa hütet sich wohl, in diesen Hexenkessel vorwitzig zu greifen. Bismarcks Wort, daß derlei Interessen nicht „die Knochen eines einzigen pommerschen Musketiers wert seien", ist die Maxime der Diplomatie geblieben: Man ist entschlossen, den Fäulnisprozeß dort nicht zu unterbrechen und die Pandorabüchse nicht verwegen zu öffnen. Es phosphoresziert dort allerdings von kleinen Revolten der Albanesen und Mazedonier, aber man ist in Europa schon allmählich gewohnt, diese ewigen Raubzüge und Guerillakämpfe als eine notwendige Begleiterscheinung des Frühlings am Balkan zu betrachten, als ein fast meteorologisches Problem, so wie Wettersturz und Frühlingsgewitter. Österreich-Ungarn als benachbarte Großmacht hat keine Eroberungsgelüste, dadurch ist die gefährliche Stelle isoliert, und trotz der beständigen Reibung der Balkanmächte kann der Funke nicht in das Gebäude der großen Staaten überspringen und die Welt entflammen. Zwischen jener Unruhe und Europas Friedenswille steht die Monarchie als eherner Wall. Ihr aufrechter Bestand hält Orient und Okzident im Gleichgewicht.

Zu einer erhabenen Friedensfeier gestaltet sich darum diese Jahrhundertwende, die selbst schon jahrhundertferne scheint von unseren ernsten Tagen. Sie hat jene große und gewaltige Ruhe der Sammlung, wie sie argen Erschöpfungen folgt oder ungeheuren Anstrengungen vorausgeht. In Wahrheit ist sie nichts als eine Atempause der Weltgeschichte, und die Stille, die wir damals als dauernde Verheißung zu genießen vermeinten, war nur die Sekunde der letzten Sammlung für den großen, den fürchterlichsten Kampf der Menschheit.

Serbien und der Panslawismus

In diese Stille zuckt plötzlich das erste Wetterleuchten. Es stammt aus dem alten Sturmwinkel Europas: aus dem Balkan.

In der Nacht des 10. Juni 1903[7] knattern Schüsse im Belgrader [Schloss] Konak. Soldaten umstellen den königlichen Palast, die Offiziere dringen ein, den Revolver in der Faust. Wer ihnen den Weg wehrt, wird niedergeschossen. Die Lakaien flüchten, nichts schützt den jungen König Alexander und die Königin Draga mehr als die verriegelte Tür ihres ehelichen Gemaches. Eine Dynamitpatrone, die einen der Verschwörer mitsprengt, beseitigt das Hindernis, und unter zahllosen Schüssen und Stichen sterben der letzte Obrenović[8] und seine Gattin. Die warmen, blutigen Leichen werden halbnackt aus den Fenstern aufs Pflaster geworfen, dann geht die Jagd der Verschwörer weiter von Haus zu Haus. Alle mißliebigen Offiziere und Politiker werden niedergeknallt, Schüsse knattern durch die Straße, und – seltsamerweise – schon klingt die Parole „Hoch, König Peter!" Die Adjutanten und Generale, die nachts noch an der königlichen Tafel saßen und mit Champagner ihren ahnungslosen Opfern zutranken, schwingen die blutigen Säbel und grüßen einen fremden Flüchtling in Genf,

---

[7] Auch bekannt als „Blutnacht"; 11. Juni lt. Wikipedia

[8] *Aleksandar Obrenović*: Mit ihm endete die Dynastie der Obrenović; König von Serbien; verheiratet mit *Draga Mašin*. Die Eheschließung und sein österreichfreundliches Verhalten führten zu der Offiziersverschwörung um Dragutin Dimitrijević, genannt Apis, und dem Mord an dem Königspaar; 1876 – 1903.

dessen Namen der Stadt und der Welt noch vor Stunden unbekannt war.

Europa schauert bei der Nachricht. Ekel und Abscheu sind aller Staaten einhelliges Gefühl. Aber dies Gefühl denkt nicht daran, sich in Tat umzusetzen, man betrachtet selbst ein so grauenhaftes Geschehnis nur als innerpolitische, nicht als europäische Angelegenheit. Die Diplomatie befürchtet, durch Einmengungen sich die Hände zu beschmutzen und hält sich abseits. Fürstenmord und Verwandtenmord ist in der Geschichte Serbiens ja an der Tagesordnung, in den hundert Jahren seines unabhängigen Bestandes hat es zehn Regenten gehabt, von denen keiner eines natürlichen Endes als Herrscher gestorben ist. Der sagenumwitterte Dušan[9] des byzantinischen Kaiserreiches war durch Vatermord zur Krone gelangt, um sie durch Mord zu verlieren, Kara Georg[10], der Befreier Serbiens vom Türkenjoch, wiederholt seltsam sein Bild, Vatermörder auch er, und ermordet wie jener. Durch eine merkwürdige jahrhundertelange Anbildung haben sich die grausamen Sitten der byzantinischen Dynastien, die brutalen Machtenteignungen der Paschas und Padischahs, in Serbien bis in unsere Tage hinein erhalten, und die Regierung des letzten Obrenović ist in seiner despotischen Raserei eine grauenhafte Analogie gewisser Vorgänge am Hofe der dekadenten römischen Kaiser, des Caligula und Claudius, nur,

---

[9] *Stefan Uroš IV. Dušan*: Aus der Nemanjić-Dynastie; gilt als mächtigster Herrscher und erster Zar von Serbien; trägt den Beinamen „Der Mächtige", und seine Herrschaftszeit gilt als „Goldenes Zeitalter" Serbiens; unter ihm wurde es eine Großmacht; verfasste eines der ersten Gesetzesbücher „Dušanov zakonik"; 1308 – 1355.

[10] *Kara Georg, Đorđe Petrović, Karađorđe*; Begründer der Dynastie Karađorđević; auch bekannt als „Schwarzer Georg"; gewählter Anführer des Ersten Serbischen Aufstandes; 1762 – 1817.

daß sie mitten in unserer europäischen Zivilisation unter der Maske der Kultur sich vollziehen. Von Sueton, aus der Biographie der Zäsaren, könnte die seine stammen, wie er, Sohn eines vertriebenen, ausschweifenden Herrschers und einer jenem feindlichen Mutter, ein Knabe noch, seine Regenten fortjagt, die Krone an sich reißt und sich, ohne das Parlament zu befragen, als großjährig erklärt. Ungeduldig, leidenschaftlich tritt er alle Rechte nieder, wechselt die Ministerien, sobald sie nicht seiner Willkür dienen und erzwingt – freilich nur durch die Hilfe des Zaren, der diesen jungen Herrscher Rußland verpflichten will und als Trauzeuge bei der schmachvollen Hochzeit dient – die Anerkennung einer mehr als zweifelhaften Frau, der Draga Mašin, als Königin. Der beispiellose Skandal ihrer Polsterschwangerschaft macht die Tragikomödie bald zur Operette, und da der ehrgeizigen Frau die geplante Kindesunterschiebung nicht gelingt, arbeitet sie darauf hin, ihren Bruder, den Leutnant Nikodem Lunjevica, als Thronerben vorzuschieben.

In diesem Augenblick, da die Thronfolgerschaft gesichert werden soll, greifen die Verschwörer ein und machen mit Säbel und Revolver dem unbequemen Mann ein Ende. Prätendenten für die Krone der Obrenović sind seit hundert Jahren die Karageorgević[11], die Nachfahren jenes Befreiers, der von dem ersten rechtmäßigen Herrscher Serbiens beseitigt wurde, wofür die Karageorgević nach orientalischem Brauch Blutrache nahmen. Da sie sich der Regentschaft nur vorübergehend, von 1842 bis 1856 bemächtigen können und sie dann durch Volksbeschluß an die Obrenović zurückgeben müssen, greifen sie zu anderen Mitteln. Am 16. Juni 1868 wird der kinderlose Fürst Michael

---

[11] *Haus Karađorđević*: Regierte abwechselnd mit dem Haus Obrenović; unter Josip Broz Tito verlor es die Macht 1945.

Obrenović im Parke von Topschider[12] ermordet. Aber die Entrüstung Europas und der Unwille in Serbien bringen die Mörder um die Beute: Der Neffe Michaels, der nachmalige König Milan[13], wird zum Herrscher proklamiert und Alexander Karageorgević wegen des Mordes zu zwanzig Jahren Zuchthaus verurteilt, aber von Ungarn nicht ausgeliefert. Erst dessen Sohn Peter hat nach der Ermordung des letzten Obrenović den Weg zum serbischen Königsthrone frei und eilt von Genf sofort her, wo er angeblich ahnungslos weilte, um sich der blutigen Krone zu bemächtigen.

Am Morgen nach der Mordnacht wehten in Belgrad von allen Dächern und Balkonen die Fahnen, aber nicht Trauerflaggen für den ermordeten König, sondern Wimpel in den hellen Nationalfarben. Das Grauenhafte der Tat schien dem Volke, das erst seit einem halben Jahrhundert der orientalischen Herrschaft sich entrungen, ganz gleichgültig. Nach wenigen Stunden war die Wahl des Peter Karageorgević dank der Agitation der Armee gesichert, doch der Diplomatie fehlte noch das Wichtigste, die Zustimmung Europas. Zwischen allen Höfen und Staatskanzleien gingen die Verhandlungen her und hin: Die Mitschuld des Königs Peter[14] war nicht erwiesen und doch

---

[12] *Mihailo III.*: Aus dem Hause Obrenović; Bruder von Milan I.; durch seine strenge Steuersetzung und seine Sympathie für Russland brach ein Aufstand aus; sein Nachfolger war Alexander Karađorđević; er wurde 1868 in Topčider ermordet; 1823 – 1868.

[13] *Milan I.*: Aus dem Hause Obrenović; König von Serbien; dankte zu Gunsten seines Sohnes Aleksandar ab; Kaiser Franz Joseph I. überließ ihm nach schwerer Erkrankung ein Haus, in dem er auch starb; 1854 – 1901.

[14] *Peter I.*: Auch Petar Oslobodilać, „Der Befreier", genannt; aus dem Hause Karađorđević; Nachfolger von Aleksandar; Enkel des serbischen Freiheitskämpfers Karađorđe; König der Serben, Kroaten und Slowenen; 1844 – 1921.

nicht abzuweisen, der einstimmig bekundete Wille des Landes konnte schwerlich übergangen werden.

Österreich-Ungarn, der Nachbarstaat, hatte die Entscheidung in Händen und zeigte durch seinen Entschluß, daß es die Unabhängigkeit Serbiens in jeder Beziehung achtete und nur Gewicht darauf legte, die freundschaftlichen Beziehungen zu erhalten. Die Antwort unseres Monarchen auf die Depesche des Königs Peter, der die Thronbesteigung mitteilte, gab gewissermaßen die Stimmgabel für alle anderen Regenten. Sie enthielt die Zustimmung, die rückhaltlose wärmste Zustimmung zur Wahl des serbischen Volkes und zugleich die schärfste Verurteilung des Königsmordes. Sie zog eine deutliche Linie zwischen der Volksversammlung und jener Prätorianergruppe aufständischer, eidbrüchiger Offiziere. Die Depesche lautete: „Erkenntlich für die freundliche Mitteilung Ihrer Thronbesteigung, lege Ich Wert darauf, Sie unverweilt Meiner vollen Sympathie und Meiner Wünsche für eine lange glückliche Regierung zu versichern. Möge es Eurer Majestät vergönnt sein, die Ihnen zugefallene Mission erfolgreich durchzuführen, indem Sie dem unglücklichen, von einer Reihe innerer Stürme schwer heimgesuchten Lande den Frieden, die Ruhe und die Achtung wiedergeben und es nach dem tiefen Falle, den es jüngst infolge eines frevelhaften und von der ganzen Welt verabscheuten Verbrechens in den Augen der ganzen Welt getan hat, wieder aufrichten! Bei der Durchführung dieser Aufgabe können Eure Majestät auf Meine Unterstützung und Freundschaft rechnen und davon überzeugt sein, daß es Mir ebenso wie Ihnen selbst am Herzen liegen wird, die schon seit langer Zeit zwischen unsern Ländern bestehenden freundnachbarlichen Beziehungen aufrechtzuerhalten und zu festigen."

Dieser Auffassung, die den Willen des Volkes anerkannte und gleichzeitig den Mord verabscheute, schlossen sich einhellig die anderen Mächte an. Zwar wurde von dieser Stunde Peter I. als König von Serbien betrachtet, aber das Mißtrauen in seine Unschuld war doch zu groß, als daß er den Höfen seinen Antrittsbesuch hätte abstatten dürfen. Jeder derartige Versuch wurde höflich abgelehnt, man achtete den Willen des Volkes, wünschte aber nicht persönliche Berührung mit dem Erben einer so blutigen Krone.

Dadurch war die Lage König Peters im eigenen Lande schwierig geworden. Mit deutlichem Fingerzeig hatten die Mächte gebieterisch gefordert, daß der jetzige König jede Beziehung zu den Königsmördern lösen müsse. Schweren Herzens war er gezwungen, alle, die ihm zum Throne verholfen hatten und nun Gönnerschaft für diesen nicht eben reinen Dienst fordern kamen, abzuweisen, ja, sogar für ihre Dienstfertigkeit zu strafen. Wenn auch die linke Hand da emsig zurückgab, was die rechte nehmen mußte, so waren diese ehrgeizigen Offiziere doch sehr entrüstet über diese Verleugnung, und es erforderte höchstes politisches Geschick, um die Zwistigkeiten zu beseitigen und das Prestige des Königs blank zu putzen, das mit dem Blut einer Frau und eines ehrgeizigen Jünglings für immer besudelt war.

In dieser schwierigen Lage fand König Peter den richtigen Mann in Pašić, dem Führer der Altradikalen. Es gelang diesem klugen, verschlagenen und rücksichtslosen Politiker, den König davon zu überzeugen, daß nur eine ganz gegensätzliche und vor allem eine demagogische Politik ihm im Lande an Zustimmung soviel zurückgewinnen könnte, was in der ganzen zivilisierten Welt durch diese blutige Tat verloren gegangen war. Ein ehrgeiziges Volk wie das serbische mußte gewonnen werden, indem man seinem Ehrgeiz ein ungeheuerliches Ziel setzte, das seine ganze Aufmerksamkeit forderte und vor allem von der nächsten, für den König so kompromittierenden Vergangenheit in die Zukunft, ins Unbestimmte lenkte. Der erste Karageorgević war ein Befreier gewesen, und diesen Namen sollte sich König Peter nochmals verdienen, hatte jener Serbien gegründet, so sollte jener Großserbien erstehen lassen, das mythische Traumbild der Balladen und Heldenlieder. Er wollte nicht bloß König von Serbien sein, sondern Zar aller Serben. Und dem leichtgläubigen, nicht sehr gebildeten Volke wurde ein Land der Verheißung gezeigt, das drittgrößte slawische Reich, das von den Karawanken bis zu den Karpaten, von der Adria bis zum Ägäischen Meere reichen sollte, das Großserbien der Vergangenheit, das Großserbien der Zukunft.

Unter dem Großserbien der Vergangenheit, auf das sich mehr die Dichter als die Historiker berufen konnten, war das Reich Stefan Dušans gemeint, der sich 1346 in Skopje (Üsküb) zum Kaiser der Rhomäer und Serben krönen ließ. In jener Zeit nach der Völkerwanderung, da hinter den germanischen Stämmen die slawischen und mongolischen Völker den Balkan überschwemmten, entstanden damals aus Eroberungszügen oftmals große Reiche, die wie Seifenblasen nach ein paar Jahrzehnten platzten und in der Geschichte der Menschheit nichts zurückließen als einen Namen ohne Inhalt und eine Jahreszahl. Diese kulturlosen Eroberer vermochten niemals das Land, das sie mit Feuer und Schwert unter ihre Krone gezwungen, mit Sitte und Sprache, den beiden Urelementen aller Kultur, zu durchdringen: Sie gaben gewissermaßen nur einen grellen Farbanstrich, ein Firnis, der im nächsten Kriegsfeuer wieder absprang. Die ganze Herrlichkeit des serbischen Kaiserreiches dauerte nicht einmal ein Jahrzehnt, dann bröckelte das mit dem Schwert eilig zusammengenietete Reich auseinander, und seine Trümmer schwemmte in der Schlacht am

Amselfeld (Kossowo-Polje 1389)[15] der türkische Ansturm für immer weg. Von der serbischen Nation blieben nur Erinnerungen in Balladen und Liedern: keine scharfumrissene Sprachgrenze, keine gesonderte Kultur, keine Kunstdenkmäler. Sie war rettungslos ertrunken in der türkischen Flut. Erst als diese an den Mauern Wiens zurückebbte, tauchten die serbischen Sprachinseln allmählich aus dem trüben Gemenge der Balkannationen auf, die – von der steten Vorwärts- und Rückwärtsbewegung siegreicher und besiegter Völker unterwühlt – längst zum sprachlichen und religiösen Chaos geworden waren. Das Paschalik und nachmalige Königreich Serbien bildete gleichsam den einzigen Kern serbischer Gemeinschaft, weil dort die beiden Elemente, Sprache und orthodoxe Religion, verbunden waren. In Bosnien waren zahlreiche Serben zwischen die Mohammedaner versprengt, nach Südungarn waren Tausende als Flüchtlinge gekommen, wo die Habsburger ihnen fruchtbare Landstriche zugewiesen hatten, in Mazedonien, diesem kochenden Völkertiegel, hausten sie sporadisch zwischen Albanern, Türken, Griechen und Bulgaren, nur das „Falkennest" Montenegro war ihnen stammverwandt. Eine genaue Statistik ihrer Volkszahl ist schwer zu erlangen, weil die Unterschiede zwischen ihnen und den Bulgaren, anderseits wieder gegenüber den katholischen Südslawen fließende sind, keinesfalls ist die Gesamtsumme der orthodoxen Serben größer als vier bis viereinhalb Millionen.

---

[15] *Schlacht am Amselfeld:* 15. Juni 1389; die Heeresführung unterlag dem Fürsten Lazar Hrebeljanović sowie Vuk Brankovićs auf serbischer Seite, unterstützt von dem bosnischen König Tvrtko I.; Sultan Murad I. wollte die serbischen Fürstentümer einnehmen und das Osmanische Reich vergrößern; Serbien war zwar geschwächt, aber aus der Schlacht gab es keinen endgültigen Sieger; „Vidovdan" wird als Gedenktag in Serbien gefeiert.

Aber ihre Statistik wurde jetzt plötzlich ehrgeizig und zögerte nicht, um sich ein künftiges Großserbien zu errechnen, eiligst auch die Kroaten und die Slowenen, obwohl sie anderen Stammes und anderer Religion sind, in ihr Traumreich einzubeziehen. Die Türken wurden einfach mohammedanische Serben genannt, die Albaner albanisierte Serben und so lange und zielbewußt Geographie und Geschichte auf den Kopf gestellt, bis sie einer ungebildeten und darum doppelt leichtgläubigen Jugend zehn Millionen vorrechnen konnte und ein Reich, das mehr oder minder halb Österreich-Ungarn und die halbe Türkei umfaßte. Auf einer Karte, die dem Werk ihres gelehrten Agitators Jovan Cvijić[16] beigegeben ist, und das sie den Panslawisten und antiösterreichischen Politikern zur Belehrung auch in französischer Sprache herausgaben, kann man diesen Größenwahn im Bilde überschauen: Fast der ganze Süden Österreich-Ungarns ist in jenes zarte Blau getaucht, das serbisches Zukunftsland bedeuten soll. Kärnten, ein Teil der Steiermark, Görz, Gradiška, Kroatien, Slowenien, Bosnien, die Hercegovina, Montenegro, das Banat, Slawonien, Albanien, Mazedonien mit Saloniki und Kavala, all das ist mit dem Blau ihrer Hoffnung getüncht, und was dort als deutsche, ungarische, türkische, italienische, griechische Bevölkerung ihrer Statistik *ad hoc* unbequem war, einfach unterschlagen oder serbische Rasse genannt, die entnationalisiert worden sei. Wo dann noch das geographische

---

[16] *Jovan Cvijić*: Serbischer und jugoslawischer Geograph und Ethnograph; seine Monographien der Balkanhalbinsel sind bis heute in den Standardwerken; er hatte eine beratende Tätigkeit bei dem Generalstab Serbiens; widersetzte sich aber der Aufforderung als Ministerpräsident zu kandidieren; trat zeitlebens nie einer Partei bei; als Vorsitzender der territorialen Sektion nahm er an den Friedensverhandlungen von Versailles teil; 1865 - 1927.

Anrecht versagte, wurde eiligst wieder das historische vorgeschoben, Stefan Dušan, der Kaiser von 1346. Nichts war ihnen zu weit und zu fern für dieses Traumbild, von dem nur eines Wirklichkeit war, Belgrad, die zukünftige Hauptstadt, und der ehrgeizige Wille eines neuen Königsresidenten, das Volk mit diesen glühenden Farben des Wunsches zu blenden und von der peinlichen Gegenwart abzulenken.

Eine Verwirklichung dieser Träume war – ein Engländer hat es zuerst prophetisch gesagt und zwar ein Österreich-Ungarn wenig freundlicher – „nur durch einen Weltbrand" zu erreichen. Daß die skrupellose Dynastie und das tapfere, kampfmutige Volk vor Blutopfern nicht zurückscheuten, war gewiß, doch das Unterfangen des kleinen Staates, die Türkei oder das zwanzig Mal stärkere Österreich-Ungarn bekriegen zu wollen, von vornherein schon eine mehr als aussichtslose, lächerliche Verwegenheit. So mußte nach dem Plane Pašić' vorerst eine langsame, beharrliche Minierarbeit begonnen werden, um Europa aus den Fugen zu bringen, und erst heute fällt Licht in die vielen krummen und dunklen Gänge, die damals von Belgrad aus angelegt wurden, um den friedlichen Bestand zu erschüttern.

Zunächst mußte – es war dies eine der notwendigsten Vorarbeiten – der Haß gegen die Nachbarstaaten im Volke und in der Jugend hochgezüchtet werden. Gegen die Türkei war dies nicht schwer: Die Türkei war der Erbfeind der Serben seit sechs Jahrhunderten. Ein halbes Jahrtausend fast hatte es gedauert, ehe die Serben den Halbmond für immer von den Zinnen Belgrads hatten niederreißen können, ehe aus dem Paschalik ein freies Reich geworden war. Alle Heldenlieder des Volkes galten dem Kampf gegen die

Janitscharen[17], der fremde Glaube gab jeder Feindlichkeit den Nimbus eines Kreuzzuges „zur Erlösung der geknechteten Brüder", und viele noch waren unter den Lebenden, die selbst unter dieser Knechtschaft gelitten hatten. Auch ohne die Kriegserklärung war der Krieg am Balkan gegen die Türken ja permanent, die Banden der Komitadschis[18] streiften ständig nach Mazedonien auf Raub aus. Es war für König Peter und seine Ratgeber darum keineswegs schwer, ihr Volk gegen diesen Erbfeind in ständiger Kampfbereitschaft zu erhalten.

Ein anderes war es freilich mit Österreich-Ungarn. Die Monarchie war Wehmutter und Taufpatin des neuen serbischen Reiches in einem gewesen, Erzieherin und Beschützerin zugleich. Die kaiserlichen Soldaten hatten unter Prinz Eugen und manchem andern Feldherrn die Türken aus Belgrad verjagt, und die freie Erde ist dort seit Jahrhunderten gedüngt mit habsburgischem Blut. Die Flüchtlinge vor der türkischen Grausamkeit erhielten Land und Schutz, die Kämpfer rege Unterstützung. Darum war es erklärlich, daß der Großvater des jetzigen Königs, der Befreier Serbiens, Kara Georg, der Monarchie die Einverleibung des neuen Staates anbot, die aber damals nicht angenommen wurde, wie auch später nicht, als Rußland in wiederholten Angeboten Österreich-Ungarn die Besetzung des serbischen Territoriums vorschlug. Österreich-Ungarns Abgesandter, der Graf Khevenhüller hatte den Bulgaren, die nach dem Sieg von Slivnitza siegreich gegen Belgrad vordrangen, Halt geboten: Immer war die Unabhängigkeit und das

---

[17] Die *Janitscharen* (wörtlich: „Feuerstelle der neuen Truppe") waren die Garde der Sultane im Osmanischen Reich.
[18] *Komitadschi*: Die Bezeichnung für Mitglieder einer politischen Untergrundbewegung bzw. eines revolutionären Komitees.

Selbstbestimmungsrecht Serbiens von ihm geachtet worden, sogar bei jener letzten und schwersten Probe, als der Kaiser und König einen vielleicht der Blutschuld nicht ganz freien Prätendenten als König anerkannte, nur um der ungetrübten Freundschaft der beiden Länder willen. Dazu kam noch die Innigkeit der Handelsbeziehungen: Österreich-Ungarn kaufte den ganzen agrarischen Überschuß des fruchtbaren Bodens, für Serbien war die österreichische und ungarische Industrie die heimische und unsere Residenzen eine Art kultureller Hauptstadt. Nicht nur durch die Donau und den Strang der Eisenbahn war den Serben die Monarchie der Weg nach Europa, sondern auch im geistigen Sinn. Ihre Schulen und Werke waren nach dem nachbarlichen Vorbild, und sie fügten sich nur dem Naturgesetz der Nähe und Dankbarkeit, wenn sie die besten und innigsten Beziehungen unterhielten, die, ohne ihrer Unabhängigkeit im mindesten Abbruch zu tun, den Wohlstand und die Wehrfähigkeit erstaunlich kräftigten. Nur durch die Freundschaft mit Österreich-Ungarn waren die raschen wirtschaftlichen und kulturellen Fortschritte Serbiens erklärlich.

Dieses traditionelle und festgefügte Verhältnis zu lockern, bedurfte es schon einiger Anstrengungen. Da im Politischen mit bestem Willen selbst von einem Pašić kein Vorwand zu finden war, wurde der erste Keil in die Handelsbeziehungen getrieben. Sie waren das feste und friedliche Band und schienen unzerreißbar, weil sie aus Notwendigkeit gewoben waren: Serbien, der Agrarstaat, gab sein Vieh und seine Frucht, Österreich-Ungarn, der Industriestaat, hatte Vorrechte in seinen Produkten. Der aufreibende Konkurrenzkampf war so beiden Staaten erspart und die Handelsbeziehungen, durch die Gewohnheit von Jahrzehnten gefestigt, schienen schon starre, eherne Geleise, auf denen sich der Verkehr klaglos abwickelte, bis die politische

Willkür alle Brücken sprengte. Kurz nach König Peters Regierungsantritt begannen die Vexationen, die bald zu Mißhelligkeiten und dem offenen Handelskriege führten.

Damit war das Korn der Erbitterung im Volke ausgesät. Der Bauer, unfähig, in seiner mangelhaften Bildung, die politischen Hinterzwecke zu erkennen, merkte nur, daß er seine Schweine und Früchte nicht verkaufen konnte oder schlechter losschlagen mußte, und wenn er um die Ursache fragte, so antworteten die Agitatoren ihm: Österreich-Ungarn. Im ganzen Lande wurde allmählich so die Meinung festgelegt, die Nachbarmonarchie wolle den kleinen Staat um seine wirtschaftliche Unabhängigkeit bringen und nach und nach als Provinz handelspolitisch erobern. Außerdem wurden Beziehungen zu all jenen Staaten angebahnt, von denen zu vermuten war, daß sie der Monarchie politisch nicht wohl gesinnt waren, mit Frankreich vor allem, das in Österreich-Ungarn immer den Bundesbruder des Deutschen Reiches sah. Um des großen Zieles willen wurde die Feindschaft mit Bulgarien plötzlich in eine sehr stürmisch bekundete Freundschaft verwandelt (deren Haltbarkeit dann freilich bei der ersten Blutprobe versagte). An Montenegro und Italien banden den König Peter familiäre Beziehungen: Seine Gattin war die Tochter des König Nikita[19] und Schwester der Königin von Italien, Deutschland wurde zu verlocken gesucht, indem man ihm ein großes industrielles Absatzgebiet auf Kosten Österreich-Ungarns zu eröffnen anbot.

---

[19] *Nikola I.*: Aus dem Hause Petrović Njegoš; König von Montenegro; Schwiegervater Peter I.; nachdem Nikola/Nikita gestürzt war, übernahm Peter I. die Krone von Montenegro; verheiratet mit Milena Vukotić, ihre Tochter wurde mit dem italienischen Thronfolger Viktor Emanuel III. verheiratet; 1841 – 1921.

Die stärkste Unterstützung fand aber das neue Regime in Rußland. Trotz des Vertrages von Mürzsteg, der zwischen Österreich-Ungarn und Rußland eine einheitliche friedliche Politik vereinbart hatte, war der alte Antagonismus dort nicht erloschen, und jede Schwierigkeit des Nachbarstaates wurde freudig begrüßt. Österreich-Ungarn war für Rußland im letzten der Hemmschuh zur Vergewaltigung des Balkans, und nichts veranschaulicht trefflicher diese innere Überzeugung als das berühmte Wort des Generals Fadejew: „Der Weg nach Konstantinopel führt über Wien." Um das mysteriöse Testament Peter des Großen vollstrecken zu können, das angeblich das russische Kreuz auf der Hagia Sophia forderte, die Aufrichtung des alten byzantinischen Kaiserreiches und damit die Vorherrschaft über Morgen- und Abendland, zu diesem letzten und geheimsten Plan des russischen Volkes mußten die kleinen Balkanstaaten erst in Rußland aufgesaugt werden und der andere Wächter der Pforte, Österreich-Ungarn, beseitigt sein. Einmal, zur Zeit des Vertrages von San Stefano, hatten sie schon die Faust auf Konstantinopel gelegt: Da war Europa dazwischen getreten, und mißmutig mußte man in Petersburg den Plan aufschieben. Der voreilige offene Ansturm war mißlungen, so rüstete man nur geheim und schürte sorgsam auch die kleinste Flamme, die der Türkei oder Österreich-Ungarn den roten Hahn aufs Dach setzen konnte.

Die offizielle russische Politik war damals gebunden durch Mürzsteg und noch viel stärker (denn Verträge sind für Rußland nie Hemmnis gewesen) durch die ostasiatische Politik. Es galt zunächst, den Schwächeren, China, zu berauben, ehe man sich an den andern wagte, an die Türkei, die ihre Lebenskraft bei Plewna reichlich bezeugt hatte. Die Abgesandten König Peters fanden zunächst bei den Diplomaten dort nur Höflichkeiten, er selbst nicht einmal Einlaß bei Hof. Aber die russische Politik war von je eine mit doppeltem Boden, neben der verantwortlichen gab es dort eine unverantwortliche, die aber in geheimnisvollem Kontakt mit den wirklichen Absichten des Kaiserreiches stand, sodaß man sich des Verdachtes kaum zu verwehren mag, die verantwortliche Politik sei dort nur eine Maske, um die wirklichen Regungen und Gesinnungen zu verbergen. So hatte sich damals gerade eine „Gesellschaft für den fernen Osten" unter Förderung der Regierung gebildet, die Handelsinteressen vortäuschte, in Wirklichkeit aber die Kriegspartei gegen Japan war und im entscheidenden Augenblick die Minister und den Zaren mit sich in den Konflikt riß.

Die Gesellschaft, an die sich die Emissäre König Peters wandten, trug eine andere Maske für ihre kriegerischen Absichten: die Maske der Kultur. Die Serben appellierten an die Panslawisten im Namen ihrer Rasse und fanden dort willig Unterstützung. Der Panslawismus, uralt in seinem Grundgedanken, bezweckt die politische Einigung aller Slawen zu ihrer gemeinsamen politischen Weltherrschaft. 1848 war zu Prag der erste Kongreß abgehalten worden, wo Palacký und Hanka die Böhmen, Gay die Kroaten, Kollár die Slowenen für die Gemeinsamkeit zu gewinnen suchte. Der zweite Kongreß fand 1867 in Moskau statt, aber die Slawophilie Rußlands, die sich die Führung ausbedachte, fand immer mehr Mißtrauen durch die Behandlung oder besser Mißhandlung der Polen, und bald wurden die Völker gewahr, daß sie zwar Panslawismus, Rußland aber Panrussismus meinten, daß, nach Puschkins Dichterwort, „alle slawischen Bäche im russischen Meere münden sollten". Eine merkliche Abkühlung entstand. Die kleinen slawischen Staaten sahen bald ein, daß sie ihre Unabhängigkeit nicht preisgeben dürften, aber das Protektorat Rußlands, der Schutz des „Mütterchens" war ihnen äußerst willkommen. Sie durften unter dieser Deckung sich allerhand Unbotmäßigkeiten erlauben und konnten immer wieder zurück unter die Röcke „Mütterchens" sich verstecken, wenn ihnen Züchtigung drohte. Rußland wieder gebrauchte sie wie die Banderillos im Stiergefecht, die den Gegner mit ihren Sticheleien in Atem halten und in Unruhe versetzen; und die panslawistischen Gesellschaften waren die geeignetste Form, um nach außen unverbindlich im Geheimen anzustacheln oder zurückzurufen. Nur verlangte Rußland eines: unbedingten Gehorsam und Unterwerfung für die eigenen Zwecke. Der Panslawismus war aus einem kulturellen Ideal ein politisches Machtmittel geworden und vor allem die beste Agitationsformel für kriegerische Vorstöße.

Unter Pašić Führung lenkte das serbische Staatsschiff nun ganz ein in die russischen Gewässer. Die Kriegspartei ließ Serbien, das einst Österreich-Ungarn befreundete, allmählich zu einer Vorhut ihrer eigenen Macht werden, und die Unterstützungen an die verantwortlichen Politiker flossen reichlich aus geheimen Quellen. Nur mußte Serbien, weil Rußland die Hände in den chinesischen Taschen hatte, seine Propaganda lautlos und vorsichtig betreiben: Es mußte der Welt gegenüber als das arme, schwache, arglose Serbien erscheinen, das sich fürchtete, von seinem gierigen Nachbarn verschluckt zu werden. Es durfte noch nicht mit dem Säbel rasseln, und die Bomben mußten im Arsenal von Kragujevac bleiben. Unterirdisch mußte die Arbeit sein. Nach dem Vorbild Piemonts – Serbien nannte sich stolz das Piemont des zwanzigsten Jahrhunderts – sollte im Nachbarland vorerst eine *Irredenta* gezüchtet werden, und „Kulturvereine", die später so berüchtigte „Narodna

Odbrana"[20], blühten eiligst auf unter dem russischen Rubeltau. In der ungarischen Unabhängigkeitspartei meinten sie Feinde der Dynastie Habsburg zu erblicken: Das genügte (gegen ihr eigenes Volksinteresse), ihr Pakte anzutragen. Während Bulgarien die Banden nach der Türkei sandte und Mazedonien plündern ließ, unterwühlte Serbien Österreich-Ungarn und die Meinung des Auslandes mit Flugschriften und Prospekten. Der Boden sollte erst gelockert werden, ehe man versuchte ihn zu sprengen. Und vor allem: Sie mußten warten, bis „Mütterchen" Rußland die Hände frei hatte.

In jener Mordnacht von Belgrad war auch die europäische Ruhe ermordet worden. Denn der unreine Ehrgeiz des neuen Herrschers schwärte im Blute des Balkans. Schon in den nächsten Jahren fühlte man das Fieber von dort sich über den ganzen Leib des Kontinents verbreiten, bis endlich nur die Waffe übrig blieb, die Eiterung auszubrennen oder selbst an ihr zu Grunde zu gehen.

---

[20] *Narodna Odbrana*: Wörtlich übersetzt: „Volksschutz"; serbische, nationalistische Organisation, die als Reaktion auf die Annexion 1908 gegründet wurde; propagierte großserbisches Gedankengut; Beziehungen zum Geheimbund „Schwarze Hand", die Attentäter rekrutierte; Verdacht an der offiziellen Beteiligung der „Narodna Odbrana" an der Ermordung von Franz Ferdinand ließen sich nicht erhärten.

Beginn der Einkreisung der Zentralmächte

Europa hatte Frieden, solange die beiden größten Kräfte gebunden waren, England, dessen Tendenz es von jeher war, die europäische Einheit durch Zwist zu zersprengen, Rußland, das mit seinem furchtbaren Gewicht ihm freien Atem raubte. Noch die ersten drei Jahre des neuen Jahrhunderts sind verhältnismäßig ruhig und politisch unbewegt.

Dann kehrt England in die Arena zurück und gefährlicher als je. Der Widerstand der verachteten kleinen Farmersleute in Südafrika, denen man mit einer Handvoll Abenteurern und einigen rasch aufgebotenen Milizen ihr Land so leicht wegzunehmen hoffte wie Indern oder Negern, war zum Burenkrieg geworden, zu einem der langwierigsten und heroischsten Kämpfe der Neuzeit. In offener Schlacht wie im heimlichen Guerillakrieg besiegt, mußte England neue und neue Söldnerheere nach Afrika treiben, und erst mit den erbärmlichsten Repressalien, mit den berüchtigten Konzentrationslagern, in denen Weiber und Kinder der Buren elend dahinsiechten, mit Bestechung und Umgarnung gelang es den Staatsmännern durchzusetzen, was das Heer mit blanker Waffe nicht zu erreichen vermochte. In dreijährigem erbitterten Kampf, der England Milliarden kostete, war schließlich ein großes Reich gewonnen, aber auch ein großes Prestige verloren.

Finanziell geschwächt, militärisch mißachtet, von den Sympathien der ganzen Kulturwelt durch den brutalen Überfall auf die kleinen, friedlichen Farmerrepubliken entfremdet, stand England jetzt allein. Aber es war nicht die *"splendid isolation"* mehr, die selbstgewählte unabhängige Einsamkeit des Stolzes, sondern ein Abseitsstehen im Schatten. Der kostspielige Krieg hatte unendliche Verheerungen im Wirtschaftsleben angerichtet, andere Staaten, Deutschland vor allem, hatten durch fleißige Friedensarbeit inzwischen viel Handel an sich gerissen, Rußland fühlte sich des lästigen Konkurrenten in Asien ledig und löste mit gutem Appetit Stück um Stück vom garen Braten Chinas los. Während England bisher groß geworden war, dadurch, daß es am Kontinent Kriege anzettelte und von jedem Gewinn einzig durch das Recht des unbeteiligten Dritten den größten hatte, so waren diesmal, während es seine Kräfte im Kampfe gegen die Republik aufrieb, die andern Staaten erstarkt und durch ihr friedliches Nebeneinandersein wirtschaftlich leistungsfähiger geworden. Die englische Alleinherrschaft in Handel und Wandel, die für ihren Stolz zur unabänderlichen Maxime der sittlichen Weltordnung geworden war, schien ernstlich bedroht durch die europäische Eintracht, den Frieden am Kontinente. Und es mußte eine neue Politik begonnen werden, um das alte Ziel zu erreichen: die unabänderliche Weltherrschaft Englands.

Die neue Zeit fand einen neuen Mann. Die schon sehr betagte loyale Königin Viktoria war inmitten des Burenkrieges gestorben, der fröhliche Prince of Wales bestieg als Eduard VII. den Thron. Weltklug, erfahren, ohne Sentiment in der Politik, an eigenen Geschäften Geschäftsmann geworden, ging er entschlossen und unbedenklich auf sein Ziel los: einen Keil zwischen die Nationen zu treiben und im Bund mit allen Schwächeren den Stärksten zu fällen. Das erhabene Wappen der *"splendid isolation"* legte er eilig ab, es hinderte beim Kampf. Kleine Zettelungen begannen, Wege und Verträge, Besuche und Versuche, aus denen ein Netz gesponnen werden sollte, bestimmt, den Stärksten zu fangen.

Einer nach dem andern sollte für seine Kraft nun büßen. Der erste Stoß war Rußland zugedacht, das mit vollen Händen in Asien zugriff, in Asien, das England, ebenso wie Afrika, Australien, als die ihm allein gehörige Kolonialdomäne betrachtete. Nun bestand für England von je die Schwierigkeit darin, seinen ärgsten Gegner zu fassen: Mit seiner Flotte konnte es dem ungeheuren, fast nur von Ackerbau lebenden Lande bloß Nadelstiche zufügen, nie aber seinen Organismus ernstlich verletzen, aber auch Rußland konnte wiederum niemals vitale Teile Englands erreichen, das so vorsichtig gewesen war, seine Kolonialgrenzen nie bis hart an das russische Reich zu schieben, sondern immer Pufferstaaten wie Persien und Afghanistan mit einer kümmerlichen Unabhängigkeit dazwischen vegetieren zu lassen. Es war also wahrhaftig der Kampf des „Walfischs mit dem Bären", wo der Walfisch nach dem Worte des englischen Ministers eben warten mußte, bis der Bär ins Wasser stiege. So lange aber Rußland noch keinen Seehandel hatte, mußte es zu Lande getroffen werden. Und dafür war der japanische Dolch.

Als ersten der großen Verträge nach jener Zeit der „erlauchten Einsamkeit" schloß England den mit Japan. Wohin seine Spitze gekehrt war, konnte jeder sehen, nur ahnten die wenigsten ihre Schärfe. Nun spürten die Russen mit einem Male einen unbekannten Gegner vor sich aus dem mystischen Dunkel des Ostens tauchen: Nicht von Westen, von Europa, wurden sie wie bei jedem Vorstoß zurückgerissen, sondern vor ihnen stand gefahrlächelnd ein fremdes gelbes Gesicht, in dessen Augen sie den englischen Haß flackern sahen. Jeder Versuch einer Einigung scheiterte an einer Hartnäckigkeit, die unverständlich gewesen wäre ohne die energischen Fingerzeige des Hintermannes, der von London aus die Marionette mit dem Dolche gegen Rußland trieb.

Der Plan gelang. Am 8. Februar 1904 schlichen sich die japanischen Torpedoboote in den Hafen von Port Arthur und rissen den russischen Panzern die Flanken auf. Der Krieg brach aus, unvermeidlich und unbarmherzig, russische Armeen und Milliarden bluteten sich aus auf den Mandschurischen Schlachtfeldern. Wie einst Europa gegen Napoleon, kämpften nun die Asiaten gegen Rußland für Englands Sache. Dieser erste der gefährlichen Gegner war erledigt für Kriegsdauer und die nächsten vier oder fünf Jahre, ohne daß *„Tommy Atkins"*[21] einen Schuß Pulver zu wagen brauchte. Und seine Abwesenheit vom Weltschauplatz wurde eiligst benützt, um eine „Strafexpedition" nach Tibet zu entsenden und dieses letzte freie Reich Mittelasiens unter seine Herrschaft zu bringen.

Der nächste Gegner, gegen den England nun sich wandte, war ein Freund, war Deutschland. Seit Beginn der europäischen Geschichte hatten nie deutsche die englischen Waffen gekreuzt, engste verwandtschaftliche Beziehungen banden die regierenden Königshäuser, Blutbande auch die Völker. In dreißig Kriegen hatte deutsches Schwert für englische Macht gefochten, gegen Frankreich wie gegen Amerika, in allen Jahrhunderten war niemals ernstlicher Zwist zwischen den beiden Staaten ausgebrochen. Mit Wohlwollen hatte man drüben, jenseits des Kanals, die Entstehung des geeinten Deutschlands gesehen, eines mächtigen Nachbars der verhaßten Großmächte Frankreich und Rußland, mit Lächeln hatte man auf die Flotte und die kleinen Kolonien geblickt, den Abfall, den sich dieser spätgeborene Staat bei der Verteilung noch gerettet.

---

[21] *Tommy Atkins*: So wurden im deutschsprachigen Raum britische Soldaten genannt.

Aber diese Sympathien schwanden rasch, als man der ungeheuren Entwicklung gewahr wurde, die dieses neugeborene Deutsche Reich durchmachte, seit es [sich] seiner Einheit bewußt war. In fernsten Gebieten fühlte der englische Handel, der bisher die einträgliche Bequemlichkeit des Monopols hatte, jetzt plötzlich einen überlegenen Konkurrenten, die Urindustrien Großbritanniens, wie die Maschinenwerke und chemischen Fabriken, sahen sich jetzt zu vervielfachter Anspannung genötigt. Vor zwanzig Jahren noch hatte Deutschland auf englischen Werften seine Kriegsschiffe erbauen lassen müssen, jetzt wuchs mit einem Male eine gigantische Handels- und Kriegsflotte empor, deren prächtigste Schiffe England das „Blaue Band" der Geschwindigkeit auf der Ozeanfahrt entrissen. Der alte Grundsatz Großbritanniens, seine eigene Kriegsflotte müsse immer stärker sein als die beiden andern größten der Kontinentstaaten zusammen, war bei der raschen Progression im deutschen Schiffbau nur mit ungeheuren Kosten aufrecht zu erhalten. Seit dem Ausspruch Kaiser Wilhelms von der Zukunft Deutschlands auf dem Wasser, der vor zwanzig Jahren noch idealistisch und phantastisch klang, war die schwarz-weiß-rote Flagge auf allen Ozeanen nach der englischen die gebietende geworden. Neben sich sah England eine neue Macht aufstehen, England, das nie eine neben sich, nur eine unter sich geduldet. Damit war innerlich die Freundschaft vernichtet.

Äußere Momente kamen dazu, diese Spannungen gerade damals zu erhöhen. Persönlich war zwischen König Eduard und Kaiser Wilhelm nicht mehr jener enge Kontakt wie zwischen Großmutter und Enkel, politische Mißverständnisse und Zeitungsungeschicklichkeiten trugen bei, die Stimmung diesseits und jenseits des Kanals aufzureizen. Deutschland hatte keinen Hehl aus seiner Volksmeinung während des Burenkrieges gemacht, bei jeder Gelegenheit gab es (wie übrigens in ganz Europa) Demonstrationen und Lieder, es regnete Spottkarten und Witzworte, die Sprache mancher Zeitung ermangelte der Höflichkeit. Wenn auch die politischen Kreise sich seit jenem ersten Telegramm Kaiser Wilhelms deutlich von jeder Sympathie für die Burenbegeisterung fernhielten und Präsident Kruger bei seinem Besuch nicht empfangen wurde, trug der Wind viel von der Volksstimme über den Kanal hinüber. Und dort sorgte die merkantile Partei, deren Geschäft mit der Beseitigung des gefährlichen Konkurrenten nur gewinnen konnte, für lebhafte Resonanz. Ohne daß Deutschland jemals England in seinen Erwerbungen oder Bestrebungen gehemmt hätte, war es drüben als die Lebensgefahr des britischen Imperiums verschrien. Ehrgeizige Politiker hatten nun leichtes Spiel.

Ein Partner war jederzeit bereit, wenn es ein Bündnis galt, das gegen Deutschland gerichtet war: Frankreich, das Land der Revanche. Es forderte vom König Eduard und seinen Ratgebern nur ein gewisses moralisches Opfer, um hier eine *„Entente cordiale"*, ein „herzliches Einvernehmen" abzuschließen. Frankreich war der Bundesgenosse Rußlands, England derjenige Japans, die beiden Sekundanten, die gegenwärtig den Kampf zu überwachen und zu unterstützen hatten, rückten lieber beide ab und tranken Bruderschaft. Vergessen sind mit einem Male die Burendemonstrationen, die die französische Regierung nur mit Mühe beim vorjährigen Besuch des Königs von England hatte niederhalten können, vergessen die beinahe blutigen Händel von Faschoda. Sobald es Deutschland gilt, war Frankreich bereit.

Die Abmachungen, die damals in Paris getroffen wurden, sind noch nicht offen gegen Deutschland gerichtet gewesen – nur schoben sie im Voraus seinen Einspruch, seine

Macht und seinen Willen beiseite. Abgesehen von einigen kleinen Kolonialberichtigungen erkennt Frankreich England das „Recht" auf Ägypten zu, während England auf eigene Ansprüche in Marokko verzichtet und die letzte große unabhängige Kolonie Afrikas dem französischen Einfluß überantwortet. Sie weisen sich darin Rechte und Reiche zu, obwohl es sich um einen souveränen Staat handelt, und teilen fremdes Eigentum, ohne irgendjemand in der Welt zu fragen, weder den eigentlichen Nachbarn, Spanien, noch Italien, Österreich-Ungarn, die Mittelmeermächte und Deutschland, das vielfache Handelsinteressen in Marokko besitzt, die selbstverständlich bei einer französischen Besitzergreifung wesentliche Verschiebungen erleiden müßten.

Selbstverständlich war diese Zuteilung der Interessensphären keine ideale und nicht bestimmt, bloß beschriebenes Papier zu bleiben. Ein paar Monate schon nach jener französisch-englischen Übereinkunft erschien der französische Gesandte René-Taillandier bei dem Sultan und verlangte eine Reihe von Reformen, die nichts anderes bedeuteten als den Anfang der „Tunifikation", der Enteignung seiner Souveränitätsrechte zu Gunsten Frankreichs. Wie Algier und Tunis sollte nun das letzte freie Stück der Nordküste Afrikas mit dem ungeheuren Hinterland an Frankreich fallen: Die sogenannten Reformen waren nur ein Vorwand, um französische Überwachungsbeamte ins Land zu schicken, die Militär nach sich gezogen hätten, um Marokko eines Tages das Schicksal Ägyptens und Algiers zu bereiten.

Der Sultan war erschreckt. Er wußte, wie schwer es für ihn war, den Forderungen Frankreichs zu widerstehen, da er nicht die Waffengewalt besaß und England ihn preisgegeben. Aber nicht nur seine eigenen Interessen waren bedroht, auch die des ganzen internationalen Handels, Spanien, Italien, Österreich-Ungarn, Deutschland, es galt mehr als die Unabhängigkeit eines afrikanischen Herrschers. Hier war zu zeigen, ob Staaten das Recht hatten, durch Verträge die Welt zwischen sich aufzuteilen und andere Staaten von gleicher Bedeutung und gleicher Kraft mit dem Fuße wegzustoßen. Es gab für Deutschland nur zwei Möglichkeiten: die, eine Vogelstraußpolitik zu treiben und zu machen, als glaube es an die „friedliche Durchdringung" Marokkos und die Aufrechterhaltung der Handelsfreiheit oder klar ein klares Wort zu sprechen. Die „offene Tür" in Marokko mußte dem deutschen wie dem Welthandel bleiben und durfte nicht ein französisches Schild erhalten ohne internationale Zustimmung: So war irgendwie zu zeigen, daß die Souveränität des Sultans nicht ein Handelsobjekt zwischen Frankreich und England sei, sondern eine europäische Angelegenheit.

Am 31. März landete die „Hohenzollern", die deutsche Kaiserjacht, vor Tanger, und Kaiser Wilhelm antwortete auf die Begrüßung des marokkanischen Vertreters, er besuche den Sultan als unabhängigen Herrscher und erwidere seine freundschaftlichen Empfindungen aufs herzlichste.

Dieser kleine politische Ausflug auf der Mittelmeerreise wirkte in Paris und London wie ein Donnerschlag. Man hatte gehofft, dank des im Dunkel geschlossenen Vertrages die Beute auch heimlich und verstohlen einheimsen zu können: Nun fiel plötzlich ein Blendlicht auf die französischen Absichten. Nichts kennzeichnete besser ihre Enttäuschung als die fassungslose Wut der Zeitungsangriffe, die plötzlich die Tonart von 1870 bliesen. Geführt war diese Campagne von Delcassé, dem radikalsten Minister des Auswärtigen, dessen Name schon seitdem Kriegsfanfare für die Welt geworden ist. Dieser extreme Nationalist vertrat energisch die Anschauung, Marokko gehöre durch seine geographische Lage einzig in die Interessensphäre

Frankreichs und Spaniens, kein anderer europäischer Staat könne und dürfe da sein Votum abgeben. Vergleich in dieser Sache wies er von vornherein ab. Von der Ministerialbank spürte man deutlich einen Willen zum Konflikt, den äußerliche Verhandlungen nur unvollkommen deckten, die Spannung wuchs und wuchs. Ein Besuch des Königs Eduard schien nur Öl ins Feuer zu gießen, auf der Börse bricht auf einen Artikel im „Matin", dem Leibblatte Delcassés, der den Krieg ankündigt, eine Panik aus. Die französische Regierung hat die Wahl, ob sie den Antrag des Magzhen, die Ordnung Marokkos einer Konferenz anzuvertrauen, annehmen wolle oder ihr Eigenrecht auf diesen Staat als zukünftige Kolonie behaupten.

Es war eine der schwierigsten Nervenproben Europas, diese Junitage 1905, und der Krieg zwischen Deutschland und Frankreich, wohl auch mit England beinahe unvermeidlich. Ein Ultimatum war schon gestellt. Da entschied in Paris der Ministerrat für den Frieden; Delcassé, der nicht nachgeben wollte, wurde über Bord geworfen, und nun hatte das Staatsschiff wieder ruhigen Kurs. Ein paar Tage später wurde ein friedlicher Aktenaustausch zwischen den beiden Staaten gemeldet und das Programm der internationalen Marokkokonferenz zu Algeciras vereinbart.

Aber Delcassé war nicht der Mann, sich so leicht über Bord werfen zu lassen, um dann in der Mißgunst der öffentlichen Meinung für immer zu ertrinken. Er hatte noch einen starken Trumpf in der Hand, und den spielte er aus: Im „Matin" wurde von „informierter Seite" enthüllt, daß England hunderttausend Mann Hilfstruppen für einen bewaffneten Konflikt versprochen hatte, die in Schleswig landen sollten. Auf dieses Versprechen gestützt, war er unerschütterlich gewesen, bis seine mutloseren Kameraden die Verantwortung nicht mit ihm tragen wollten, ihn im Stiche gelassen hätten.

Jetzt erst nach dieser grausamen Enthüllung war es klar, wie skrupellos England die beiden Staaten in den Krieg hatte treiben wollen und wie es durch militärische Versprechungen – die es freilich nur dem Minister persönlich machte und sich hütete, schriftlich festzulegen – den Schwächeren aufreizen und zum Weltkrieg verführen wollte. Schauernd erkannte Europa jetzt erst die Gefahr, an der es haarbreit sich vorübergerettet hatte –, denn weder in Deutschland noch in Frankreich war vordem dem Volke bewußt gewesen, daß sie so nahe vor einem mörderischen Zusammenstoß standen. Beide Völker waren ahnungslos und ahnten nichts von den Wolfsgruben, mit denen König Eduards Reisen und Audienzen die europäische Politik gespickt hatten. Die Entrüstung brach in beiden Ländern aus. Natürlich wurde jetzt von England her und auch von französischer Seite eilig dementiert, aber Jean Jaurès[22], der große Sozialistenführer, bestätigte mit seiner unantastbaren Autorität die Exaktheit jener Behauptungen.

Nun wußte Deutschland, woher der scharfe Wind wehte, den es seit ein paar Jahren überall spürte, wohin es sich wenden mochte. Und zum ersten Mal empfand es jetzt den Druck des eisernen Ringes, der, wie Gerhard Hauptmann so schön sagte, ihm um die Brust gelegt wurde und den es zersprengen mußte, um nicht aufzuhören zu atmen. Es war ein leises vorahnendes Klirren von Waffen in der Welt. Die

---

[22] *Jean Jaurès*: Bekanntester Vertreter des Reformsozialismus; französischer Historiker; Mitbegründer der Französisch Sozialistischen Partei; setzte sich vor dem Ersten Weltkrieg inbrünstig für den Pazifismus und gegen den drohenden Krieg ein; wurde unmittelbar vor Kriegsbeginn von dem französischen Nationalisten Raoul Villain ermordet, der nach dem Ende des Weltkrieges freigesprochen wurde – seiner Frau wurden die Gerichtskosten angelastet. Vgl. auch Stefans Zweigs Artikel in der „Neuen Freien Presse" nach dessen Ermordung, 1916.

beiden Armeen hatten in jenen Tagen schon Vorsorge getroffen, die englische Flotte lag wie zufällig versammelt, und indes die Menschen ahnungslos ihren Geschäften und Werken nachgingen, züngelte schon die Flamme der englischen Politik am Gebälke des europäischen Friedens. Schon damals hätte ein gefährlicher Zufall die Welt in Brand setzen können, und nur dem beiderseitigen Willen, nicht aber England war es zu verdanken, daß dies Unheil – wie man damals hoffte, vermieden, oder wie wir heute wissen – verzögert werden konnte.

Auch die Verhandlungen am Tische in Algeciras waren noch sehr unruhig. Aber keiner der Vertragschließenden wollte nun, da Europa [sich] der Gefahr bewußt geworden war, den Frieden leichtfertig mehr opfern. Im Wesentlichen waren Deutschland und Frankreich über die Grundlagen schon einig, ehe sie nach Algeciras gingen, vor allem garantierte Frankreich feierlich die Unabhängigkeit und Souveränität des Sultans, den Kaiser Wilhelm als freien Herrscher begrüßt hatte, sowie wirtschaftliche Freiheit, während ihm wieder Überwachungsrechte mannigfacher Art eingeräumt wurden. Im Einzelnen wurden die Diskussionen lebhaft, nie aber geriet der Kongreß in wirkliche Gefahr. Was schließlich als Resultat übrig blieb, war eine ziemlich dehnbare Machtbefugnis Frankreichs und des benachbarten Spaniens. Der Konflikt war nicht aus der Welt geschafft, sondern nur erstickt. Und so wie durch Serbien im Osten war nun auch im Westen ein eiterndes Problem geschaffen, das eines Tages ausgebrannt werden mußte, wenn die Diplomatie zögerte, es rechtzeitig auszuschneiden.

An jenem Beratungstische war zum ersten Mal die europäische Konstellation zutage getreten, die sich dank der gefährlichen Emsigkeit König Eduards zur herrschenden entwickeln sollte. Frankreich wurde vollinhaltlich unterstützt von England und Rußland, seinen Verbündeten, Spanien interessierte sich nur für seine eigenen Rechte. Weniger festgefügt zeigte sich der Dreibund. Italien, das in den Mittelmeerangelegenheiten mehr auf Frankreich und England zu geben meinte und im Begehren Frankreichs nach Marokko die Sicherheit seiner Gleichgültigkeit gegen Tripolis sah, vertrat den französischen Standpunkt. Deutschland hatte nur einen Freund, den wackeren Sekundanten, wie Kaiser Wilhelm dankend in seiner Depesche sagte: Österreich-Ungarn. Der Bund zwischen Habsburg und Hohenzollern war auch dort als ehern und unzerstörbar vor der Welt bekräftigt, und nicht zum Geringsten sicherte das Bewußtsein dieser Festigkeit – sowie die Schwäche Rußlands – den Frieden. Aber um diese beiden Länder, die einzigen Europas, die keinen Machtzuwachs begehrt und gefordert hatten, war, weil sie die Rechte freier unabhängiger Staaten schützten, allmählich ein Kreis der Machtgierigen gerundet. König Eduard, der sah, daß jenes Bündnis mit Frankreich noch nicht ausreiche, um Deutschland zu demütigen, begann, neue Helfer zu werben. Nach Spanien ging die erste Reise, wo dem jungen König eine englische Prinzessin angetraut wurde, auch Rom wurde besucht, mit der offenkundigen Absicht, in der losen Fügung des Dreibunds eine vollständige Abspaltung Italiens zu erzielen, mit Rußland wurden jetzt, da es ungefährlich gemacht worden war, Verhandlungen wieder aufgenommen. In Frankreich züngelten in allen Zeitungen die Flämmchen auf, die Kriegspartei wurde unruhig, seit sie in England einen Werber und Agitator ihrer Absichten wußte. Immer enger spürten Deutschland und Österreich-Ungarn die Einkreisung; aber sie hielten die Hand fest am Schwert und ließen unbesorgt Argwohn und Neid um sich wuchern, ihres Rechtes gewiß und ihrer vereinten Stärke.

Von Mürzsteg bis zur türkischen Revolution (1903 – 1907)

Niemals war die Tatsache offenkundiger, daß alle Unruhe des Balkans immer nur von Rußland künstlich erregt worden war, als in jenen Jahren, da das Zarenreich keine Zeit und keine Kraft hatte, um seine Zerstörungspläne gegen die Türkei durchzuführen. Während des russisch-japanischen Krieges bricht die immer lodernde, immer zuckende Flamme der Balkanaufstände plötzlich in sich zusammen: Es fehlt die Schürung von Petersburg, der panslawistische Atem und vor allem der Rubel, der alle jene Guerillakriege ins Rollen brachte. Alle Freiheitsbestrebungen sterben plötzlich ab, und Mazedonien, eben noch in voller Gärung, bietet, während Rußland alle seine Kräfte aufrafft, um den gelben Gegner niederzuringen, das Bild vollkommener Ruhe.

Freilich: Die russische Diplomatie wünschte diese Ruhe nur so lange, als sie selbst außerstande war, von einer Unruhe zu profitieren. Und sie wünschte vor allem, daß alles unverändert bleibe, bis sie wieder Kraft genug habe, sich einzumengen und nach Aufwühlung des ganzen Landes für sich im Trüben zu fischen. Um jeden Preis musste verhindert werden, daß während der Abwesenheit Rußlands von der europäischen Arena Österreich-Ungarn oder eine andere Großmacht seine Stellung im Balkan befestige. Frankreich, England, Italien, Deutschland hatten bestenfalls wirtschaftliche Interessen, so ging die Bemühung dahin, Österreich-Ungarn durch Verträge die Hände zu binden, solange Rußland die seinen nicht frei hatte. Man mußte jetzt freundlich sein und die Krallen einziehen. Und das panslawistische Programm wurde hinter den Ofen gehängt, solange das asiatische noch nicht erledigt war.

Aufstände in Mazedonien boten einen angenehmen Vorwand, mit Österreich-Ungarn anscheinend loyal zu verhandeln. Diese Aufstände waren nach einem bestimmten System angelegt: Banden aus Bulgarien und Serbien, Komitadschis genannt, brachen in türkisches Gebiet ein, sengten und brannten die Heimstätten friedlicher Mohammedaner nieder, ermordeten nicht nur Gendarmen, sondern auch Frauen und Kinder. Setzten sich aber die Türken zur Wehr oder entsandten sie Soldaten gegen jene Banden, so wurde von den kleinen Staaten – die natürlich das Überschreiten ihrer Grenzen durch diese bewaffneten Haufen nie merkten – verzweifelt in die Welt geschrien, die Türkei mißhandle ihre christlichen Untertanen. Selbstverständlich waren diese Bandenbewegungen auch genug gut organisiert, um sofort eingestellt werden zu können, sobald Europa die Geduld verlor und energisch Ruhe forderte.

Das Frühjahr 1903 war von Bulgarien und Serbien für eine besondere Aktion ausersehen: Ein Albanesenaufstand war inszeniert als Einleitung einer einheitlichen aufständischen Bewegung. Aber Rußland wünschte die Sache vertagt, um in Japan freie Hand zu haben. Für den Fall aber, daß dennoch irgendetwas sich ereigne, während seine Truppen in Ostasien beschäftigt waren, sollte Österreich-Ungarn festgelegt werden. Und im Herbst 1903 erschien der Zar in Wien.

Zu Mürzsteg, am 2. und 3. Oktober 1903, wurde Österreich-Ungarn die Fessel angelegt. Die Diplomatie war von Graf Goluchowski[23] vertreten, der nur Frieden um jeden

---

[23] *Agenor Maria Adam Graf Gołuchowski*

Preis wünschte und nichts von den asiatischen Plänen Rußlands ahnte oder in ihnen nur die Sicherung der östlichen Grenze empfand. Rußland als Freund zu haben, war man so ungewohnt in Österreich-Ungarn, einen Zaren von einer *„Harmonie parfaite"* der österreichisch-russischen Ansichten sprechen zu hören, wie der Bürgschaft des Friedens, und man ließ sich vertrauend die Hände binden. Der Kaiser und König Franz Joseph war großherzig genug, Treue zu erwarten, wo er Treue bot: Nie war Österreich-Ungarn unter seiner Regierung einem Bundesgenossen untreu geworden, nie hatte es, auch wenn seine Nachbarn in den größten Schwierigkeiten waren, das Schwert auch nur in der Scheide gelockert, nie war die geringste offensive Aktion unternommen worden. Ihm war das ungetrübte Glück seiner Landeskinder wichtiger als jeder persönliche kriegerische Ehrgeiz, und jede Gelegenheit, den Frieden zu festigen, fand an ihm einen eifrigen Förderer, so auch dieser Vorschlag Rußlands. Die Reformpläne in der Türkei waren nur der Vorwand, das Wesentliche war die beiderseitige Verpflichtung der Mächte, nichts im Balkan anders wie einverständlich zu unternehmen und den Status quo aufrecht zu erhalten. Ein bestimmter Termin dieser Aufrechterhaltung war nicht gegeben, er lautete in Wirklichkeit: Solange es Rußland gefiel, sich an das Programm gebunden zu erachten.

Durch diesen Vertrag gesichert, konnte Rußland nun seine abseitigen Pläne verfolgen. Und vier Monate später war schon der Krieg an Japan erklärt. Nun erst verstand man bei uns den Sinn von Mürzsteg, aber eine übermäßige Ehrlichkeit in der diplomatischen Auffassung, ein Vertrauen auf die Dankbarkeit Rußlands – trotz zwanzigfacher Gegenbeispiele in der Geschichte – ließ einen Augenblick versäumen, der niemals wiederkehren sollte. Deutschland wie Österreich-Ungarn, obwohl jenes das Zarenreich als

Verbündeten seines Todfeindes, dieses als seinen slawischen Neider kannten, ließen sich durch die Freundschaftsversprechungen Nikolaus II. täuschen und setzten die Ehre, ihr Wort zu halten, höher als die eigene Existenz. Deutschland opferte sogar das letzte von Sympathie, das es in England besaß, für die Unterstützung der russischen Flotte auf, Österreich-Ungarn ließ sich die handelspolitischen Herausforderungen Serbiens gefallen, ohne auch nur den Griff nach dem Schwert zu tun, der damals seine Wirkung nicht verfehlt hätte. Und es wäre dabei nicht einmal notwendig gewesen, dem kämpfenden Rußland in den Rücken zu fallen. Auch nach dem Frieden von Portsmouth war das riesige Reich noch auf Jahre an allen Gliedern gelähmt: Die Armee war desorganisiert, die Finanzen zerrüttet, der Ausbruch der Revolution hatte die Fundamente der öffentlichen Ordnung fortgesprengt, und drohende Symptome wie die Meuterei an Bord des „Petropawlowsk" zeigten die vollkommene Paralysierung seiner Angriffskraft. Die brutale Niederwerfung aller geistigen Bestrebungen hatte die letzten Sympathien Europas dem Zarismus entfremdet, und selbst die slawischen Balkanvölker, die mit dem Prestige Rußlands ihre eigene Macht vermindert sahen, waren vom Enthusiasmus für das „Mütterchen" abgekommen. Österreich-Ungarn war also in diesen Jahren von 1903 bis etwa 1908 nicht nur die überlegene, sondern sogar die einzige Großmacht am Balkan. Auch innerlich war seine Situation günstig, der Ausgleich zwischen Österreich und Ungarn war endlich geschlossen, keine Aktion, auch nicht die verwegenste, hätte damals Widerstand gefunden. Aber der Ehrgeiz Österreich-Ungarns war vornehmlich auf den inneren Frieden gerichtet; man wollte die Jahre der Stille nützen, um im Ausgleich der Nationen die Festigkeit des Staates zu sichern.

Von Nachbarländern begehrte Österreich-Ungarn nichts: Venezien war für alle Zeit und ohne Reue an das angeblich nun befreundete Italien gegeben, auch mit Deutschland, dem letzten Gegner, war es in Blutbruderschaft verbündet. Nirgends war Erweiterung des slawischen Besitzes begehrt, auch Kolonien – die Welt war ja verteilt – durfte es nicht mehr erhoffen. Aber die wirtschaftliche Großmachtstellung der Monarchie erheischte Absatzgebiete, und während alle anderen Staaten mit Ausnahme des ständig benachteiligten Deutschland sich gewaltige Überseereiche eroberten, war ihr merkantiles Territorium gleich groß geblieben. Aber dieses Territorium, die Levante, beherrscht durch Tradition des Handels, die Vorherrschaft der Flotte, mußte Österreich-Ungarn gesichert bleiben. Die Türkei hatte längst erkannt, wer ihre uneigennützigsten Freunde waren, sie hatte Deutschland, dem einzigen Staate, der ihr nie Erde entrissen, die Bagdadbahn konzessioniert, die ihm die wirtschaftliche Übermacht dort sicherte, und war auch bereit, Österreich-Ungarn freundlich entgegenzukommen. Abdul Hamid, der vorsichtigste und klügste Sultan seit Jahrhunderten, wußte, was ihn die englische, die französische und russische Freundschaft gekostet hatte und zog es vor, die wirtschaftliche Annäherung an uneigennützige Staaten zu vollziehen. Die Levante war von je die Domäne Österreich-Ungarns gewesen und sollte es bleiben, mehr als je: Das war der gemeinsame Wunsch beider beteiligter Staaten. Doch der erste Anlaß, bei dem die Monarchie ihr Anrecht betonen zu müssen glaubte, weckte bereits einen Entrüstungssturm.

Graf Aehrenthal, der seit Ende des Jahres 1906 die äußere Politik Österreich-Ungarns leitete, kündigte am 27. Jänner 1908 in den Delegationen den Bau der Sandschakbahn[24] an. Nach dem Berliner Vertrage stand der österreich-ungarischen Regierung das Recht zu, Bahnverbindungen durch den Sandschak Novi Pazar zu legen, und wenn sie durch dreißig Jahre davon keinen Gebrauch gemacht hatte, so war dies Recht ebensowenig verjährt wie der Vertrag. Die neue Bahn sollte einerseits an die bosnischen Linien anschließen, andererseits an die türkische Linie Mitrovitca – Saloniki, also direkt an das Ägäische Meer. Der wesentliche Vorteil für Österreich-Ungarn wäre gewesen, daß hier ein direkter Weg gegen die Levante geöffnet war, indes bei den bisherigen Verbindungen unsere Waren Serbien zu passieren hatten, eben dasselbe Serbien, das seine Gegnerschaft gegen die Monarchie gar nicht mehr verhüllte und gerade dem Handel die größten Schwierigkeiten in den Weg legte. Für die Wirtschaftspolitik der Monarchie war es ein Lebensinteresse, direkt mit seinem größten Konsumenten in Verbindung zu stehen, auch militärisch war es von hoher Wichtigkeit für beide Staaten, in ununterbrochenem, unkontrolliertem Verkehr zu sein. Staatsmännisch war aber damit zugleich ausgedrückt, daß bei einem Zerfall der Türkei, an dem Rußland und die Balkanstaaten so emsig arbeiteten, Österreich-Ungarn nicht gleichgültig bleiben werde und die Richtung seines Willens „au delà de Mitrovitca" gegen das Ägäische Meer sich freikämpfen müßte, wollte es nicht eingeschnürt werden, um politisch und wirtschaftlich zu verkümmern.

Ein Protest gegen diesen Bahnbau war selbstverständlich ausgeschlossen: Das Recht Österreich-Ungarns war

---

[24] *Sandschak-Bahn*: Auch Sandžak-Bahn genannt, war die ursprünglich geplante Orient-Bahn; sie sollte die Verbindung Wien – Sarajevo – Sandschak – Saloniki herstellen; 1912/13 wurde Sandschak zwischen Serbien und Montenegro aufgeteilt.

vertraglich unanfechtbar, die Zustimmung des Sultans, des einzig Beteiligten, gegeben. Selbst die feindliche Diplomatie vermochte in dem durchaus legalen Vorgange keinen Span zu finden, um Entrüstungsflammen zu entfachen, aber das inoffizielle Ausland, die Presse, schlug mächtig Lärm. Eine Initiative Österreich-Ungarns, des totgeglaubten Staates, wurde als eine unerhörte Anmaßung empfunden: Man verstand gar nicht, daß auch die Monarchie, genauso wie die andern Nationen, wirtschaftliche Aspirationen haben könnte. Es hagelte Angriffe; Frankreich machte das böse Deutschland verantwortlich, England war mißmutig, Italien eifersüchtig, selbst Deutschland sah ungern die Brudermonarchie auf eigene Faust handeln.

Am meisten wetterte natürlich Serbien, dem in der Erregung zum ersten Mal das Einbekenntnis seiner Absichten auf Bosnien und den Sandschak entschlüpfte. Es protestierte, als sei diese Bahn durch ihr eigenes Land gelegt, und der Schienenstrang durchquere ihre Äcker und Felder. Eine solche Auffassung konnte in Rußland, zu dem sie sich um Hilfe wandten – vorläufig – noch nicht gebilligt werden. Denn Rußland war noch ermattet vom Kriege; wenngleich über das Lebenszeichen Österreich-Ungarns sehr verärgert, mußte es Ruhe halten. Die einzige Antwort, die Iswolski, der Gegenspieler Aehrenthals, fand, war eine Kompensationsbahn, die Donau-Adria-Bahn, die von Nisch nach einem albanischen Hafen führen sollte. War es Österreich-Ungarns Tendenz, Serbien zu umgehen, so wollte auch Serbien wieder einen Weg ans Meer, der nicht an den schwarz-gelben oder rot-weiß-grünen Grenzpfählen vorbeiginge. Graf Aehrenthal lehnte nicht ab, schon weil er wußte, daß dieses Projekt technisch soviel wie unausführbar und einzig als Fußangel ihm vorgelegt war. Und schon begannen die Ingenieure im Sandschak die Tracierungsarbeit.

Da zeigte der Balkan, dieser Hexenkessel seltsamer und widerstreitender Völkerschaften, eine neue Blase, die lärmend zerplatzte. In Albanien und Mazedonien war der gewohnte Frühjahrsaufstand gewesen – die Schneeschmelze ist dafür das alljährliche Signal –, man hatte wieder Militär zu seiner Bekämpfung gesandt, aber diesmal machte unvermuteterweise das Militär mit den Rebellen gemeinsame Sache, ein Komitee für „Ordnung und Fortschritt" wird unter den Offizieren gebildet, und die Armee marschiert auf Konstantinopel, um die einst versprochene, vom Sultan aber wieder unterschlagene Verfassung zu erzwingen. Abdul Hamid beeilt sich, nachzugeben. Er bewilligt ein Parlament, sodaß die Türkei nach Rußland als der letzte Staat in Europa das System der Volksvertretung adoptiert. Eine Reihe anderer Rechte, wie die der Freiheit der Religionsausübung und der unverletzbaren persönlichen Freiheit, werden anerkannt, um damit den Einmischungsbestrebungen und den heuchlerischen Klagen der Balkanstaaten ein Ende zu machen. Es hatte den Anschein, als wollte die alte, absterbende Türkei aus ihrer jahrhundertelangen Apathie erwachen und sich als moderner, zukunftsträchtiger Staat organisieren.

Daß aber dieser Trieb nicht von innen gekommen war, aus einem national-religiösen Bedürfnis, sondern daß die Drahtzieher der türkischen Revolutionen außen saßen, mußte bald zutage treten. England und Frankreich hatten mit Mißmut gesehen, daß der deutsche Botschafter der mächtigste Mann bei der Hohen Pforte geworden war. Abdul Hamid hatte seine wirklichen Freunde Deutschland und Österreich-Ungarn erkannt und suchte sich mehr und mehr dem französischen Finanzeinfluß zu entringen, der durch Jahre unter dem Vorwand der Kontrolle die ergiebigsten Industrien ausgebeutet. Er konnte nicht vergessen, was England, was Rußland vom lebendigen Leib seiner Nation gerissen. Und dieser Machteinfluß der beiden Zentralmächte am Goldenen Horn[25] war ständig im Wachsen: Um ihn zu brechen oder ins Wanken zu bringen, mußte der ganze türkische Staat erschüttert werden. Heute ist es erwiesen, daß es französische und englische Agenten waren – das Balkankomitee –, das die „Jungtürken" spielte, und tatsächlich schien die Regierung in ihren Tendenzen plötzlich verändert. Der Einfluß der Zentralmächte schien gefährdet: Es dauerte lange, ehe die Türkei – zu spät – ihre Verblendung erfuhr, die sie mit dem Verluste fast des ganzen europäischen Besitzes bezahlte. Graf Aehrenthal erkannte die Gefahr, die in dieser plötzlichen Veränderung lag. Er wußte, daß längst Errungenes durch die Frage der parlamentarischen Vertretung wieder in Diskussion gestellt werden sollte. Alle Vereinbarungen drohten plötzlich wieder fraglich zu werden, aber er war fest entschlossen, nicht noch einmal Verhandlungen über Gesichertes zu beginnen. Die Sandschakbahn hatte als Barometer gedient: Die Stimmung stand auf Sturm, war aber dennoch wandelbar. Und er kannte Österreich-Ungarns Kraft und die Schwäche seiner Gegner: So beschloß er zu handeln.

---

[25] *Goldenes Horn:* Bosporusbucht vor Istanbul.

Die Annexion
1908

Unter den zahlreichen Programmpunkten der neuen türkischen Verfassung war es einer insbesonders, der für Österreich-Ungarn eine offene Klarstellung der bestehenden Verhältnisse erheischte, nämlich die Forderung nach einer parlamentarischen Vertretung aller dem Ottomanenreich zugehörigen Länder. Hier lag für spätere Zeiten die Gefahr von Auseinandersetzungen, denn im Berliner Vertrag war es Andrássy nicht gelungen, bei den Mächten durchzusetzen, daß Bosnien und die Hercegovina der Monarchie einverleibt würden. Einzig das Mandat der Okkupation und Verwaltung (*occuper et administrer*) konnte damals erlangt werden, und wenn es auch auf ewige Zeiten ausgestellt war und nach allem menschlichen Ermessen von niemandem abgefordert werden durfte, so war es der Türkei durch einen klugen und fast erpresserischen Handstreich in der letzten Sekunde gelungen, von Andrássy ein geheimes Schriftstück zu erlangen, das bescheinigte, „daß die Souveränitätsrechte des Sultans über Bosnien und die Hercegovina in keiner Weise durch die Tatsache der Okkupation berührt werden sollten". Bei den schwankenden Verhältnissen im Großwesirat war nun zu fürchten, daß eine Partei im türkischen Parlament einmal die für Österreich-Ungarn längst definitiv gewordene Besetzung wieder in Diskussion bringen könnte, was niemandem erwünschter gewesen wäre als den Serben, die nur die Gelegenheit ersehnten, um den Zustand in Bosnien als einen provisorischen und vor allem als einen der Bevölkerung sehr antipathischen hinzustellen. Die Zweideutigkeit einer rechtlich klaren Sache war ein Stein des Anstoßes auf dem Wege der österreichisch-ungarischen Politik, und ihn wegzuräumen mußte daher wichtigste Sorge der Staatsmänner der Doppelmonarchie sein.

Der günstigste Augenblick war versäumt, der russisch-japanische Krieg. Zu jener Zeit wäre jeder Einspruch illusorisch gewesen. Nun aber war ohne Konzessionen kaum die Erwerbung dessen zu erlangen, was Österreich-Ungarn eigentlich schon besaß. Der einfachste Weg, mit dem nominellen Besitzer, der Türkei, zu verhandeln, war versperrt. Denn kein neues Regime hatte jemals gewagt, als erste Regierungshandlung eine Abtretung vorzunehmen, wenn auch eine bloß fiktive. So beschloß Aehrenthal mit Iswolski zu verhandeln, der diese günstige Gelegenheit nicht vorübergehen lassen wollte, eine für Rußland höchst lästige Fessel, die ihm dereinst von den Westmächten angelegt worden war, die Sperrung der Dardanellen für russische Kriegsschiffe, abzuschütteln. In Buchlov, dem Sommersitz des Grafen Berchtold, fand jene historische Zusammenkunft statt, in der beide Staatsmänner versprachen, einander tatkräftig zu fördern, wenn sie ihre Ansprüche geltend machen würden, und zwar Österreich-Ungarn eine Annexion Bosniens, Rußland die Dardanellendurchfahrt. Auch mit Tittoni, dem Vertreter Italiens, waren zweifellos Vereinbarungen getroffen, auf Deutschlands Bundestreue war zu zählen, und um der Türkei das Nachgeben zu erleichtern, entschloß sich Graf Aehrenthal, ihr mit einer freiwilligen, allerdings nicht unbedenklichen Konzession entgegenzukommen: Der Aufgabe des Sandschaks Novi Pazar, über den Österreich-Ungarn Hoheitsrechte hatte und durch den die nun für weiteres aufgegebene Bahn eben hätte traciert werden sollen. Dieser Maßnahme war militärischerseits im Herbst 1908 nur unter der Voraussetzung beigestimmt worden, daß der Krieg mit Serbien in gewisser Aussicht stand, in welchem Fall der Sandschak natürlich sofort und zwar mit ausreichenden Kräften wieder besetzt worden wäre.

Nach dieser diplomatischen Vorbereitung, die mit gewiß unverhältnismäßig großen Zugeständnissen verbunden, aber wenigstens, soweit Verträge sichern, eine vollkommene war, entschloß sich Graf Aehrenthal zur Tat. Die Unabhängigkeitserklärung Ferdinands von Bulgarien, des bisherigen Vasallen der Türkei, gab den Auftakt. Und am 6. Oktober 1908 erschien das folgende Handschreiben des Kaisers und Königs: „Durchdrungen von der unerschütterlichen Überzeugung, daß die hohen kulturellen und poltischen Zwecke, um derentwillen die Österreichisch-Ungarische Monarchie die Besetzung und Verwaltung Bosniens und der Hercegovina übernommen hat und die mit schweren Opfern erzielten Erfolge der bisherigen Verwaltung nur durch Gewährung von ihren Bedürfnissen entsprechenden verfassungsmäßigen Einrichtungen dauernd gesichert werden können, für deren Erlassung aber die Schaffung einer klaren und unzweideutigen Rechtsstellung der beiden Länder die unerläßliche Voraussetzung bildet, erstrecke Ich die Rechte meiner Souveränität auf Bosnien und die Hercegovina und setze gleichzeitig die für Mein Haus geltende Erbfolgeordnung auch für diese Länder in Wirksamkeit. Zur Kundgebung der friedlichen Absichten, die Mich bei dieser unabweislichen Verfügung geleitet haben, ordne Ich gleichzeitig die Räumung des Sandschaks Novi Pazar von den dahin verlegten Truppen meiner Armee an. Franz Joseph *m. p.*"

Gespannt lauschte man in Österreich-Ungarn auf das Echo. Man war einigermaßen auf Sturm gefaßt seit jenem Zwischenfall mit der Sandschakbahn, aber der Tumult, der sich erhob, übertraf alle Erwartungen und vor allem, er kam aus einer Windrichtung, die niemand erwartet hatte, von England. Selten war in der Weltgeschichte das Verhältnis zweier Staaten zueinander ein derart harmonisches gewesen, wie dasjenige Österreich-Ungarns und Englands, nie hatte ein Zwist sie in Waffen entzweit, niemals die geringste Mißhelligkeit zwischen ihnen geherrscht, England war es gewesen, das die Initiative zum Berliner Kongreß übernommen, England, das sich dem Grafen Andrássy vorher verbürgt hatte, die Annexion – und nicht nur die Okkupation – auf diesem Kongresse mit allem diplomatischen Nachdruck zu unterstützen, England war es selbst, das Stück um Stück große Teile des Ottomanischen Reiches tatsächlich oder nominell dem eigenen Bestande eingefügt hatte. Aber plötzlich war England wie immer, wenn es ihm paßte, „moralisch", sah in der Titeländerung eines schon längst Tatsache gewordenen Rechtes einen Diebstahl, eine noch nie dagewesene Verletzung des Berliner Vertrags, der, wie Crispi zu Bismarck schon vor zwanzig Jahren sagte, nur mehr aus Fetzen bestand. Aehrenthal war der Machiavell Europas, und aus allen Organen des großen Friedensbeschützers Edward Grey tönten Sturm und Drohung.

Daß England damals die Rolle des Chorführers übernahm, war in jenen Tagen noch nicht recht zu verstehen. England war damals inmitten seiner Einkreisungspolitik gegen Deutschland und hatte im Stillen gehofft, Österreich-Ungarn, den letzten und treuesten Verbündeten – denn Italien war schon gewonnen – von ihm abzuziehen. Ein Geheimnisvolles war da geschehen: In der Sommervilla von Ischl hatte König Eduard im Sommer 1908, zwei knappe Monate vor der Annexion, noch Vorschläge gemacht, deren Wortlaut man nicht kennt, wohl aber deren Sinn. Österreich-Ungarn sollte von Deutschland abrücken, und es ist kein Zweifel, daß hohe Belohnung dafür ihm versprochen war. Die Antwort unseres Monarchen war die einzig ehrenhafte und würdige: eine restlose Abweisung, die König Eduard dauernd verstimmte und diesen Besuch in Österreich-Ungarn zu seinem letzten machte, indes er in keinem Jahr versäumt hatte, nach Marienbad zu kommen. Nun war die Gelegenheit da, Österreich-Ungarn zu zeigen, was es versäumt habe, indem es einen so hohen Protektor abwies: Wollte es seine Gunst nicht, so sollte es die Schwere seines Unwillens fühlen. Die Presse wurde mobilisiert, ohne jede Umschweife mitgeteilt, daß England seine Zustimmung zur Annexion verweigerte, das berüchtigte Balkankomitee unter Noël Burton, dessen Aufgabe es bisher gewesen, die Austreibung der Türkei aus Europa mit Sack und Pack – *„with bag and baggage"* – nach der Gladstonischen Formel vorzubereiten, tat plötzlich Buße, erklärte seine Hetzbücher gegen das ottomanische Reich für bedauerliche Irrtümer und pilgerte zum Yildiz-Kiosk, um Buße zu tun und gegen Österreich-Ungarn zu hetzen.

Die Türkei, der Hauptbeteiligte, war anfangs überrascht worden und schien bereit, sich mit Österreich-Ungarn gütlich zu einigen. Die freiwillige Abtretung des Sandschaks war eine zur Aussöhnung dargereichte Hand, und da es der Stärkere war, der sie bot, wäre es für den Schwächeren vor der Welt nicht beschämend gewesen, einzuschlagen. Österreich-Ungarn hatte sich seit der Okkupation als der zuverlässigste Freund erwiesen, und man wußte das am Goldenen Horn. Aber England stellte sich hinter die Diplomaten und steifte ihnen den Rücken, es war in fremdem Interesse, hier Mißhelligkeiten zu stiften und einen Ausgleich zu verhindern, der alle Proteste zum Wort zerblasen hätte. Es war offenkundig Englands Tendenz, Österreich-Ungarn in Schwierigkeiten zu bringen, und die türkischen

Unterhändler erkannten bald die Möglichkeit, hier zu erpressen und damit sich ein Prestige vor dem neu zusammengestellten Parlamente zu erringen. Aus dem anfangs leisen Widerspruch wurde allmählich ein lautes Zetergeschrei; nicht ohne Unterstützung von Seiten der konkurrierenden Mächte wurde ein Boykott österreichischer und ungarischer Schiffe und Waren begonnen, dem nur durch energisches Vorgehen zu begegnen gewesen wäre. Drohende Schritte gegen die Türkei durfte aber Österreich-Ungarn nicht unternehmen, solange es nicht der Meinung der Großmächte sicher war. Und das konnte es wahrhaftig nicht sein. Von keiner Seite fand es Unterstützung. Deutschland war gerade am Wege gewesen, die Einkreisung, die seine Grenzen schmerzhaft bedrückte, zu lockern, indem man England und Rußland nähertrat, als der Entschluß zur Annexion den Vertretern der Einkreisungspolitik einen billigen Vorwand bot, das Netz um die beiden Staaten wieder zusammenzuschnüren. Die Banken hatten viel Geld in der Türkei investiert, die Zukunft der Bagdadbahn hing viel vom Wohlwollen der Machthaber am Bosporus ab, so war Fürst Bülow gezwungen, zu erklären, daß die Annexion erfolgt sei ohne jede vorherige Mitteilung an den befreundeten Bundesstaat und er sie „ungefähr zur gleichen Stunde erfahren habe wie Rußland und England", womit er öffentlich die Legende zerstörte, als handle Österreich-Ungarn nur als Vorposten Deutschlands. Im Ganzen wurde die Annexion als eine unwillkommene Störung der Stunde betrachtet, und erst die Gehässigkeit der Slawen machte jenseits der Grenze klar, wie notwendig ein Zusammenhalt der beiden Staaten war. Frankreich war natürlich unfreundlich gegen den Bundesgenossen Deutschland, allerdings aber merkwürdig weniger gehässig und viel konzilianter als England. Die Kriegsangst von

1906 stak dem Lande offenbar noch zu tief in den Knochen, und wenn sie drüben den Grafen Aehrenthal einen neuen Delcassé nannten, so traf dieser Tadel ihre eigenen Ambitionen. Von Italien, dem Bundesstaat, wäre freundliche Zustimmung zu erwarten gewesen, umso mehr, als Tittoni den Plänen Aehrenthals vorher seine Zustimmung gegeben hatte. Aber die jahrzehntelange Arbeit der *Irredenta*[26] war nicht vergeblich geblieben: Das ganze Land empörte sich gegen die Annexion. Als ob man neues Land und faktischen Machtzuwachs erworben hätte, forderte man als „Kompensation" das Trentino, die Blätter gebärdeten sich kriegerisch, und das Ministerium war genötigt, trotz seiner strikt am Semmering und in Salzburg gemachten Zusagen und des kurz vordem erneuerten Dreibundes seine Erklärung vom 6. Oktober, daß die Veränderung durch die Annexion nur die faktische Anerkennung eines bisherigen Zustandes sei, rückgängig zu machen und die Zustimmung zu jener Konferenz zu erklären, die Iswolski wollte und Österreich-Ungarn verweigerte. In offener Sitzung wurde die Sympathie für Serbien und Montenegro bekannt, die eben damals der Monarchie mit dem Messer drohten, und die Vereinbarungen mit Rußland stolz notifiziert. Wieder war das Gleiche zutage getreten wie in der Konferenz von Algeciras – was Fürst Bülow zu nachsichtig eine Extratour nannte –, nämlich daß Italien in der entscheidenden Stunde immer vom Dreibund abrückte und Politik der Volksstimmung trieb, statt jener der offiziellen Vereinbarungen und beschworenen Bündnisse.

Am kompliziertesten, erregendsten aber war das Verhältnis Österreich-Ungarns zu Rußland in jenen Tagen,

---

[26] *Irredenta*: Nach dem 1878 gegründeten politischen Verein *Italia Irredenta* („Unerlöstes Italien"); Bestrebungen vom Mutterland getrennter Volksgruppen, sich diesem anzugliedern.

weil es hier neben den allgemein politischen Gegensätzen ein persönliches Duell der beiden hervorragendsten Diplomaten vor den Augen Europas gab. Iswolski[27] hatte mit dem Grafen Aehrenthal für diesen Fall eine absolut bindende Vereinbarung des Verhaltens: die rückhaltlose Zustimmung, ebenso wie Graf Aehrenthal im Voraus das Einverständnis zur Eröffnung der Dardanellen gegeben hatte. Kaum daß Iswolski nun vom Gelingen des österreich-ungarischen Planes erfuhr, wollte er nun seine Kompensation durchsetzen – aber in London scheiterte der Wunsch nach Eröffnung der Dardanellen am starren Widerstand der Engländer. In Rußland, wo man von seinen Zugeständnissen und seiner vorherigen Billigung keine Ahnung hatte, wühlte die panslawistische Presse Schlammwolken gegen Österreich-Ungarn auf, und es fehlte dem verantwortlichen Minister der Mut, für sein gegebenes Wort nun auch öffentlich einzustehen. Da er sich von England und Frankreich gestützt fühlte, leugnete er jedes Zugeständnis als eine Düpierung und verweigerte – obwohl er anscheinend beweisende Dokumente in Aehrenthals Händen wußte – die Anerkennung Rußlands anders als auf einer Konferenz. Nun stand Österreich-Ungarn auf dem Standpunkte, daß es über die Annexion als fertige Tatsache Diskussionen nicht mehr dulde und über Kompensationen nur mit jenen Staaten verhandle, die ein Anrecht hätten, und dies sei einzig die Türkei. Man hatte bei uns jene Konferenz in Algeciras noch zu deutlich im Auge, wo selbst der italienische Bundesgenosse auf die andere Seite gerückt war und man dann zu zweit – Deutschland und Österreich-Ungarn – der geschlossenen Majorität ge-

---

[27] *Alexander Petrowitsch Iswolski*: Russischer Diplomat, 1910 – 1917 Botschafter in Paris; deutschfeindlich; wesentlich an der Vorbereitung zum Ersten Weltkrieg beteiligt; 1856 – 1919.

genüberstand und nur die Wahl hatte, nachzugeben oder das Schwert zu ziehen. Iswolski blieb fest, keine Mahnung an Versprechungen konnte ihn von seinem Vorhaben abbringen, aber auch Graf Aehrenthal wußte, daß es ein Zurück nimmer gab von einem Akte, den Seine Majestät unterzeichnet, und vor allem keine Nachgiebigkeit gegen Drohungen, wenn es die Ehre galt. Er war noch vor zwei Jahren Botschafter in Petersburg gewesen, kannte zu gut die Stimmung des russischen Volkes und den Zustand der Armee, um die panslawistischen Drohungen zu überschätzen.

Wirklich gefährlich, weil nicht diplomatisch, sondern impulsive, bis zum Wahnwitz siedende Volkserregung war aber die Situation in Serbien. Seit König Peter zur Herrschaft gekommen, hatte man dem sanguinischen und leichtgläubigen Volke suggeriert, Bosnien sei sein Besitz und schon reife Frucht vom morschen Stamme Österreich-Ungarns. Und nun zeigte Österreich-Ungarn seine Kraft, behauptete und betonte als sein Eigen, was ehrgeizige Träume schon als dem Großserbien zugehörig gesehen. Selbst die künstlichste Statistik konnte nicht mehr als ein Drittel der Einwohner für orthodoxe Serben erkennen, aber nach den Belgrader Berichten waren es „unterdrückte serbische Brüder", die dort „im Joche" Österreich-Ungarns schmachteten. Ein Schrei ging durch das ganze Land, als hätte man Serbien beraubt und nicht ein nur mehr nominelles Stück der Türkei der Monarchie einverleibt. Die Anrechte waren freilich sehr dunkle, sie waren eher zu spät gekommene Ansprüche an den Berliner Kongreß von 1878 statt an die Annexion von 1908, gerade dreißig Jahre zu spät gekommene. Dort hätten Serbien und Montenegro vielleicht behaupten dürfen, der Aufstand in Bosnien und der Hercegovina gegen die Türkei sei von ihnen angezettelt worden, serbische Freischaren hätten als erste das Land erobert. Aber der Kongreß hatte nicht das Vertrauen in die staatsmännische und kulturelle Verwaltungsfähigkeit der Kleinstaaten, Europa wollte Ruhe und Sicherheit am Balkan, so wurde Österreich-Ungarn zum Hüter bestellt. Was in diesen dreißig Jahren dort an Kultur geleistet worden ist, hätte auch weniger legale Anrechte als die Österreich-Ungarns zu rechtlichen gemacht. Und nichts konnte Serbien in dieser Stunde berechtigen, sich als der Benachteiligte auszugeben – nichts als der von den Karageorgević und ihren Ministern dem Volke ohne innere Ansprüche suggerierte Rechtstitel über Länder, die außerhalb Serbiens lagen. Die Annexion war ein Eingriff nicht in die Besitzsphäre, sondern in die Wunschsphäre der Karageorgević, diese aber umfaßte ja auch Mazedonien, Albanien, Montenegro, Dalmatien, Kroatien und erstreckte sich bis ungefähr Graz und Triest. Auf diese Wunschsphäre Rücksicht zu nehmen, lag natürlich nicht in den Interessen der Monarchie. Aber der Ausbruch der Leidenschaften in Belgrad überstieg jede Erwartung und jedes Maß. Die Offiziere durchzogen mit geschwungenen Säbeln die Straßen, eine Totenlegion wurde gebildet, vor der österreich-ungarischen Gesandtschaft staute sich der Pöbel, um von dort dann zur türkischen zu ziehen und ihr – in plötzlich erwachter Zuneigung – Sympathiekundgebungen darzubringen. Die Skupschtina, die sich versammelte, wollte sogleich den Krieg erklären – sechsundsechzig Stimmen fanden sich dafür gegen die dreiundneunzig der Bedächtigeren, die schließlich den Ausschlag gaben. Es wurde beschlossen, Protest einzulegen bei Österreich-Ungarn, wo Graf Aehrenthal die Annahme des Schreibens glatt verweigerte, weil er einen Einspruch einer nicht beteiligten Macht nicht duldete –, Agenten wurden an alle Höfe gesandt und vor allen Pašić und der Kronprinz selbst nach Petersburg. Dieser junge Kronprinz Georg spielte sich sofort zum Führer der Kriegspartei auf, hielt Ansprachen, die schwerste Beschimpfungen der Monarchie mit lächerlichen Drohungen vermengten und zeigte nicht übel Lust, selbst die Herrschaft zu übernehmen, falls sich sein Vater nicht fügte. Von Montenegro scholl reges Echo herüber, auch König Nikita hielt feierliche Ansprachen, in denen er offen erklärte, „die schwarz-gelbe Farbe werde nie die Grenze bilden" und Montenegro von der Hercegovina trennen. Beide serbische Staaten forderten die Verweigerung der Annexion von den Großmächten, was ihnen zunächst gelang, nachdem sie dagegen versprochen hatten, sich friedlich bis auf weiteres zu verhalten – und außerdem „Entschädigungen" an sie für einen Besitz, den sie nur erträumt hatten. Dies alles wies darauf hin, wie mißlich die Auflassung unserer Stellung im Sandschak gewesen.

Die Lage der österreichisch-ungarischen Diplomatie war in diesem Augenblick eine sehr schwierige. Deutschland zeigte den Willen, sich möglichst wenig aktiv zu engagieren und die Angelegenheit als spezifisch österreichisch-ungarische zu belassen, wie man sie in Wien als Handlung eigener Initiative begonnen hatte. Iswolski war seinem Versprechen untreu geworden, Tittoni nicht minder, alle Großstaaten, außer Deutschland, weigerten geschlossen die Zustimmung, was die Ansprüche der Türkei natürlich aufs äußerste ermutigen mußte. Die unberechenbare Volksleidenschaft in Serbien erforderte kostspielige militärische Maßnahmen an der Grenze, auch in Galizien mußten geheimnisvolle russische Truppenverschiebungen mit eigenen Vorkehrungen gepaart werden, die italienische Grenze bedurfte trotz des unterzeichneten Dreibundblattes sorgfältiger Bewachung. Das alles war erregend und kostspielig. Dazu kam noch der Boykott der österreichungarischen Waren und Schiffe in der Levante, veranstaltet vom jungtürkischen Komitee, aber rege von England und Italien unterstützt, die mit ihren eigenen Erzeugnissen den österreichisch-ungarischen Handel für immer zu verdrängen hofften. Direkte Vorstellungen halfen nichts, und militärisch war Österreich-Ungarn in dieser Stunde eingekreist von Mißgunst und Haß, ohnmächtig gegen die Türkei, selbst an eine Flottendemonstration durfte nicht gedacht werden, weil die italienische Volksstimmung zu wenig zuverlässig war, um alle Schiffe aus der Adria zu entsenden. Auch die inneren politischen Verhältnisse waren wenig erfreulich, und der Tag des sechzigjährigen Regierungsjubiläums mußte mit dem Standrecht in Prag gefeiert werden. So hatten Serbien, die Türkei und Montenegro es leicht, die Monarchie herauszufordern, die als eminent friedlicher Staat die äußersten Konsequenzen vermeiden wollte.

Die erste Erleichterung in diesem Zustand brachte ein tragischer Zufall, das Erdbeben von Messina im Dezember 1908, das mit seinen furchtbaren Verwüstungen und Schäden auch der kriegerischen Partei in Italien die Lust zu momentaner Einmengung benahm. Frei im Süden, konnte Österreich-Ungarn nun energischer mit Rußland verhandeln, und mitten in diesen Pourparlers über die Konferenz vermochte sich Graf Aehrenthal den formellen Verzicht der Türkei zu erringen, der jeden fremden Einspruch erledigte. Vierundfünfzig Millionen wanderten leider mit dem Sandschak zurück an die Türkei, aber der Boykott war zu Ende, und vor allem, keine Großmacht hatte jetzt mehr einen Vorwand, Österreich-Ungarn einen Besitz zu bestreiten, der doppelt durch das sittliche Recht wie das legale ihm zugesichert war. Frankreich war überdies des Konfliktes müde, in England flaute das Interesse merklich ab, sobald die freie Dardanellendurchfahrt eingesargt war, und auch Rußlands Intervention und Wunsch nach einer Konferenz war illusorisch geworden. Mit dem Dokument vom 23. Februar 1909, in dem die Pforte ihre Zustimmung gab, schien der Konflikt beendet: Der angeblich so frevelhaft Beraubte reichte dem Räuber friedlich und freundschaftlich die Hand, die Zuschauer, die sich auf einen mörderischen Zweikampf gefaßt hatten, durften enttäuscht abziehen. Der Streit war zu Ende, da die Streitenden sich geeinigt hatten.

In Serbien aber brach auf die Nachricht von der vollzogenen und durch den Verzicht der Türkei vollkommen rechtsgültig gewordenen Annexion eine Erregung aus, die bei weiten jene der ersten Tage übertraf. Nun war es nicht nur der Kronprinz mehr, der seine provokatorischen Reden hielt, auch der Ministerpräsident ließ sich zu Äußerungen von solcher Gewalttätigkeit hinreißen, daß Österreich-Ungarn durch den Gesandten, Grafen Forgach, Aufklärungen fordern mußte. In offener Skupschtinasitzung[28] wurde erklärt, Österreich-Ungarn müsse aufhören, ein Balkanstaat zu sein, es müsse sich entschließen, die Rolle einer östlichen Schweiz einzunehmen. Während man aber im Lande offen von einer Zermalmung der schwachen und morschen Monarchie sprach, Volk und Armee in einen fanatischen Größenwahn hetzte, spielte man nach außen das schwache Lämmlein, daß vom Wolfe Österreich-Ungarn überfallen sei und erklärte ständig die „absolute Unterwürfigkeit unter den Willen Europas", während man ihm in Wirklichkeit schroffen Trotz bot.

Europa war nämlich der ständigen Beunruhigung durch das serbische Geschrei nach der „Luftröhre" – dem Korridor zu einem montenegrinischen Hafen, der durch abgetrenntes bosnisches Gebiet führen sollte – herzlich

---

[28] *Skupschtina:* Das serbische Wort skupština bedeutet Versammlung; u. a. wird es als jugoslaw. Bundesversammlung bzw. Parlament übersetzt.

müde. Nachdem Österreich-Ungarn mit der Türkei sich verständigt hatte, war für Frankreich und England kein Grund mehr zur Intervention, Italien war durch das Erdbeben von Messina von der äußern Politik abgelenkt und zufriedengestellt durch eine kleine politische Kompensation Österreich-Ungarns an Montenegro; vor allem hatte aber Deutschland, der Quertreibereien müde, sich entschlossen auf Österreich-Ungarns Seite gestellt. Nun mußte auch Rußland sich endlich entschließen, europäische Politik statt bloß slawische zu treiben, und alle Mächte intervenierten gemeinsam in Belgrad und rieten, von jeder territorialen Kompensation Abstand zu nehmen, weil sie eine unerfüllbare und ungerechte Forderung sei.

Aber seltsamerweise antwortete man in Belgrad auf diese Vorschläge ganz Europas ausweichend, man stellte dort die zu leistenden Kompensationen einer Konferenz anheim. Offenkundig war dieser Widerstand Serbiens gegen alle Großmächte von irgendeiner Seite erwünscht, und in Wien kannte man den Drahtzieher nur zu gut: Es war Herr von Hartwig, der russische Gesandte. Das bewährte System der russischen Politik mit dem doppelten Boden funktionierte auch hier wieder vortrefflich: Während am lichten Tag vor allen Diplomaten Serbien feierlich beschworen wurde, gegen Österreich-Ungarn doch nachgiebig zu sein, wurde ihm heimlich der Nacken gesteift und alle möglichen Provokationen ersonnen. Die Noten des Wiener Auswärtigen Amtes ließ man tagelang unbeantwortet liegen, man wußte in Rußland, daß jeder Tag Mobilisierung in Österreich-Ungarn Volksvermögen aufzehrte und wollte den für die Nachbarmonarchie so peinlichen Zustand möglichst verlängern.

Wochen und Wochen war dies gelungen, denn in Österreich-Ungarn wollte der Monarch seinen Lebensabend in

Frieden beschließen, und alles wurde vermieden, was zu einem Ausbruch hätte führen können. Mit kaum verständlicher Geduld ließ man den Kronprinzen vom Balkan die Ehre der Monarchie begeifern, unsern Gesandten höhnen, unsere Noten unerledigt auf den Tischen der serbischen Staatslenker schimmeln –, aber endlich riß die Geduld, hüben und drüben, in Deutschland und in Österreich-Ungarn. In Wien war man nun entschlossen, zu biegen oder zu brechen. Und in Berlin hatte man endlich erkannt, wo die Wurzel des Widerstandes war, und daß nicht in Belgrad, sondern in Petersburg das *Aut–aut* gestellt werden müßte. Unser Schwert lag schon blank, nun klirrte zum ersten Mal auch das deutsche vernehmlich in der Scheide.

Diese letzten Märztage des Jahres 1909 werden in Wien unvergeßlich bleiben. Zum ersten Mal – und unendlich drohender als im Juli 1906 – fühlte man, daß die ganze europäische Atmosphäre mit Schwüle und Stickluft geladen war. Nicht die wenigsten waren es, die bei uns wünschten, lieber früher als später möge diese Wetterwolke sich entladen: Die Kanonen starrten geladen hinüber nach Belgrad, ganz Österreich-Ungarn wartete nur auf das entscheidende Signal. Das Ultimatum lag schon ausgefertigt bereit und konnte jede Stunde übergeben werden, die Zeitungen sprachen unverhohlen aus, daß die Entscheidung auf des Schwertes Spitze ruhe. Am 25. März, einem Feiertage, brachte die „Neue Freie Presse" jenen berühmten Artikel Heinrich Friedjungs, der alle Anwürfe Österreich-Ungarns gegen Serbien zusammenfaßte und – offenkundig in hohem diplomatischen Auftrag verfaßt – das *Aide-mémoire*, die Motivierung des Ultimatums und der Kriegserklärung war. In Wien verstand man sofort den Ernst der Situation, elektrisch vibrierte die ganze Stadt, das ganze Reich.

Und am nächsten Tag war alles vorbei, der scharfe Wind hatte die Wolke weggefegt. Die Blase des serbischen Hochmuts war über Nacht geplatzt und nichts zurückgeblieben als ein wenig Schmutz und Geifer in den Zeitungen. Über Nacht war der Kronprinz Georg, das irrwitzige Haupt der Kriegspartei, zur Abdankung von der kronprinzlichen Würde gezwungen worden, angeblich wegen Mißhandlung eines Dieners – als ob im serbischen Konak Tätlichkeiten als Verbrechen gelten würden. Aber er war – von einer unsichtbaren Hand – weggestoßen aus der europäischen Politik, und fast gleichzeitig kam die Kunde von der Anerkennung der Annexion in Rußland. Nun mußte auch Serbien den Nacken beugen und in einer Note vom 31. März zähneknirschend erklären: „Serbien anerkennt, daß es durch die in Bosnien geschaffenen Tatsachen in seinen Rechten nicht berührt wurde und verpflichtet sich, die Richtung seiner gegenwärtigen Politik gegen Österreich-Ungarn zu ändern und künftighin mit diesen letzteren auf dem Fuß freundnachbarlicher Beziehungen zu leben." Die Banden mußten aufgelöst, die Rekruten nach Hause gesandt werden. Auch Österreich-Ungarn durfte sich endlich der Ruhe und Entspannung freuen: Unter schweren Opfern an Geld, Energie und Nervenverbrauch war dieser Erfolg errungen, aber er hatte der politisch etwas gleichgültigen Bevölkerung der Monarchie zum ersten Mal den Ernst der europäischen Situation gezeigt, den Pfahl im Fleische und zugleich mit dem politischen das Selbstbewußtsein des ganzen Reiches gekräftigt. Alles Unsichere war geregelt, das Reich durch die Annexion gerundet, alle fremden Ansprüche für immer zu Boden geschlagen. Nun hatte Serbien keine Argumente mehr als seine letzten und verzweifelten: die Bomben aus dem Arsenale von Kragujevac.

Die vollendete Einkreisung Deutschlands und Österreich-Ungarns 1908 – 1912

In Treue waren nun durch diese letzte Prüfung Deutschland und Österreich-Ungarn aneinandergehämmert, ein einziger eherner Block. Aber rings um sie erhob sich jetzt mit verdoppelter Stärke fremder Groll und Neid. Österreich-Ungarn war diplomatisch siegreich mit einem ganz neuen und kraftspendenden Selbstbewußtsein aus dem Kampfe um die Annexion hervorgegangen, und die materiellen Opfer erwiesen sich nun als gering gegen den ungeheuren moralischen Gewinn. Deutschland wieder als wahrhaftiger Friedensstaat hatte einen unglaublichen wirtschaftlichen Aufschwung genommen. Während England Milliarden im Burenkriege, Rußland im japanischen Kriege ausgeben mußten, Frankreich sich an Kolonialabenteuern schwächte, Italien durch jenen Erdstoß blühendes Land in ein Trümmerfeld gewandelt sah, hatte die deutsche Nation ruhig und zielbewußt ihre Macht ausgebaut, günstige Handelsverträge sicherten seinem Handel vorteilhafte Entfaltung, und das Nationalvermögen hatte sich in nie geahnter Weise erhöht. Deutlich begann die Welt diesen Staat in seinem wahren Range zu spüren: als die Hauptmacht Europas, das Zentrum seiner Kultur und Kraft.

An diesen Erfolgen mußte die englische Mißgunst selbstverständlich in vervielfachter Proportion wachsen. Die Riesenschiffe der Hamburg-Amerika-Linie beherrschten immer mehr den Ozean, den jene seit je als ihr Macht-gebiet betrachteten, längst war die berühmte Technik und Industrie von der deutschen geschlagen und, obwohl keine Mühe gespart wurde, durch Warnungsmarken „Made in Germany" die Verbreitung deutscher Produkte zu hindern, so erzwangen sie sich doch überall Platz und Geltung. Und da in England die Geldinteressen von je die entscheidenden für den Gang der Politik waren, so beschloß die Regierung unter der Initiative König Eduards, die ganze Stoßkraft der englischen Feindseligkeiten einzig gegen Deutschland zu wenden und die Einkreisung allmählich in eine Erdrosselung zu verwandeln.

Die Vertreter der beiden wichtigsten Bundesstaaten waren willfährig zu jedem Beginnen. Delcassé und Iswolski waren beide persönlich gekränkt und wollten ihr politisches Prestige um jeden Preis zurückgewinnen: Selbst der europäische Krieg mit Hunderttausenden oder Millionen Opfern schien ihnen nicht zu hoher Einsatz im Spiel um einen Ruhm als Heros oder Herostrat. Delcassé konnte nicht vergessen, daß er gefallen war, als Deutschland nur ganz leise an das Schwert klirrte, Iswolski, der gegen Österreich-Ungarn diplomatisch den Kürzeren gezogen hatte und dies vor den Augen der ganzen Welt, sah in einem Vernichtungskrieg gegen Österreich-Ungarn die einzige Satisfaktion seiner Niederlage. Beide suchten im eigenen Lande Helfer und fanden sie leicht in den Ehrgeizigen, Delcassé vor allem in Poincaré, einem der geschmeidigsten und skrupellosesten Politiker Frankreichs, der geradewegs auf die Stelle des Ministerpräsidenten zusteuerte und vielleicht schon damals die des Präsidenten der Republik für sich erträumte. Mit Iswolskis Hilfe, der mit großen Geldmitteln einen Teil der französischen Presse für die slawischen Zwecke gewann, wurde die *Entente* mit Rußland, die bisher wesentlich defensiven Zwecken gegolten hatte, eingehärtet und in eine Angriffswaffe verwandelt. Rußland mußte stark werden: Dazu wurden neuerlich Milliarden hinüber gesandt, diesmal aber unter bestimmten Bedingungen nicht nur finanzieller, sondern auch strategischer Natur. Das Bahnnetz an der deutschen Grenze sollte ausgebaut werden, französische Offiziere leiteten die Reorganisation der Armee, hüben und drüben arbeiteten die Kriegsparteien einander geschäftig in die Hände. England goß emsig Öl ins Feuer dieser neuentfachten Kriegsbegeisterung – die in Frankreich zum großen Teil durch die Vorherrschaft auf dem Gebiet der Aviatik aufgeflammt war – und war außerdem emsig tätig, neue Bundesgenossen zu werben und die alten von Deutschland abzuziehen. In Ischl war König Eduard damit so gründlich abgefallen, daß er einen Versuch nicht mehr erneuerte. Aber in Spanien, wo der junge König eine englische Prinzessin geheiratet hatte, erreichte seine Initiative eine Aussöhnung mit Frankreich, und auch sein Besuch in Italien – wo man hintereinander alle Gegner Österreich-Ungarns, den Zaren, den König Peter von Serbien und den Fürsten Nikita von Montenegro empfangen hatte – schien nicht ganz wirkungslos zu sein. Der Dreibund war gelockert, während die *„Entente cordiale"* – Frankreich, England, Rußland mit all ihren Annexen – sich immer mehr straffte und für den Augenblick des Abschnellens noch Italien hinüberzuziehen hoffte.

In Deutschland spürte man deutlich und immer deutlicher die Umschnürung. Und der Kaiser in seiner energischen Initiative versuchte für seine Person die Gefahr zu bannen, indem er eine offene Aussprache mit den Gegnern suchte. In jenem Interview des „Daily Telegraph" erklärte er öffentlich und deutlich, daß er England in den schwersten Stunden zur Seite gestanden sei, sogar einem Antrag Frankreichs und Rußlands zu einem gemeinsamen Angriff widerstrebt hatte und selbst im Gegensatze zur Volksstimmung auch weiterhin den Frieden aufrechtzuerhalten hoffte. Aber diese offen hingereichte Hand blieb unbemerkt, im Gegenteil, das Interview erzeugte einen Sturm des Unwillens im Reiche und außerhalb, weil es den Gegensatz der Volksstimmungen so betonte. Und seit jenem Tage war das Mißtrauen zwischen den Nationen nur noch gesteigert. England verzichtete ganz auf seine bisherige Politik: Man ließ zu, daß Rußland Finnland und Persien knechtete, Frankreich mehr und mehr Marokko unter dem Vorwand der Polizeirechte vergewaltigte, man versprach Italien Tripolis, das der Türkei gehörte, und nur Deutschland fand überall, wo es nur vordringen wollte, einen wohlerklärlichen Widerstand.

Eine kurze Entspannung brachte der Tod König Eduard VII. am 6. Mai 1910. Dieser weltkluge und ehrgeizige Monarch hatte es verstanden, in wenigen Jahren das am meisten vereinsamte und unbeliebteste Reich zum Drehpunkt der europäischen Politik zu machen. Mit Ausdauer und Geschick hatte er das Netz geflochten, das, dichter und dichter um Deutschland gesponnen, kaum mehr mit Diplomatie zu entwirren, sondern einzig mit dem Schwerte zu zerschneiden war. Sein Nachfolger Georg V. hatte zwar nicht mehr jene aggressive Feindlichkeit der Gesinnung, aber die gefährliche Politik war schon auf festem Geleise und überlebte unter der Leitung Edward Greys ihren Schöpfer. Sie vermied jetzt nur jene Offenheit, die König Eduards Haltung bei all ihrer Gefährlichkeiten doch loyal gemacht hatte und legte sich ein neues System heuchlerischer Unverbindlichkeiten zurecht, die Maske der Neutralität, unter der besser der Haß gegen Deutschland sich decken konnte.

Einsichtige und weitblickende Warner hatten schon zur Zeit des Abschlusses des Algecirasvertrags hervorgehoben, daß mit der ungewissen Vorrechtstellung Frankreichs in

Marokko ein Brandherd im Hause des europäischen Friedens fortglimme. Wie schon so oft papierene Verträge, so würde auch dieser von Frankreich mißachtet werden, sobald es den Augenblick für günstig erachte, und ihr für die Moral unserer Zeit bedenklicher Pessimismus über den Wert feierlich unterzeichneter und beschworener Verträge sollte leider Recht behalten: Früher als jemand es vermuten konnte, machte sich Frankreich von neuem an die Tunifizierung Marokkos. Die Polizeistellung, die es Deutschland mit Hilfe Englands, Rußlands und Italiens in Algeciras abgzwungen, war eine gute Deckung der militärischen Absichten, und die mit Geld erkaufte Gefügigkeit des Sultans schien rechtlich jedes Vorgehen zu beschützen.

Das Jahr 1911 sollte wieder eines der großen Gewitterspannungen werden. Die Schwüle am politischen Himmel ballte jetzt öfter solche Gewitterwolken zusammen: Die letzte vom Balkan her hatte sich im Jahre 1909 noch gnädig verzogen. Aber nicht minder gefährlich drohte nun und grollte die vom marokkanischen Wetterwinkel, es funkelte schon gefährlich am Horizont, und schon schien der Blitz niederfahren zu wollen.

Die Ursache war diesmal die Ungeduld der nationalistischen Kreise in Frankreich, sich Marokkos zu bemächtigen. Die Algeciras-Akte gaben ihnen zwar alle Möglichkeiten einer *„Pénétration pacifique"*, aber von England ermutigt und das schon merklich erstarkte Rußland an der Seite, wollten diese Ehrgeizigen Marokko sofort Frankreich angegliedert sehen. Delcassé war aus seiner Versenkung wieder emporgetaucht und fungierte offiziell als Marineminister, in Wirklichkeit steuerte er auch die Außenpolitik, die von einem Strohmann, Monsieur de Selves, geleitet zu sein schien. Der parlamentarische Berichterstatter von Poincaré – die Kriegspartei hatte das Heft in Händen. Zuerst fand man den Vorwand von Aufständen, um Militär in die Schoja zu senden. Dann erzwang man vom Sultan, daß er um Schutz bitte. Wiederum wurden Soldaten gesandt. Das *„Comité du Maroc"* dirigierte die Presse: In den schwärzesten Farben wurde die Situation der Europäer dargestellt und plötzlich – mit erstaunlicher Analogie zu den seinerzeitigen Schreckensmeldungen im Boxeraufstand von der Ermordung der Gesandtschaften in Peking – Bedrohung, ja, sogar Niedermetzelung der Franzosen in Fès, der Hauptstadt Marokkos, mitgeteilt. Von überallher wurden zwar diese Nachrichten sofort dementiert und die absolute Ruhe und Sicherheit in Fès konstatiert, aber die Regierung Frankreichs, ganz in den Händen der Nationalisten, ließ die Komödie beginnen. Am 19. April 1911 wurde General Moinier „zum Entsatze von Fès" mit einer großen Truppenmacht abgesandt, und als er am 21. Mai – ohne einen Schuß abgefeuert zu haben – in der durchaus ruhigen Stadt einzog, jubelte die ganze französische Welt über die Rettung der Europäer.

In Deutschland, wo man Berichte über die absolute Ungefährlichkeit der Situation hatte, sah man besorgt das Eindringen der Franzosen, die offenkundige Verhöhnung des Vertrags. Ernste Anfragen wurden am Quai d'Orsay im liebenswürdigsten Sinne beantwortet, eine Besetzung sei nicht geplant, die Truppen würden sofort zurückgezogen werden, sobald die Beruhigung des Landes wieder eingetreten sei. In Deutschland kannte man diese Art Termine: Seit dreißig Jahren saßen die Engländer so in Ägypten, und ebenso provisorisch hatte Rußland jetzt Nordpersien besetzt. Vergeblich versuchte man in der offiziellen „Norddeutschen Allgemeinen Zeitung" auf die Tatsache aufmerksam zu machen, daß mit der eigenmächtigen Kündigung des Vertrags auch die andern Signatare wieder freie Entschließung hätten, aber man war in Paris plötzlich schwerhörig geworden. Auch Spanien verstand den Sinn der französischen „Hilfeleistung" und beantwortete sie schleunigst durch Truppenlandungen in Sarrant und Tétouan. England schwieg. Italien schwieg. Sie waren durch Geheimverträge gebunden, und so war es an Deutschland, in Anbetracht der Pariser Schwerhörigkeit, etwas deutlicher zu sprechen.

Am 1. Juli 1912 erschien das deutsche Kanonenboot „Panther" im Hafen von Agadir, an der Westküste Marokkos. Nach dem Vertrage von Algeciras waren diese Häfen Kriegsschiffen gesperrt, und Deutschland wollte damit offen zeigen, daß, wenn Frankreich den Vertrag nicht achte, es sich gleichfalls nicht gebunden fühle und in Anbetracht der neuen Forderungen die seinen gleichfalls erneuere. Der Kanzler gab durch die Entsendung symbolisch zu verstehen, wenn sich auch Frankreich mit seinen Bundesgenossen über die Annexion Marokkos geeinigt habe, so müsse es sich ebenso entschließen, Deutschland aufrichtige Mitteilung von seinen Absichten zu machen und seine Zustimmung zu erlangen suchen. Deutschland läßt sich nicht düpieren und durch diplomatische Noten über die tatsächliche Okkupation der größten Kolonie in der Nähe Europas täuschen, entweder erhebt es Einspruch oder es wird abgefunden, so verstand man hüben und drüben sofort diesen Akt. Und in Deutschland war die öffentliche Meinung ganz auf Seiten der Regierung: Man war müde, die Welt vor den Augen aufgeteilt zu sehen und selbst hungrig und verhöhnt im Winkel zu bleiben.

In Frankreich tobte die Presse, aber die Regierung verstand den Ernst der Situation. Statt wie die ärgsten Hetzer es wollten, auch französischerseits Kriegsschiffe nach Agadir zu schicken und englische dorthin zu bestellen – wie leicht konnte eine Kanone, ein Gewehrschuß dort den Weltkrieg entladen –, beschloß man lieber mit der deutschen Regierung zu verhandeln. Und da man in Berlin mehr nicht gewünscht hatte, war die Einigung schon unterwegs.

Die erste Störung kam von der Seite, von der sie für Deutschland zu erwarten war: von England. Sir Grey teilte sofort dem deutschen Botschafter mit, daß England nirgends an der marokkanischen Küste eine Erwerbung Deutschlands dulden werde. Während es Frankreich ganz Marokko einfach zugeteilt hatte, verweigerte es – aus eigener Machtvollkommenheit – Deutschland eine Kohlenstation am Ozean. Damit war die feindliche Gesinnung deutlicher als je bekräftigt, und sie steifte den französischen Unterhändlern natürlich sehr den Nacken. Die zweite Störung kam durch Indiskretionen über die Verhandlungen in der französischen Presse, die übermäßig die Volkserregung anfachten, die dritte von einer Drohrede Lloyd-Georges. Kriegerische Vorkehrungen wurden getroffen. Die englische Flotte konzentrierte sich, in Frankreich und Deutschland wurde die Armee geschliffen „wie ein Rasiermesser", in den diplomatischen Beziehungen zwischen England und Deutschland trat eine merkliche Erkaltung ein, seit am 21. Juli der deutsche Botschafter glatt erklärt hatte, daß er die Marokko-Angelegenheit als eine einzig zwischen Frankreich und Deutschland spielende betrachte und Verhandlungen „zu dritt" ablehne. In diesem Sommer war die Kriegsgefahr für Europa so nahe wie noch nie. Zwei Mal standen, wie man später erfuhr, die Verhandlungen scharf vor dem Abbruch; gleich dem Reiter über dem Bodensee erfuhr das Volk Frankreichs und Deutschlands erst Monate nachher, über welchen Abgrund es mit knapper Not hinweggekommen war. Immer war es England gewesen, das dazu drängte, immer waren es die beiden hauptbeteiligten Staaten, die wirklich die Opfer eines Krieges zu tragen hatten, die vor der entsetzlichen Verantwortlichkeit zurückscheuten. Frankreich hatte einen Teil seiner Armee noch im marokkanischen Gebiet, Rußland war noch nicht verläßlich genug, Deutschland wiederum scheute den Krieg – den es vielleicht damals schon als notwendig erkannte in Anbetracht der Gesinnungen Englands – schon um der Ursache willen: Das Marokkogebiet lag für Deutschland zu fern, um je beim Volke als Kampfpreis gewürdigt zu werden. Es fehlte hüben und drüben der rechte Anlaß, und mit Erfolg betonte auf beiden Seiten die sozialistische Partei, daß wegen einer afrikanischen Kolonie die zwei höchsten Kulturnationen nicht die Waffe gegeneinander erheben dürfte. Daß es in Wahrheit England war, das diese Zwietracht wollte, wurde beiden erst später bewußt, diesmal aber entschied glücklich ein dumpfes Gefühl zur Nachgiebigkeit. Und besonders Deutschland war es, das dem Frieden ein gewaltiges Willensopfer zu bringen hatte.

Am 4. November wurde endlich das Marokkoabkommen zwischen Deutschland und Frankreich unterzeichnet. Frankreich erhielt vollkommen freie Hand in dieser seiner neuen Kolonie, Deutschland einen Zipfel französischen Kolonialgebietes am Kongo. Der neue Vertrag hatte den einzigen Vorteil, daß er den Streitfall definitiv regelte und der eine Brandherd Europas nun endgültig erstickt war. Aber anderseits hatte der Konflikt diesseits und jenseits des Rheins das Nationalgefühl in seiner Reizbarkeit erhöht, daß beide Parteien von ihrem Erfolge enttäuscht waren, Frankreich, weil es reales Besitztum an den „Feind" gab für Ansprüche und Betätigungen, Deutschland, weil das ertauschte Sumpfgebiet in einem lächerlichen Mißverhältnis zu der pathetischen Entsendung des „Panther" und der europäischen Erregung stand. Der Kolonialsekretär gab seine Entlassung, um seiner Mißbilligung sichtbaren Ausdruck zu geben, und bis in die untersten Kreise des Volkes arbeitete sich die Überzeugung ein, daß Deutschland vor England und Frankreich zurückgewichen sei.

Der Krieg war vermieden – zum dritten Mal in diesem Dezennium, das ein Jahrhundert, ja, eine Ewigkeit des Friedens vermessen hatte ankündigen wollen –, aber die Spannung war nur vermehrt, die eiternden Wunden mit Papier und Worten verklebt. Deutschland wußte, daß seine Gegner ihm nirgends einen Zollbreit neuen Landes gönnen wollten, indes sie über seinen Kopf hin die letzten freien Staaten der Welt sich zuteilten. Enger und enger preßte sich das vielmaschige Netz an, das König Eduard gewoben und an dem kaufmännische Mißgunst, politischer Ehrgeiz und nationale Rachsucht emsig weitergesponnen. So straffte sich die Hand zum Schlag. Flottenvermehrungen, neue Armeeprogramme in allen Staaten zeigten deutlicher als alle Erregung der Zeitungen und Menschen, daß man den Weltkrieg nahen fühlte und sich eilte, ihm bereit zu sein. Milliarden wanderten wieder von Frankreich nach Rußland, in Persien einten sich die Hände der ewigen Widersacher England und Rußland zu gemeinsamem Griff, und mit dem Gefühl der nahenden Entscheidung wuchs gigantisch in allen Nationen Sorge und Grauen vor dieser europäischen Katastrophe. Und diese elementare Furcht, diese edle menschliche Furcht vor dem Untergang der zeitgenössischen Kultur, nur sie allein hatte diesmal den Krieg im Keim erstickt im letzten, allerletzten Momente. Mit Marokko schien die Zwietracht zu ruhen. Aber die Schwüle war zu groß: Und fast zur gleichen Stunde flammte am andern Ende Europas der zweite Brandherd auf, der Balkan. Italien war es, das die Pandorabüchse eröffnet hatte: die Liquidation des türkischen Reiches, von der schon Bismarck prophezeit hatte, daß sie den größten Krieg Europas verschulden werde.

Tripolis und der Balkankrieg
1912 – 1913

Während noch unter erregter Teilnahme der ganzen Welt Deutschland und Frankreich jene entscheidende Erledigung der Marokkoangelegenheiten vorbereiteten, die den europäischen Frieden auf Jahre hinaus sichern sollte, war wiederum an anderer Stelle ein Stein ins Rollen gekommen, und auch er sollte wieder, da die Einigkeit der Mächte so locker fundiert war, zur Lawine werden, die Völkerschicksale mit sich riß. Auf dem Kongreß zu Algeciras hatte sich Italien zum Dank für seine den Mittelmeermächten Frankreich und England hilfreiche Haltung, die eigentlich mit seiner Dreibundverpflichtung wenig in Einklang stand, einen Wechsel ausstellen lassen. Der Wechsel lautete auf fremden Besitz, auf Tripolitanien, aber er trug die doppelte Gegenzeichnung der beiden wichtigsten Bürgen, Frankreich und England, die das Eigentum der Türkei wie eigenen Besitz an Italien abtraten. Nun, da Frankreich daranging, sein Teil der Beute unter Dach zu bringen, schien in Italien der günstigste Moment, den Wechsel einzulösen.

Es war nur eine einzige Schwierigkeit für die italienischen Diplomaten zu überwinden, nämlich einen triftigen Rechtsgrund nach außen hin zu finden. Die Türkei war durchaus friedfertig, und als, von Agenten provoziert, kleine Mißhelligkeiten zwischen Arabern und italienischen Kolonisten sich einstellten, kam eigens der türkische Thronfolger zu Besuch nach Rom, um seine herzlichen Absichten gegen die italienische Nation kundzugeben. In Tripolis herrschte

Ruhe, und es wäre harte Arbeit gewesen, einen Vorwand zu kriegerischem Anlaß stichhältig zu machen: Außerdem befürchtete die italienische Regierung bei Forderungen an die türkische das Unangenehmste, nämlich Nachgiebigkeit in allen nur halbwegs mit dem Völkerrecht vereinbarten Fragen, sodaß jener brutale Eingriff, den sie beabsichtigte, immer unentschuldbarer geworden wäre.

Darum stellten sie die Tat vor das Wort. Ein Expeditionskorps wurde ausgerüstet, und als die Soldaten schon eingeschifft waren, blitzte plötzlich aus heiterm Himmel – am 28. September – ein Ultimatum an die Türkei, binnen vierundzwanzig Stunden mitzuteilen, ob sie die militärische Besetzung Tripolis' und der Cyrenaika durch Italien ruhig zugestehen wolle, widrigenfalls die Botschafter ihre Pässe zu beheben hätten. Damit war allen Konzessionen der Türkei von vornherein die Spitze abgebrochen und eine Ablehnung dieser Forderungen erzwungen, die mit der Ehre auch des geringsten Staates mit bestem Willen nicht zu vereinbaren war. Zwei Tage später eröffnete die italienische Flotte das Bombardement auf die Forts von Tripolis und bohrte ein paar türkische Kanonenboote in den Grund, die – unkund des Überfalls – die herannahenden italienischen Schiffe mit Wimpelgruß freundlich bewillkommt hatten.

Der Eindruck dieses brutalen Überfalls war in Europa der denkbar unangenehmste, und selbst die Österreich-Ungarn feindlichen Mächte lehnten die Analogie der Annexion Bosniens ab, denn in jenem Falle hatte die Monarchie sich ein Land zu Eigen gemacht, das es seit drei Jahrzehnten mustergültig im Auftrage der Großmächte verwaltet und zu kultureller Blüte gebracht hatte, ein Land, das ihm formell schon längst zugesprochen war und das die Türkei nie mehr als ihr Eigen zu betrachten gedachte. Tripolitanien hingegen war eine reguläre freie Provinz, deren Ertrag sich auf jährlich fünfzigtausend Pfund belief, die niemals gegen die türkische Herrschaft sich aufgelehnt hatte und ausschließlich von Moslimen bewohnt war. Der einzige Anspruch Italiens war die geographische Nähe und – ein Argument, das zu sehr die Lächerlichkeit fürchtete, um von der offiziellen Politik benützt zu werden und einzig demagogischer Propaganda diente – die Zugehörigkeit vor zweitausend Jahren zum Weltreich der Zäsaren, ein Rechtsanspruch, der gleicherweise auch für Frankreich, das einstige Gallien, für Germanien und Britannien Geltung gehabt hätte.

Offiziell wurde von den Großmächten kein Einspruch erhoben – die meisterhafte Diplomatie Italiens hatte ja beide europäische Machtgruppen sich zu verpflichten verstanden –, aber die öffentliche Meinung war allerorts erregt. In England war man wie immer, wenn ein anderer Staat als England eine Gebietsvermehrung erreicht, moralisch entrüstet und im englisch-ethischen Empfinden verletzt. Frankreich vergaß, daß es selbst eben eine andere gigantische Kolonialprovinz sich zu Eigen gemacht hatte und ärgerte sich über die „lateinische Schwester", die sich jetzt gleichfalls mit afrikanischen Schätzen brüsten konnte. Für Deutschland, den Bundesgenossen, war dieser Überfall am peinlichsten, denn seit einigen Jahren war es ihm gelungen, am Goldenen Horn sich diplomatisch festzusetzen, und Wilhelm II. galt in der mohammedanischen Welt seit seiner Reise nach Jerusalem und dem Besuche in Tanger als der Protektor des Islam. Seine Situation war die denkbar schwierigste, weder durfte es sich gegen Italien erklären, um die Zahl seiner politischen Gegner in Europa nicht zu vermehren, noch gegen die Türkei, wo es ungeheure wirtschaftliche Werte investiert hatte. Seine Tätigkeit mußte darum eine bloß ausgleichende sein und beschränkte sich meist auf Interventionen in humaner Hinsicht. Dem Eingreifen des deutschen Botschafters zum Beispiel war es zu verdanken, daß die Türkei den Aufenthalt der italienischen Zivilpersonen im Lande während des ganzen Krieges gestattete –, ein Vorgang, der dann im Weltkriege von 1914 weder von England noch von Frankreich, den Kulturstaaten und Herren der Zivilisation nachgeahmt wurde.

Österreich-Ungarn nahm die Gelegenheit wahr, Italien seine loyale Gesinnung zu beweisen. Nachdem es die ihm wichtige Zusicherung empfangen, daß die Flotte kriegerische Aktionen gegen die Türkei in der Adria – im heutigen Albanien – nicht unternehmen würde, begleitete es den Verlauf absolut neutral und – sehr im Gegensatz zu Italiens Haltung während der Annexion Bosniens – eher in wohlwollender Neutralität. Es lag eigentlich im Interesse der Monarchie, daß sich das italienische Expansionsbedürfnis, das bisher – von den *Irredenten* mißleitet – einzig das Trento und Albanien ersehnt hatte, statt nach Norden gegen Süden wandte, wo ihm ungeheure Möglichkeiten offenstanden. Die Interessensphären der beiden Adriamächte, die im Balkan leicht einmal hätten kollidieren können, waren nun dauernd getrennt, und eine engere Verknüpfung des in den letzten Jahren locker gewordenen Bundes schien – schon durch das enge Einvernehmen Aehrenthals mit dem Leiter der italienischen auswärtigen Politik San Giuliano – gewährleistet.

Der Verlauf der italienischen Expedition entsprach vorerst nicht den Erwartungen der Nation. Schon knapp nach der Landung erlitten die italienischen Truppen empfindliche Schlappen durch die türkischen Regimenter und die mit ihnen vereinigten Beduinen, und selbst nach der Besetzung der Küstenstädte gelang es nicht, weiter als einige Kilometer in das ungangbare und sandige Land vorzudringen. Der militärische Widerstand erhöhte sich eher, statt er sich durch die Verluste verminderte, seit Enver[29] Pascha den Kleinkrieg organisierte und die Senussis[30], ein fanatischer Kriegerstamm, auf Befehl des Sultans zu Hilfe gekommen waren. Einen direkten entscheidenden Stoß gegen die Türkei zu führen, war den Italienern unmöglich: Die Engen der Dardanellen mit ihren modernen Forts boten einem Einbruch Trotz, ein Einmarsch in Albanien war durch die Verpflichtungen gegen Österreich-Ungarn, eine Unternehmung in Kleinasien durch den Einspruch Frankreichs und Englands unmöglich. Dazu kamen politische Schwierigkeiten mit der französischen Regierung infolge der Kaperung zweier französischer Dampfer, die Munition den Türken bringen wollten –, denn wenn auch Delcassé Italien Tripolis zugesprochen hatte und offiziell die Unternehmung gut hieß, so wühlten doch die Militärkreise unterirdisch dagegen. Von Tunis aus wurde ein regelrechter Waffenschmuggel organisiert, und die französische Regierung – die seit dem Marokkovertrag vom 5. November ihr Eigen sicher hatte – tat nichts, um dem neuen afrikanischen Nachbarn die Situation zu erleichtern. Das Endresultat war eine verstärkte Spannung und anderseits ein verstärktes Empfinden vom Werte und der Richtigkeit des Dreibunds in Italien – das ja übrigens immer vorhanden war, wenn Italien sich in Nöten befand.

Die Drahtzieher der deutschen Einkreisung – Delcassé, Iswolski, Grey – empfanden diese Wandlung mit Mißbe-

---

[29] *Damad İsmail Enver*: Auch Enver Pascha genannt; Politiker, Generalleutnant und Kriegsminister des Osmanischen Reiches; gehörte zu den Hauptbeteiligten des armenischen Völkermordes; 1881 – 1922.

[30] *Senussi:* Wurden nach ihrem Begründer Muhammad Ibn Ali Sanusi benannt; seit 1833 in Nordafrika Anhänger eines kriegerischen islamischen Ordens.

hagen. Das Bündnis Deutschlands mit Österreich-Ungarn, das mehr als zehn Millionen wohlgerüsteter Soldaten darstellte, schien ihnen im Kampfe nur herausgefordert werden zu dürfen bei einer zumindest doppelt numerischen Überlegenheit. Schon hatten sie hoffen dürfen, dank der steten Bemühungen und Lockungen König Eduards Italien dem Dreibund entfremdet zu haben, gewisse Anzeichen – der Jubel beim Empfang des Zaren, der demonstrativ österreichisch-ungarisches Gebiet auf seiner Reise vermieden hatte, die Begrüßung König Peters von Serbien – ließen sogar darauf schließen, daß Italien der Monarchie in den Rücken fallen werde, und nun entging ihnen plötzlich dieser starke militärische Machtfaktor. Es war natürlich, daß sie nach Ersatz, nach einer gleichstarken Waffe, Umschau hielten, die Österreich-Ungarn bei einem Kampfe in den Rücken gestoßen werden konnte, und da sie nicht vorhanden war, so zögerten sie nicht, sie zu schmieden.

Diese neue Waffe war der Balkanbund. Hartwig, der russische Gesandte in Belgrad, der beinahe serbischer dachte als die Serben, führte bloß Iswolskis und der Slawophilen Aufträge durch, wenn er mit allen Mitteln die widerstreitenden Interessen der kleinen Balkankönigreiche zu einer Angriffswaffe vereinigte. Frankreich und Rußland hatten noch sechshunderttausend Mann oder eine Million nötig, um den Krieg gegen Deutschland und Österreich-Ungarn beginnen zu können: Und es galt nun, den ehrgeizigen Kleinstaaten Versprechungen zu machen, um sie für den fremden Zweck zu gewinnen. Serbien war von jeher zu allem bereit, was gegen Österreich-Ungarn ging, Montenegro der gehorsame Trabant Rußlands. Um Bulgarien, dessen König aus der österreich-ungarischen Armee zum Fürstenthrone stieg und der seine Krone zum großen Teil der Monarchie dankte, zu gewinnen, mußte die „slawische

Brüderlichkeit" wieder entdeckt werden. Die französischen Finanziers taten den Rest, und knapp nach dem Staatsbesuche Poincarés in Petersburg entstand heimlich dieser Dreistaatenbund, dem sich in ungleich mehr lockerer Form auch Griechenland anschloß, freilich nur, wenn es gegen die Türkei gehen sollte. Denn dies war der letzte Sinn des Bundes: gemeinsam gegen alle Nachbarn vorzugehen und geschlossen gegen sie zu kämpfen. Im Falle eines Sieges fiel ihnen Beute zu, im Falle einer Niederlage deckte sie „Mütterchen" Rußland.

Daß dieser Balkanbund nur für Rußland und im Einverständnis mit dem Zaren geschlossen wurde, ist inzwischen durch die Publikation des Vertrages in einer Pariser Zeitung offenbar geworden und ebenso, daß seine Ziele durchaus keine kulturellen waren, sondern einzig die Ablösung großer Gebietsteile der Türkei und Österreich-Ungarns beabsichtigten. Am 29. Februar war zwischen Serbien und Bulgarien die Vereinbarung geschlossen, die nicht nur ein militärisches Einvernehmen im Einzelnen feststellte, sondern auch die feindlichen Intentionen gegen die Türkei, Österreich-Ungarn und Rumänien bekundete. Es heißt darin wörtlich: „Falls Österreich-Ungarn Serbien angreift, ist Bulgarien verpflichtet, jenem unverzüglich den Krieg zu erklären und mindestens zweihunderttausend Mann nach Serbien zu senden, die offensiv und defensiv zusammen mit dem serbischen Heere zu kämpfen haben. Dieselbe Verpflichtung hat Bulgarien Serbien gegenüber, wenn Österreich-Ungarn, unter was für einem Vorwand und ohne Zustimmung der Türkei, seine Truppen in den Sandschak Novi Pazar einrücken läßt, sodaß Serbien ihm den Krieg erklärt; oder wenn Serbien zur Wahrung seiner Interessen in den Sandschak Truppen einmarschieren läßt und hiedurch einen Konflikt mit Österreich-Ungarn herbeiführt."

Hiemit war die Monarchie vom Balkan abgesperrt. Serbien verbot ihr jede Einmengung und sicherte sich allein das Recht, Veränderungen vorzunehmen, ganz nach seinem Gutdünken. Es konnte – durch Besetzung des Sandschak – jederzeit einen Konflikt mit Österreich-Ungarn provozieren, wann ihm die Stunde gut dünkte, und war dabei Bulgariens Hilfe sicher. Und vor allem derjenigen Rußlands. Ausdrücklich enthielt der Bündnisakt den Paragraphen, daß „eine Kopie dieses Vertrags und seines geheimen Anhangs an die russische Regierung und den Zaren abgesandt werden sollte, der bei Meinungsverschiedenheiten die schiedsrichterliche Instanz zu bedeuten hätte". Auch die Teilung der Beute war in diesem Vertrage festgesetzt und – es ist wichtig, dies zu bemerken – dem Zaren bereits bekannt. Iswolski hatte nun ein Instrument in Händen, das gleicherweise gegen die Türkei oder Österreich-Ungarn gewendet werden konnte, das er im Geheimen dirigierte, indes nach außen hin die russische Politik als die Beschützerin des Friedens gefeiert werden konnte. Die Minen unter den Frieden waren gelegt: Sie konnten von ferne, von Petersburg oder Paris, entzündet werden, ohne daß jemand den eigentlichen Urheber gewahr würde. Günstiger schien es den Verbündeten, den Krieg zuerst gegen die Türkei und dann erst gegen Österreich-Ungarn zu führen. Die Türkei hatte zwar gegen Italien große Erfolge: Der Krieg kostete sie wenig, da er im Lande gar nicht geführt wurde und die Küsten durch die Intervention Frankreichs und Englands geschützt waren, während Italien für den Kolonialkrieg ungeheure Summen ausgeben mußte, die mit den kleinen militärischen Erfolgen durchaus in keinem Verhältnis standen. Es mußte Italien daher nur erwünscht sein, wenn die Pression auch von anderer Seite käme und die europäische Türkei, in ihren vitalen Kräften bedroht, in Afrika einen Widerstand aufgeben mußte, den sie allein, trotz einer ungeheuren Militärmacht und der mobilisierten Kriegsflotte, nicht niederzuringen vermochte. Zweifellos empfing Montenegro über die Adria her geheime Ermutigung. Und tatsächlich: Im Frühling und Hochsommer loderten die Flammenzeichen in Mazedonien wieder auf.

Es schien nur wieder der alljährliche Frühjahrsputsch der von Bulgarien und Serbien bezahlten Banden zu sein, aber in Österreich-Ungarn sowohl als in der Türkei beunruhigten die plötzlichen Sendungen von großen Quantitäten Sprengstoffen aus Frankreich, die unter dem Titel von Bergwerksexplosivkörpern konsigniert waren, sowie die zahlreichen Kanonentransporte. Es konnte trotz der Geheimhaltung den beiden Staaten nicht verborgen bleiben, daß sich etwas Feindseliges in jenem gefährlichsten Winkel Europas vorbereitete. Noch war das Ziel der Machinationen nicht klar – und noch weniger das Einverständnis Rußlands –, aber jedenfalls mußte die Monarchie rechtzeitig ihre Interessen wahren, die auch diejenigen des Friedens waren.

Am 15. August regte Graf Berchtold – der nach dem Tode des Grafen Aehrenthal das Erbe einer europäischen Verantwortung übernommen hatte – einen Meinungsaustausch unter den Mächten an, um Zugeständnisse und Reformen von der Türkei gegen ihre Fremdvölker zu erlangen und jeden aggressiven Schritt der Balkanstaaten unmöglich zu machen. Die Antwort der Mächte war lau: Es schien offenkundig im Interesse Frankreichs, Rußlands, und Italiens, hier Komplikationen zu schaffen, die für Österreich-Ungarn, den Nachbarstaat, eine Quelle von Verlegenheiten werden könnten. Aber Graf Berchtold, der anscheinend den Umfang der Gefahr kannte, erneuerte seine Bemühungen. Nach einer eingehenden Besprechung mit dem Kanzler des Deutschen Reiches, Bethmann Hollweg, kündigte er zunächst in den Delegationen die Situation am Balkan als gefährlich an und wiederholte seine Vorschläge an die Mächte in dringender Form. Er zögerte nicht – umso mehr als Serbien, Bulgarien, Montenegro und nun auch Griechenland mobilisierten – eine Aktion der Mächte offen zu fordern.

Nun fühlten Frankreich und Rußland, daß sie vor der Welt den Schein eines Friedenswillens zu retten hatten. Und in Paris wurde von Poincaré jenes Programm formuliert, das zu den perfidesten Dokumenten der Unaufrichtigkeit in der neueren Geschichte wird zählen müssen. Es war eine Mahnung an die Balkanstaaten – dieselben, die Frankreich seit Monaten mit Waffen und Munition versorgte –, den Frieden zu halten, die Reformen den Mächten zu überlassen und enthielt den famosen Passus: „Sollte der Krieg zwischen den Balkanstaaten und der Türkei dennoch ausbrechen, so würden die Mächte keine aus dem Konflikt sich ergebende Veränderung im territorialen Status quo der europäischen Türkei zulassen."

Damit sollte vor der Welt den Balkanstaaten abgewinkt werden. Die europäische Autorität verweigerte ihnen jede Besitzerweiterung auf Kosten der Türkei – so schien es wenigstens. Aber Serbien, Bulgarien und Montenegro wußten, was diese Drohung wert war, denn dieselben Mächte – Frankreich und Rußland –, die hier öffentlich ihnen abmahnten, hatten jenen Geheimvertrag gebilligt, in dem die Teilung der Türkei bis ins kleinste festgesetzt war und der Zar für die Schwierigkeiten bei der Beute die Rolle des Schiedsrichters willig übernommen hatte. Sie wußten, daß Frankreich und Rußland nur ihren Sieg wünschten, um ihnen dann nach dem Grundsatz: „*J'y suis, j'y reste*", „Hier bin ich, hier bleib ich" die schon voraus geteilte Beute zuerkennen zu können. Österreich-Ungarn und Deutschland aber, die diese Drohung im Interesse des Friedens ernst meinten, würden dann die peinliche Rolle der Mißgünstigen spielen, die den geeinten christlichen Völkern, den Kulturbringern des Ostens, die mit Blut errungenen Gebiete durch Berufung auf tote Buchstaben neidisch entwenden wollten.

Die Balkanstaaten übernahmen es, die Komödie der Friedensabsichten weiterzuspielen. Sie schienen sich beugen zu wollen, sandten Forderungen an die Türkei statt der Kriegserklärung, aber als die Vertreter Österreich-Ungarns und Rußlands am 8. September 1912 die Note in Cetinje überreichten, mußte ihnen der König Nikita mitteilen, daß er eben – welch ein verhängnisvoller Zufall! – der Türkei bereits den Krieg erklärt hatte. Man hatte den Kleinsten, den Unverantwortlichsten, vorausgeschickt: Gerade diesen Taster, den geläufigsten der russischen Diplomatie, der schon im Krimkriege so vortrefflich funktionierte, hatte Iswolski gedrückt, um die Mine anzuflammen, die den Frieden Europas menschenmörderisch vernichten sollte.

Die Balkankriege,
die Londoner Konferenz und Albanien
1913

Einen papiernen Wall – den *„status quo"* – hatte Europa auf den heuchlerischen Vorschlag der französisch-russischen Diplomatie hin vor der Türkei aufgerichtet. Aber schon die ersten Siege der Balkanstaaten stießen ihn durch. Die Bulgaren siegten bei Kirkilisse und Lûle-Burgas, die Griechen bei Janina, die Serben bei Kumanovo, die ottomanischen Armeen waren zerschmettert, Adrianopel umstellt, der Vormarsch auf Konstantinopel schien nur mehr eine Frage der Zeit. Nun wäre es – den unwahrscheinlichen Fall als tatsächlich gesetzt, daß jener Vorschlag des *„status quo"* ein ehrlicher gewesen war – an Frankreich und Rußland, den proponierenden Mächten, gewesen, den Balkanstaaten Einhalt zu gebieten und auf der Unverletzlichkeit der Türkei zu bestehen. Aber Poincaré und Iswolski, die nur ihre Zerstörung wünschten, damit sich der mit Mühe zusammengekittete Balkanbund dann gegen Deutschland und Österreich-Ungarn wende, waren so weit von der Unterstützung ihres eigenen Vorschlages entfernt, daß sie schon einen neuen aushecken, der Österreich-Ungarn von jedem Einspruch abhalten sollte.

Österreich-Ungarn hatte mit seltsamer Geduld zugesehen, wie serbische und montenegrinische Truppen den Sandschak besetzten, dieselben Kasernen, wo noch vor fünf Jahren die kaiserlichen und königlichen Truppen als Landesherrscher ihre Stellung hatten. Nicht ohne Grund mußten darum Serbien und die Balkanmächte befürchten, die Monarchie werde die Kriegserklärung an die Türkei mit einem sofortigen Einmarsch in den Sandschak – ihre einstige vom Berliner Kongreß zugesprochene Einflußsphäre – beantworten, und damit wäre die Möglichkeit eines Konfliktes leicht gegeben gewesen. Aber so gesichert die Rechtsstellung Österreich-Ungarns in diesem Falle war, das Friedensbedürfnis – das oft, allzu oft erwiesene – der Monarchie überwog, und ohne Einspruch ließ man in Wien die Besetzung des Territoriums zu, das – obwohl ökonomisch wenig wichtig – für Österreich-Ungarn von außerordentlicher politischer Bedeutung war. Denn dieser früher österreichisch-ungarische, dann wieder türkische Landstrich trennte einerseits als Keil die beiden serbischen Länder Montenegro und Serbien, andererseits war er eine Brücke nach der Türkei. War diese in Feindeshand, so konnte zu Lande kein Handel mehr mit der Türkei, dem Ottomanenreich, geführt werden, die Grenze war verloren, der Plan der Sandschakbahn, das Symbol der österreichisch-ungarischen Handelsvorherrschaft in der Levante, für immer erledigt. Das damalige Geschehenlassen des Einmarsches der Serben und Montenegriner war ein so großes Zeichen von Friedfertigkeit bei der Monarchie, daß es fast als Schwäche gedeutet werden mußte, und selbst die verwegensten panslawistischen Blätter konnten in der geduldig zuwartenden Haltung der Monarchie nichts finden, was mit kühnster Verdrehung als feindlicher oder bloß unfreundlicher Akt hätte gedeutet werden können.

Aber das genügte offenbar in Petersburg nicht. Man wollte, daß Österreich-Ungarn auch in Hinkunft ausgeschaltet sei und daß es sich in den vom Zaren sanktionierten serbisch-bulgarisch-montenegrinischen Teilungsplan überhaupt nicht einmenge, sondern geduldig im Schmollwinkel warte, bis diese Mächte genügend gekräftigt seien, um von ihm selbst Territorien abfordern zu können. Rußland hatte unter der Hand die Teilung vorgenommen, nun plante man, Österreich-Ungarn jede Möglichkeit einer schüchternen Bemerkung abzuschneiden. Die Formel wurde wieder in Paris gefunden, sie klang sehr schön und lautete, die Mächte sollten ihr *„désintéressement"*, ihre Gleichgültigkeit gegen alle Veränderungen am Balkan, erklären (nachdem sie einen Monat früher dort jede Veränderung feierlich verboten hatten). Die Boulevardpresse instrumentierte diesen Vorschlag mit süßer Musik: Man möge die jungen Staaten ihr Werk der Kultur vollenden lassen – die Carnegie-Kommission bereiste inzwischen schon das Land, um die beispiellosen Greuel der Komitadschis festzustellen –, das siegreiche Christentum müsse unterstützt werden und die Sache der Freiheit, denn der Balkan gehöre einzig den Balkanvölkern. In diese Friedensschalmeien mengte sich nur merkwürdig dissonierend der Pariser Jubel über den „Sieg Creusots gen Krupp" – die Geschütze der Balkanstaaten hatte Frankreich, die der Türkei Deutschland geliefert – und die triumphierende Ankündigung einer baldigen Abrechnung. Aber die Formel hieß *„désintéressement"*.

In Österreich-Ungarn zögerte Graf Berchtold nicht, höflich – allzuhöflich – die perfide Einladung abzulehnen. Jeder wußte, daß sie nur lanziert war, um Österreich-Ungarn und Deutschland, die Ablehnenden, als die Friedensstörer von Europa zu denunzieren, die Friedensstörer in einem Kriege, den die Proponenten der „Gleichgültigkeit" angezettelt und finanziert hatten. Gleichgültigkeit von Österreich-Ungarn in Balkanangelegenheiten zu fordern, war so kühn, wie wenn man von Frankreich Gleichgültigkeit gegen Marokko geheischt hätte, im Falle, daß – etwa Spanien – sich seiner hätte bemächtigen wollen. Aber es galt, Sand in die Augen der Welt zu streuen, damit sie nicht die pulvergeschwärzten Hände derer bemerkten, die gegen den Frieden die vernichtende Bombe geschleudert.

Außer Österreich-Ungarn und dem getreuen Deutschland waren aber auch andere Staaten nicht gesonnen, sich das Recht, mitzureden, wenn die europäische Türkei durch einen Federstrich Iswolskis geteilt werden sollte, nehmen zu lassen. Rumänien hatte wohl mindestens ebenso wie das kleine Montenegro Anspruch, ein Balkanstaat genannt zu werden und zeigte sich durchaus „ungleichgültig". Wie perfid aber und bloß auf den äußeren Effekt berechnet der Pariser Antrag war, empfand man sogar in Italien, das zwar einen Krieg mit der Türkei geführt hatte und eben erst das Protokoll von Lausanne unterzeichnete. Dort war längst auf offener Tribüne der Kammer die Vereinbarung mit Österreich-Ungarn mitgeteilt worden, daß diese beiden Staaten niemals – selbst bei einer Katastrophe der Türkei – in der Adria eine dritte Macht dulden würden. Es war also deutlich und vor aller Welt deutlich festgestellt, daß eine Teilung des türkischen Erbes die Grenzmächte Österreich-Ungarn, Italien und Rumänien sehr „interessiert" antreffen würde und der Vorschlag Poincarés nichts als eine verlogene Geste war, um die Schuld von Verwicklungen, die die russisch-französische Kriegspartei nicht ohne Mühe in die Welt gesetzt, auf Österreich-Ungarn und natürlich den Sündenbock aller Kriege, auf Deutschland abzuwälzen.

Graf Berchtold parierte den gefährlichen Stoß gegen die Interessen Österreich-Ungarns mit einem geschickten Gegenstoß. Er wies den Vorschlag des *„désintéressement"* ab, faßte aber die Pariser Phrase „der Balkan den Balkanvölkern" so an, daß sie sich gegen ihre eigenen Protektoren wendete. Nachdem er den Verzicht auf territoriale Neuerwerbungen Österreich-Ungarns neuerlich betont hatte, billigte er die Zuteilung nationaler Gebiete an die National-staaten: der Bulgaren in Mazedonien an Bulgarien, der Serben an Serbien und – der Albaner an ein neuzugründendes Albanien. Sollte tatsächlich das Prinzip der Nationalitätenfreiheit von nun ab am Balkan regieren, so durften die Albaner nicht unter die serbische oder bulgarische Herrschaft geknechtet werden. Die Adriaküste durfte nicht serbisch werden, sondern albanisch, wenn dies Land der Türkei entrissen werden sollte.

So unwillig auch bei den Slawophilen Petersburgs und Moskaus dieser Vorschlag gehört wurde, es war doch rechtlich gegen ihn kein Einspruch zu erheben. Daß die Balkanstaaten, die ja nach außen hin pompös verkündet hatten, sie wollten keinen Landgewinn, sondern nur die Befreiung der Geknechteten, diese Gebiete sich längst als Beute gegenseitig – unter der Patronanz des Zaren – zugesprochen, das durfte ja jetzt noch nicht gesagt werden. Die Glorie der uneigennützigen Befreier mußte ihnen bleiben, bis – die Beute zum Teilen reif war. Der Vorschlag des Grafen Berchtold störte empfindlich diese geheimen Kreise, er fuhr mitten hinein in das Netz dieser Abmachungen und riß es durch, so daß eines der wichtigsten Beutestücke – Albanien – zu Boden fiel. In Serbien brach das obligate Wutgeheul los, aber daran war man nun nachgerade in Europa gewöhnt. Man wusste, dass diese Janitscharenmusik nur darauf berechnet war, die Nerven zu irritieren und daß ein Fingerzeig von Petersburg genügte, um diese künstliche Aufwallung sogleich zum Schweigen zu bringen. Alle diese pathetischen Phrasen, daß Serbien ersticken müsse ohne einen Zugang zum Meer, ohne adriatische Küste, blieben nur Worte: Aber sie füllten die Luft mit Lärm und Unruhe.

Die Schaffung eines unabhängigen Albanien, diese von Deutschland und Rumänien unterstütze Forderung Österreich-Ungarns und Italiens, war nicht abzuweisen. Die russische Diplomatie beschloß nun, nicht offenen Widerstand zu leisten, sondern dieses Albanien zu einem unlebensfähigen Staat zu machen. Den Traditionen ihrer Politik gemäß war es unerwünscht, endgültige und ruhige Zustände am Balkan zu haben: Er sollte ein ewig brodelndes Feuer bleiben, an dem sich die Früchte ihrer Politik gar braten könnten. Albanien, wie sie es planten, sollte ein verkümmertes, schwächliches Staatswesen werden, ein Objekt der Vergewaltigung für seine Nachbarn: Von seinem Rumpf sollten alle Gliedmaßen abgerissen werden, die wichtigsten Städte amputiert, die Blutzirkulation des Handels behindert. Nur mit dieser Absicht nahmen sie die Einladung zu dem Kongreß in London an, wo unter dem Vorsitz Edward Greys der Friede der Türkei mit dem Balkanbund und die Schaffung des neuen Staatengebildes beraten werden sollten.

Dieser Londoner Kongreß war nichts als ein verhängnisvolles Feilschen zwischen dem Dreibund und der Tripelentente um Albanien. Stück um Stück seiner Grenzen wurden verteidigt und erobert, wobei die Nachgiebigkeit Österreich-Ungarns die Ansprüche Rußlands – das angeblich bloß für die Sache des bedrohten Slawentums kämpfte – nur immer aufs Neue reizte. Alles, was vorläufig erreicht wurde, war, daß Serbien der direkte Zugang an die Adria verwehrt blieb, aber um die beiden wichtigsten Städte Djakova und Skutari wogte noch immer der Kampf, als jenes zweite Programm des Kongresses – der Friede zwischen den Balkanstaaten und der Türkei – in Trümmer ging.

Was für Österreich-Ungarn diese Verhandlungen zur Qual machte, war die stete und kostspielige Bereitschaft zum Kriege, die ihr nun zum dritten Male von den Nachbarn im Norden und im Osten aufgezwungen wurde. Da ein loyales Paktieren mit Rußland nicht möglich war, mußten große Teile der Armee auf erhöhten Stand gesetzt werden: Gegen Serbien standen Truppen aufgestellt und auch in

Galizien, wo Rußland gerade jetzt den Zeitpunkt für geeignet hielt, um seine berüchtigten „Probemobilisationen" vorzunehmen. Die Reservisten mußten zum Teil einberufen werden, wichtige Konferenzen des Grafen Berchtold und des Chefs des Generalstabes S. d. J. Freiherrn Conrad von Hötzendorf in Bukarest, die Besuche des deutschen Kaisers – alle diese öffentlichen Anzeichen mehrten jenen entsetzlichen Ungewißheitszustand, der sich fortwirkend auf ganz Europa verbreitete. Man fühlte wieder die Wolken sich ballen, wieder war Serbien der Wetterwinkel, und allmählich wuchs die Spannung zur Erbitterung, umso mehr als geradezu zum Hohn auf Österreich-Ungarn serbische Regimenter nach Durazzo marschierten und die Offiziere ihre Säbel dort zum Schwur des Verbleibens mit dem Wasser der Adria netzten. Die Armee fieberte. Wieder war sie in Bereitschaft an der Grenze, sie wußte, daß jenseits ein unversöhnlicher Feind war und konnte mühsam nur den Willen bezähmen, endlich einmal mit dem Schwert diesem Umschleichen und Bedrängen zu wehren.

Wieder war es unseres Monarchen und Österreich-Ungarns oft bewährte Friedensliebe, die zuerst einen Schritt gegen die Gegner tat, das erste Wort des Vertrauens sprach. Mit dem russischen Hofe waren seit jenem politischen Duell Aehrenthal – Iswolski die Beziehungen abgebrochen, noch war der ganze Komplex der Fragen unerörtert. Da sandte Franz Joseph den Prinzen von Hohenlohe, den Gatten seiner Großnichte, mit einem Brief an den Zaren. Der Inhalt dieses Schreibens ist nicht bekannt, aber sein Sinn ist offenkundig: Er bot ein loyales Verhandeln an, statt des drohenden mit dem schußbereiten Gewehr, der greise Monarch zeigte wiederum öffentlich seinen feierlich bekundeten und seit beinahe fünfzig Jahren kraftvoll aufrecht erhaltenen Willen zum Frieden der ganzen Welt mit dieser spontanen und hoheitsvollen Geste. Die erste sichtbare Wirkung war eine Entspannung an den Grenzen Galiziens. Österreich-Ungarn und Rußland demobilisierten die dort zusammengezogenen Truppen. Aber in Bosnien und an der serbischen Grenze blieb der drohende Kriegszustand.

Die Ereignisse auf dem Kriegsschauplatz waren inzwischen reger gewesen als die Diplomaten in London. Die türkische Armee war hinter die letzte Verteidigungslinie zurückgedrängt, Adrianopel, ihre größte Festung, stand vor dem Fall, Skutari, das heroisch unter Hassan Riza Pascha sich verteidigte, wurde nun auch von den Serben belagert, da die Montenegriner allein sich als zu schwach gezeigt hatten, dieses Bollwerk Albaniens zu gewinnen. Schon schien es, als sollte dem König von Bulgarien gegeben sein, was die Zaren von Rußland seit hunderten Jahren ersehnten: Das griechische Kreuz auf der Hagia Sophia zu erneuern –, da bat Konstantinopel abermals um Frieden. Alle Bollwerke waren gefallen, nur das letzte kleine, Skutari, hielt stand.

Aber diese kleine Festung Skutari war in diesem Augenblicke der Mittelpunkt Europas. In endlosen Verhandlungen hatte Österreich-Ungarn sie Rußland endlich für Albanien abgerungen, hatte sogar auf alle anderen Wünsche verzichtet um dieses letzten willen –, mit einer ungeheuren letzten Anstrengung für den Frieden hatten die Mächte in London sich geeinigt, aber der Balkan, voll von Perfidie und Tücke, bot einen neuen Widerstand. Widerstand des Schwächsten gegen den Stärksten, Widerstand – es klingt zu lächerlich – Montenegros gegen das geeinte Europa. Die Botschafterkonferenz einschließlich Rußlands hatte die Aufhebung der Belagerung von Skutari befohlen, aber König Nikita geruhte nicht, die Gesandten zu empfangen. Er vertraute auf die Nebenregierung in Rußland, die Slawophilen. Die Mächte sandten Kriegsschiffe – sieben Panzer blockierten das kleine

Antivari, aber die Herren von Cetinje betrachteten mit Feldstechern die seltene Flottenparade als ein ergötzliches Schauspiel. Und was die Waffen nicht vollbringen, bewirkt endlich der Verrat. Essad Pascha, der den früheren Kommandanten Skutaris, Hasan Riza [Pascha], ermorden ließ, um zur Macht zu gelangen, kapituliert gegen freien Abmarsch mit seiner ganzen Besatzung: Nikita hat ihn verlockt mit der Fürstenkrone Albaniens.

Europa ist düpiert, und in Rußland scheint großer Wille vorhanden, diese höchst willkommene Düpierung zu dulden. Aber jetzt entschließt sich endlich Österreich-Ungarn, zu handeln. Es ist müde, seine Gesandten vor dem Konak in Cetinje antichambrieren zu lassen, mit knapper Not ist sein Militärattaché einem Attentat entgangen, der Jubel in Serbien zeigt nur zu deutlich, daß man zu lange gezögert. Endlich, Ende April 1913, blitzt das Ultimatum an Montenegro. Wieder ist die letzte äußerste Maßregel von Nöten, um sich Achtung zu verschaffen. Schon sind die Truppen marschbereit, schon die Kanonen gegen den Lovćen gerichtet. Da erinnert sich endlich König Nikita, daß ein Viertel seines Heeres in diesem Kriege vernichtet ist und gibt nach. – Aber es ist noch immer nicht der Friede. Zu viel Zündstoff haben die Agenten von Paris und Petersburg auf dem Balkan angehäuft, zu viel Gier ist in den „armen, kleinen" Balkanstaaten. Selbst die ungeheuren Eroberungen, der ganze Landbesitz der Türkei können ihre überhitzten Ansprüche nicht sättigen. An Österreich-Ungarn wagen sie sich noch nicht, die europäische Türkei ist schon ihr Eigen –, so wendet sich ihre Gier gegeneinander. Zusammengestellt nicht durch die idealen Ziele, die von Paris und Petersburg in der Welt verkündet wurden, sondern durch Habsucht und fremde Interessen, geraten sie noch auf dem Schlachtfeld in Streit. Die berühmte slawische Brüderschaft ist plötzlich vergessen, gegen Bulgarien kehrt sich Serbien, dem Griechenland Gefolgschaft leistet.

Der zweite Balkankrieg entbrennt. Und plötzlich enthüllt Rußland sein wahres Gesicht. Die panslawistische Lüge wird plötzlich zur Fratze: Statt die slawischen Staaten zu fördern, denkt man in Petersburg nur daran, den Feind Österreich-Ungarns, Serbien, zu stärken. Und gegen Bulgarien, den slawischen Staat, hetzt Iswolski nun Rumänien –, gegen das während des ersten Krieges ebenso mobilisiert wurde wie gegen Österreich-Ungarn und die Türkei. Fünf Gegner stürzen sich auf Bulgarien, das die Hauptlast des Krieges gegen die Türkei getragen und nun zusammenbricht. Die Rumänen stehen knapp vor Sofia – der verblendete Minister Danew konnte sich noch im gefährlichsten Momente die Konzessionen an König Carol trotz der dringenden Ratschläge Österreich-Ungarns nicht abringen –, und so mußte Bulgarien in den Frieden von Bukarest willigen. Wie alle Staaten bisher erkennt nun Bulgarien den Wert der russischen Versprechungen. Zerfetzt wird dort der Bundesvertrag, der unter den Augen des Zaren unterfertigt war, fast die ganzen Territorien, die bulgarische Soldaten mit ihrem Blute gedüngt haben, fallen an das triumphierende Serbien und Griechenland, in Adrianopel, das mühsam erstürmte, zieht Enver Pascha ein und heftet den Halbmond wieder auf das Minarett. Kein Großstaat, am wenigsten Rußland, steht dem verlassenen König der Bulgaren bei, dem man in Petersburg nicht verzeiht, daß er sich zum Zaren erhob und Konstantinopel für sich begehrte –, nur Österreich-Ungarn erhebt Protest gegen die Vergewaltigung. Aber es kann allein die Vernichtung und Erniedrigung Bulgariens nicht hindern.

Zähneknirschend, mit Tränen in den Augen, unterfertigen die bulgarischen Unterhändler das verhängnisvolle Blatt.

Hunderttausende sind gefallen, aber das Ziel ist nicht erreicht, der Balkan ist nicht beruhigt. Bulgarien gibt nach, aber nur für den Augenblick, Serbien, statt befriedigt zu sein, blickt in größenwahnsinniger Gier schon nach der österreichisch-ungarischen Grenze, Albanien ist in vollem Aufruhr. Die Waffe Iswolskis, der Balkanbund, ist gesprengt: Er wird nie mehr gegen Österreich-Ungarn gewandt werden. Aber auch Österreich-Ungarn darf nicht triumphieren: Sein erbitterter Feind, Serbien, ist nun doppelt so stark wie vordem, eine wertvolle Bundesgenossenschaft, die Freundschaft Rumäniens, ist gefährdet, der Anschluß an die Türkei verloren. Das russische Prestige hat gelitten seit dem Verrat von Bukarest, die Türkei ist gedemütigt, aber nicht gebrochen, Griechenland vergrößert, aber um die albanischen Häfen verkürzt, Italien beunruhigt durch die plötzlich auftauchende Mittelmeermacht. Unruhiger ist die Welt als je zuvor. Die Pandorabüchse des Balkans ist von der verwegenen Hand Iswolskis geöffnet worden: Zu schließen hat sie keiner vermocht, nun strömen ihre giftigen Dämpfe aus und beunruhigen die Atmosphäre Europas. Enger haben sich die großen Staatenkomplexe Rußland, Frankreich, England zusammengeballt, enger auch Deutschland und Österreich-Ungarn, die Reibungsflächen sind vermehrt, die Gefahr vergrößert. Im deutschen Parlament bringt der Reichskanzler einen Milliardenkredit für Rüstungen ein, das französische antwortet mit der Annahme der dreijährigen Dienstzeit. Es ist eine schwüle Stunde, dichter und dichter ballt sich das Gewölk. Und alles deutet auf eine furchtbare Erinnerungsfeier des europäischen Zustandes vor hundert Jahren: der Völkerschlacht von Leipzig, da alle Staaten gegeneinander in Waffen standen, nur, daß es diesmal das Herz Europas, das in Nibelungentreue geeinte Deutschland und Österreich-Ungarn ist, das sich, einer gegen alle, zu verteidigen hat.

Die Ermordung des Thronfolgers
1914

Der Balkankrieg hatte keine Entspannung gebracht. Nur deutlicher waren die beiden Mächtegruppen geworden, nur reger waren die Regisseure des Krieges in Frankreich und Rußland am Werke: Es war ihnen gelungen, das Gleichgewicht der Welt in Schwebe zu bringen, eine einzige brüske Bewegung vermochte nun das Unheil zerschmetternd niederstürzen zu lassen. Überall war die Glut von ihnen künstlich glimmend erhalten worden: Rußland hatte Bulgarien verraten, Rumänien gegen Österreich-Ungarn mißtrauisch gemacht, Serbien mit Größenwahn vergiftet und das neugeschaffene Reich Albanien sollte ein Keim der Zwietracht zwischen Österreich-Ungarn und Italien werden. Immer neue Schwierigkeiten wurden ersonnen, um die Wahl eines Fürsten zu verzögern und dort die Anarchie aufwuchern zu lassen, die der russische Minister nicht ganz ohne Ahnung der geheimen Tätigkeit seiner Agenten prophetisch angekündigt hatte. Jede kleine Angelegenheit bei der Gründung des jungen Staatenwesens wurde künstlich kompliziert und dem neuen, endlich bestellten Herrscher, dem Fürsten zu Wied, eine Reihe von Revolten auf den Hals gehetzt. Die Monarchie hatte diesen Staat als Gleichgewichtsfaktor, als Element der Ruhe mitten zwischen die ewig feindlichen, ewig gärenden Balkanstaaten setzen wollen, Rußland und Serbien trachteten ihn als einen Keil zu verwenden, der das Einvernehmen Österreich-Ungarns und Italiens auseinandersprengen sollte. Kleine Staaten waren für Rußland seit je nur Preller,

Sturmböcke, um das Gefüge des nachbarlichen Reiches zu lockern und um dann, wenn dieses ins Wanken geriet, selbst hervorzutreten und in dem Zusammenbruch sich das Beste zu rauben. So war Bulgarien gegen die Türkei, Rumänien wieder gegen Bulgarien vorgeschickt worden: Nun sollte von Albanien und Serbien die systematische Unterwühlung der Monarchie beginnen. Österreich-Ungarn von Norden, Süden und Osten gefaßt, Deutschland von Westen, Osten und Norden umklammert –, die Falle war vorbereitet, und vielleicht existierte schon damals in den Archiven ähnlich wie in jenen der Balkanstaaten vor dem Kriege mit der Türkei der ausgearbeitete Teilungsplan, in dem der lebendige Körper der Monarchie schon in großen und kleinen Fetzen zerteilt war.

Allerdings, der Überfall war noch nicht sofort geplant. Rußland, obzwar in den zehn Jahren seit dem japanischen Krieg und der Revolution unendlich gekräftigt, mußte noch militärisch rüsten, vor allem in jenem Sinne, den der französische Generalstab verlangte, im Sinne einer erhöhten Mobilisationsgeschwindigkeit. Die gewaltigen Kräfte des gigantischen Reiches konnten erst allmählich an Ort und Stelle geschafft werden, während es Frankreich darum zu tun war – diese Fragen wurden ganz offen diskutiert –, daß von beiden Seiten gleichzeitig gegen Deutschland gestoßen werde und ihm beide Flanken gewaltsam eingedrückt. Es war zu einer solchen raschen Konzentrierung vor allem der Ausbau des Bahnnetzes in Polen nötig, für das Frankreich wieder eine Milliardenanleihe gerne bewilligte. Vorläufig wurden nur die bekannten „Probemobilisierungen" eingeübt. Im Jahre 1916 sollte der Aufmarsch fertig sein, im gleichen Jahre, wo der Handelsvertrag mit Deutschland ablief –, für diesen Termin kündigten ganz unverhohlen die Pariser Blätter die Abrechnung mit den

Zentralmächten an, denn dann könnte ja Serbien schon wieder erstarkt sein, und vielleicht könnten der rollende Rubel und die französischen Anleihen inzwischen Italien und Rumänien für die Einkreisung gewinnen. Man wollte ja den Sieg möglichst bequem haben und – nach bewährtem System – möglichst auf Kosten der Bundesgenossen.

Das offizielle Rußland brauchte also noch zwei Jahre, um seine kriegerischen Vorbereitungen zu vollenden. Deshalb wieder pathetische Reden über den Frieden und freundschaftliche Besuche in Berlin. Inzwischen hatte das inoffizielle Rußland die Unterminierung des Terrains durchzuführen, die Slawophilen wurden vorausgeschickt, die an den Grenzen der Monarchie ihre „allslawischen", in Wahrheit aber panrussischen Kongresse abhielten, nationale Vereine stifteten, die unter unpolitischer Maske systematisch Spionage und Aufwiegelung trieben. Die Ruthenen wurden durch ihre Popen bearbeitet, die als Kinder armer Leute umsonst in russischen Seminaren herangebildet wurden, um dann als Emissäre des Zarenreiches wieder nach ihrer Heimat zurückgesandt zu werden. Zeitschriften, Kirchen wurden – angeblich mit dem Gelde der Ruthenen in Amerika, in Wirklichkeit aber mit den Rubeln der Geheimfonds – gegründet, und der Graf Bobrinsky, derselbe, der so kühn war, beim Prozeß in Marmaroschsiget zu sagen, die Slawophilen seien der Monarchie nicht feind, kündigte ihnen die Befreiung vom polnischen Joche und die „russische Flagge auf der Höhe der Karpaten" an. Ganz Galizien wurde so systematisch von Agenten und Spionen unterwühlt, in der Bukowina die bekannten russischen „Kulturvereine" gegründet; zwei Mal in kurzer Frist mußte der russische Militärattaché Wien verlassen, weil er in sehr unangenehme Spionage-Affären verwickelt war. Überall arbeitete das unoffizielle Rußland, die Stellung der Monarchie zu unterhöhlen, unausgesetzt mußte die Staatsanwaltschaft dieser gefährlichen Maulwurfsarbeit nachgehen, die unterirdisch durch das ganze Grenzgebiet gezogen war, und jede ihrer Maßnahmen wurde jenseits der schwarzgelben Pfähle als „Unterdrückung der slawischen Brüder" verkündet. Der Rubel rollte, von unverantwortlichen Händen gestreut, aber die ungeheuren Mittel, die zur Vergiftung und Agitation der österreichisch-ungarischen Staatsuntertanen ausgegeben wurden, strömten aus den Geheimfonds der Regierung. Das alte System der russischen Politik mit dem doppelten Boden – maßlose skrupellose Agitation bei friedlicher Beteuerung – feierte ihre Triumphe, und erst im Kriege wurde das ganze fürchterliche Ausmaß jener jahrelangen „friedlichen" Betätigung offenbar. – In Frankreich hingegen arbeitete die Kriegspartei ohne Maske, im Gegenteil, sie zeigte mit einer gewissen Ostentation ihren Willen zur endgültigen Abrechnung, indem sie Poincaré an die höchste Stelle der Republik berief, Poincaré, der das russisch-französische Bündnis neu gekräftigt hatte und die deutsche Einkreisung als das Erbe König Eduards leidenschaftlich gefördert. Auch Delcassé tauchte wieder aus der Versenkung auf, die dreijährige Dienstzeit wurde bewilligt –, obwohl Jaurès prophetisch sich diesen Vorbereitungen widersetzte. Die Kriegspartei hielt das Steuer, der Wind von England her wehte günstig, so nahm das französische Staatsschiff mit voller Geschwindigkeit den Weg in die Gefahr. Seit dem Balkankriege waren die Militärs von der absoluten Überlegenheit der Creusot-Geschütze gegen Krupp überzeugt, die Aeroplane – die *„oiseaux de France"*, wie sie triumphierend genannt wurden – schienen die Herrschaft in der Luft zu verbürgen, heftiger und heftiger drängte darum die Armee gegen die endliche Entscheidung. Wer sich dem Kriegsklüngel widersetzte, wurde niedergetreten. Gegen Caillaux, der während der Marokkoaffäre ein loyales Verhältnis mit Deutschland anbahnen wollte und jetzt noch der friedlichen Auseinandersetzung das Wort redete, wurden maßlose Gehässigkeiten und Verleumdungen vorgebracht, Jaurès systematisch als Verräter verhöhnt und – da kein Anwurf seine moralische Makellosigkeit treffen konnte – im Augenblicke der Entscheidung dann auch tatsächlich durch Mord beseitigt.

In England, wo alle Fäden dieser Verschwörung gegen Deutschland zusammenliefen, zeigte nach außen nichts die ungeheure und bewußte Feindseligkeit. Sir Edward Grey wußte, daß er vor dem Parlamente es nicht verantworten könnte, den Krieg zu betreiben: So mußte er erst im Geheimen appretiert werden. Mit Rußland – dem bei der Mehrzahl der Engländer verhaßten – schloß er eine Flottenkonvention, die er im Parlamente nicht mitzuteilen wagte, es war, wie alle die Verträge Englands, nur ein Brief und kein Vertrag, aber so bindend wie jenes Versprechen der einhunderttausend Mann in der Marokkoaffäre. Und während noch das ganze Land an die absolute Unabhängigkeit Großbritanniens glaubte, war es längst verstrickt mit geheimen Verpflichtungen in alle slawophilen und chauvinistischen Verschwörungen. Und es bedurfte der ganzen Verwegenheit heuchlerischer Politik, um noch Uneigennützigkeit und Unparteilichkeit von der Ministerbank immer und immer wieder zu bekunden, da man längst gemeinsame Militärpläne mit der Ost- und Westmacht und selbst dem neutralen Belgien in den Generalstabskreisen hatte, die Rollen schon ausgegeben waren und man nur das Signal – von hüben oder drüben – erwartete, um endlich dem leidigen Handelskonkurrenten Deutschland das Bein zu stellen.

Deutschland und Österreich-Ungarn kannten die Gefahr. Ein Milliardenkredit, leider nur in Deutschland freudig und einhellig bewilligt, bewies, daß man gesonnen sei, kein Opfer zu scheuen, um aufrecht zu erhalten, was vor vierundvierzig Jahren die deutsche Einheit mit ihrem Blute erkauft hatte und was deutscher Fleiß in diesen wenigen Jahrzehnten auf dem Weltreich sich an Besitz und Ehre erobert. Aber gleichzeitig mühte sich Kaiser Wilhelm neuerlich um Verständigung, vor allem um eine mit England; selbst im empfindlichsten Punkte der deutschen Weltpolitik, der Bagdadbahn, wurde eine Einigung mit bedeutsamen Opfern gewonnen, höfische Besuche zeigten neuerlich den Willen, die leitenden Kreise der Kriegshypnose ihrer Ratgeber zu entziehen. Auch Österreich-Ungarn stärkte seine Wehr, aber hier verbürgte nach aller irdischen Voraussicht der Friedenswille des Kaisers unblutige Lösung aller Konflikte und Unveränderlichkeit des europäischen Bestandes. Selbst in den feindlichen Äußerungen war jeder kriegerische Zusammenstoß jenseits der Regierung Franz Josephs gedacht, weil er gewissermaßen das sicherste Symbol des Friedens war, und man wußte, daß seinem persönlichen Ansehen in Europa noch in letzter Stunde ein Versuch zur Erhaltung der Einigung gelingen möchte.

So rüsteten die Großstaaten, aber sie zögerten noch. Die Politik des Dreierverbandes wartete auf die geeignete Stunde. Aber ein Staat in Europa wollte nicht warten, er war zu ungeduldig: Serbien. Die raschen Siege über die Türken, der Triumph über die Bulgaren hatte das leicht erregbare Volk trunken von Selbstgefühl gemacht. Ein Jahr, ein einziges, hatte die Grenzen des Reiches fast verdoppelt, die eine Hälfte des verheißenen Programms, die Zerstörung der Türkei, war aus einem Fieberraum plötzlich Wirklichkeit geworden; kein Wunder, daß ihnen auch der zweite Teil des Versprechens König Peters, die Vernichtung Österreich-Ungarns, als eine Kleinigkeit erschien. Die Vorbereitungen hatten ja seit jenem verhängnisvollen Annexionsjahr – und sehr im Gegensatz zu dem Versprechen des März 1909, freundnachbarliche Beziehungen zu pflegen – nicht ausgesetzt, sie waren zwar heimlicher geworden, aber umso skrupelloser. Während unter der Leitung Hartwigs, eines Schülers Iswolskis, die literarische und politische Propaganda ganz offen geführt wurde, Spione nach Bosnien kamen und Gegenspione sogar in die österreichisch-ungarische Gesandtschaft, um Papiere zu verkaufen, die nachher triumphierend als Fälschungen erklärt werden konnten, während dieser gefährlichen, aber noch immer erklärbaren Tätigkeit der Politiker wurde eine andere nicht minder emsig vorbereitet, die bedeutend mehr Grund hatte, das Tageslicht und vor allem die europäische Meinung zu scheuen. Es waren dies die Agitation der „Narodna Odbrana" und die Komitadschischulen.

Im Jahre 1908, während der Annexion, hatten emsige Offiziere, vor allem Milan Pribičević, ein aus der österreichisch-ungarischen Armee desertierter Serbe, irreguläre Freischaren, die Komitadschis, für den möglichen Krieg mit Österreich-Ungarn heranzubilden unternommen. Etwas abgelegen von Belgrad, in der Heimlichkeit kleiner Städte, wurde mit angeworbenen Burschen ein mehrmonatlicher Kurs eröffnet, in dem die hoffnungsvollen Eleven im Bombenwerfen, Revolverschießen, Minenlegen, Zerstörung von Eisenbahnen, Brücken und Tunnels unterrichtet wurden. Die Zeugenaussage eines Mitattentäters hat später gezeigt, mit welcher Sorgsamkeit die Irregulären von Offizieren der serbischen Armee zu dieser verbrecherischen Tätigkeit instruiert wurden und wie genau die Regierung die Einzelheiten dieser Ausbildungsschulen kannte.

Die Anerkennung der Annexion schien dann diesen Schulen ein Ende zu machen. Aber die Agitatoren der „Narodna Odbrana" waren anderer Meinung, sie vertraten den Standpunkt, daß dies Bombenwerfen und Revolverschießen auch im Frieden geübt werden sollte und zwar – in Bosnien. Während der Krise hatte man mit Reden und Broschüren Lärm gemacht; jetzt sollten Explosionen, Attentate und Prozesse dauernd das österreichisch-ungarische Problem für die Welt in Erinnerung erhalten. Die jungen Leute waren zum Teil leicht zu überreden, denn der politische Mord gilt in Serbien als nationale Großtat, und der Attentäter, der nach der Schlacht von Kossowo dem Sultan Murad in seinem Zelte den Dolch ins Herz stieß, wird heute noch in Festen und Liedern gefeiert. Der Begründer der Dynastie Karageorgević gilt dort als Held, weil er seinen Vater auf der Flucht ermordete, und die Offiziere, an deren Händen das Blut der letzten Obrenović klebte, bekleideten die höchsten Stellen im Staate. Geld tat bei den meist existenzlosen Leuten das übrige, und so war es nicht zu verwundern, wenn im Jahre 1910 ein Attentat auf den Chef der Landesregierung in Bosnien und der Hercegovina, G. d. I. Freiherrn von Varešanin [von Vares] – bedenklich nahe nach dem Besuch des Kaisers und Königs Franz Joseph – zwei auf den Banus von Kroatien und noch eine Anzahl anderer nicht immer gelungener Mordanschläge auf hervorragende Vertreter der österreichisch-ungarischen Regierung unternommen wurden.

Bei der Auswahl der Attentäter zeigte sich aber stets die berechnende Perfidie der Drahtzieher in Belgrad. Niemals ließen sie einen dieser Morde von einem Angehörigen Serbiens unternehmen, immer wurden Bosnier und Kroaten ans Messer geliefert. Für die Welt sollte ja der Anschein geboten werden, als stöhne Bosnien unter der österreichisch-ungarischen Fremdherrschaft, als seien diese Attentate nur Explosionen einer übermächtigen Volkserregung, der Serbien mit Mitleid, aber ohne jede Anstachelung nahestünde. Die wichtigste Arbeit der „Narodna Odbrana" bestand darum darin, junge, meist halbwüchsige Burschen, am liebsten Gymnasiasten, die als Halbgebildete den pathetischen Verheißungen leicht erliegen konnten, nach Belgrad hinüberzulocken. Dort wurde ihnen – die Organisation umfaßte ja alle Gesellschaftskreise – eine äußere Lebensstellung sofort geboten, sie mit Ehren umschmeichelt, selbst beim Ministerpräsidenten Pašić und dem Prinzen Georg hatte mancher dieser jungen Fanatiker Zutritt, gleichzeitig aber wurden sie in den edlen Künsten des Bombenwerfens und Revolverschießens herangebildet. Sandte man sie – mit falschen Papieren und sehr guten Empfehlungsschreiben – in die Monarchie zurück, so war ihre Aufgabe dort die Propaganda oder – die Tat. Immer aber mußten es Österreicher oder Ungarn sein, die zur Tat bestimmt waren –, Serbien sollte vor den Augen der Welt das unantastbare Land der Freiheit scheinen, Österreich-Ungarn der Tyrann der slawischen Völker. Und um immer neue Desperados zu gewinnen, wurden in Belgrader Zeitungen diese Attentäter als Befreier ihrer Brüder, als Nationalhelden gefeiert. Am 18. August 1910, dem achtzigsten Geburtstag des Kaisers Franz Joseph, brachte die „Politika" ein großes Bild – Bogdan Žerajić[31], der zwei Monate vorher das Attentat auf den Landeschef von Bosnien verübt hatte, und schrieb dazu, daß „sein Name im Volke wie etwas Heiliges genannt wird" und feierte den „Helden" in einem

---

[31] *Bogdan Žerajić*: Attentäter des Gouverneurs von Bosnien und Herzegovina: Marijan Freiherr Varešanin von Vareš; Vorbild von Princip.

Gedicht. Es galt ja, diesem Helden Nachfolger zu werben, und da wurde keine Mühe gescheut.

Das offizielle Serbien betrieb diesen Vorgängen gegenüber eine Vogelstraußpolitik. In den Lehrbüchern wurde zwar gedruckt, daß Bosnien, Kroatien und Dalmatien zu Serbien gehörten, für das Kriegsministerium ein Bild gemalt, das die Einbringung der „geraubten" Provinzen darstellte, aber bei jeder Anfrage erklärte der Ministerpräsident, daß sich dies nicht gegen Österreich-Ungarn wende. Auch hier wollte man den Zersetzungsprozeß Österreich-Ungarns erst beschleunigen, statt offen mit dem Beil gegen seine Grenze anzurennen, nur waren die Mittel eben radikalere, „serbischer" als sie jemals in Europa gegen einen Großstaat versucht worden waren. Man brauchte Attentate, da man Komitadschibanden nicht zu senden wagte, wie einstens gegen die Türkei, mit Gewalt wollte man gerade diejenigen aus dem Wege räumen, die das Stagnieren der österreichisch-ungarischen Kraft mit Energie bekämpften und durch neue Fermente seinen gewaltigen Organismus zu erneutem verstärkten Leben erweckten.

Der unwillkommenste und gefährlichste von diesen Erneuerern Österreich-Ungarns war den Feinden der Monarchie Erzherzog Franz Ferdinand von Österreich-Este, der Thronfolger. Irgendwie war – mehr durch Wunsch gezeugt als durch Logik – in den übelgesinnten Nachbarstaaten die Meinung entstanden, der Bestand der österreichisch-ungarischen Monarchie sei an Franz Joseph I. gebunden, und mit seiner Regierung würde auch der Kaiserstaat zu Ende sein. Man wußte, mit welcher hingebungsvollen Liebe alle Völker an diesem Patriarchen des Reiches hingen und wie selbst bei den Leidenschaftlichsten die Ehrfurcht vor seiner Person das Wort und die übermäßige Erregung bändigte. Wohl bewußt, daß – so lange der Monarch seiner

Armee und seinen Völkern gebot – jeder Angriff gegen die Monarchie die Vielfalt der Nationalitäten in eine wundervolle Einheit patriotischer Leidenschaft verwandeln würde, setzten sie anfangs ihre Hoffnung auf die Stunde, da andere Hände das Szepter des Reiches fassen würden. Aber der Thronfolger hatte in den letzten Jahren, mit immer mehr Einfluß und Macht bekleidet, deutlich gezeigt, daß er nicht gesonnen sei, die Größe der Monarchie preiszugeben, aus allen seinen Handlungen war deutlich die Energie ersichtlich, Österreich-Ungarn zu festigen, zu erhöhen und zu erneuern. Er förderte die Armee, schuf die Marine beinahe neu, an allen ökonomischen und nationalen Fragen nahm er lebhaft Anteil. Seine Freundschaft mit Kaiser Wilhelm bot die Garantie, daß nach wie vor das Bündnis mit dem Deutschen Reich der unveränderliche Grundpfeiler der österreichisch-ungarischen Politik sein werde, seine Ehe mit Herzogin Sophie von Hohenberg aus dem alten czechischen Geschlechte der Chotek sicherte ihm die Sympathie der Slawen. Bei allen Manövern gegenwärtig, jede Neuerung und Veränderung verfolgend, Historiker und Kunstliebhaber, ein Verehrer der alten Tradition bei allem Willen zur Erneuerung, zeigte er deutlich, daß er die Berufung auf den Habsburgerthron auch als eine große Verpflichtung empfand, als eine Aufgabe, die er mit Ernst, Arbeit, Leidenschaft und Strenge zum Wohle der Monarchie durchzuführen gesonnen war. Unverkennbar war sein Wille, nichts von dem erlauchten Erbe preiszugeben, sondern im Gegenteil, den Wert des Übernommenen durch Hingebung und Entschlossenheit zu mehren.

Dieser starke und arbeitsfreudige Thronerbe war darum ein Hemmnis für alle, die auf den Untergang und die Zermürbung der Monarchie hofften. Und auf ihn lenkte sich in Serbien die erbitterte, in ihren Mitteln zügellose Agitation der „Narodna Odbrana". Für Unbequeme hatte die serbische Tradition immer nur ein Mittel: den Mord. Die Obrenović waren aus dem Wege geräumt, der Putsch gegen die Njegusch[32], die Dynastie Montenegros, war zwar mißlungen, konnte aber wiederholt werden, dem Fürsten von Albanien hatte man den roten Hahn auf das Dach gesetzt: Nun mußte das Serbien der Karageorgević noch die Gefährlichsten treffen: die Habsburger.

Sorgfältig wurde das Verbrechen ausgearbeitet und besonderes Gewicht auf das Symbolische gelegt. Der Thronfolger mußte in Bosnien fallen, damit die „Bestrafung" für den „Raub" ersichtlicher sei, auch der Tag sollte den Mord ins Heroische erheben, der Jahrestag von Kossowo, der Schlacht auf dem Amselfelde, da der serbische Nationalheld den Sultan Murad, den Zerschmetterer des ersten Großserbien erdolchte. Damit das Attentat nicht mißlinge, wurde gleich eine ganze Gruppe von Mördern ausgesandt. Princip und Čabrinović[33], zwei junge Leute im Sold der

---

[32] *Petrović*; Dynastie in Montenegro; auch Njegosch bzw. Njegoš als Beinamen, nach dem Ort Njeguši („Njegusch" oder „Njegosch").

[33] *Gavrilo Princip*: Einer der bosnisch-serbischen, nationalistischen Attentäter und Vollzieher des Mordes in Sarajevo; galt als Volksheld und wird teilweise noch heute verehrt; er wurde aufgrund seiner Minderjährigkeit und trotz seiner Aussagen, dass er sich keiner Schuld bewusst wäre, er einen Tyrannen ermordet hätte und dass er Österreich hasste nur zu 20 Jahren schwerem Kerker verurteilt; die Tuberkulose überlebte er nicht; 1894 – 1918. Genauso erging es *Nedeljko Čabrinović* und *Trifun „Trifko"*. *Čubrilović* bekam 16 Jahre Strafe, kam nach dem Zerfall der Monarchie frei, studierte und wurde unter Josip Broz Tito Minister für Forstwirtschaft. *Veljko Čubrilović, Miško Jovanović* und *Danilo Ilić* wurden der Beihilfe zum Mord schuldig gesprochen und im Februar 1915 durch Hängen am Würgegalgen hingerichtet. *Ivo Kranjčević*, er versteckte die Waffen, wurde zu 10 Jahren schwerem Kerker verurteilt; *Cvetko Popović* bekam 13 Jahre wegen Hochverrats – aufgrund dessen er minderjährig war. *Muhamed Mehmedbašić* konnte als Einziger fliehen; wurde in Montenegro verhaftet,

„Narodna Odbrana", wurden ausgewählt, der Major Vojislaw Tankosić der serbischen Armee und der Komitadschiführer Milan Ciganović versahen sie mit Reisegeld, übten sie sorgfältig im Browning-Schießen, und das königlich serbische Militärarsenal in Kragujevac lieferte die Bomben. Die Sorgfalt ging so weit, daß ihnen auch Zyankali mitgegeben wurde, damit sie sofort Selbstmord verüben könnten und die Spuren zurück nach Belgrad verwischt würden. Es sollten ja „unterdrückte Bosnier" sein, die das Attentat ausführten.

Die Schwierigkeit bestand nun darin, die Mörder und vor allem die Bomben über die österreichisch-ungarische Grenze zu schaffen, die damals – Erzherzog Franz Ferdinand inspizierte die Manöver in Bosnien – besonders scharf bewacht war. Aber die königlich serbischen Behörden boten dem wichtigen Unternehmen gerne hilfreiche Hand. Die Grenzwachen wurden von den geheimnisvollen Leitern der „Narodna Odbrana", die noch von Höhergestellten gedeckt wurden, angewiesen, den „Patrioten" den Übergang auf Schleichwegen zu ermöglichen; und der offizielle Verwaltungsapparat funktionierte vortrefflich. Der Finanzwachmann in Loznica, Šabac und anderen Übergangsorten sah zwar das reichhaltige Arsenal von Bomben und Revolvern, aber sein Lächeln billigte nur den geheimnisvollen Zweck in Bosnien. Glücklich über der Grenze wurden die Verschwörer einzeln von den eingeweihten Vertrauensmännern der „Narodna Odbrana" in Bosnien übernommen, und erst der 28. Juni vereinigte sie wieder in Sarajewo zu gemeinsamer Tat.

---

nachdem er mit seiner Tat prahlte; wurde aber aufgrund der Angst vor Serbien nie nach Österreich ausgeliefert; er entkam und wurde erst aufgrund des von ihm und Dragutin Dimitrijević ausgeführten Mordkomplotts verhaftet und zu 15 Jahren verurteilt.

Die Bombe des Čabrinović verfehlte ihr Ziel, aber Princip machte seinen Lehrern, den Majoren Tankosić und Milan Pribičević Ehre: Sein Browning traf den Erzherzog und traf auch eine wehrlose Frau zu Tode. Noch andere Verschworene warteten auf dem Wege, aber die Tat war getan, des neuen Österreich-Ungarns Haupt gefällt, und das Serbien der Karageorgević feierte wieder einen seiner grauenhaften Triumphe. Der Ring war geschlossen von jener Mordnacht im Konak von Belgrad bis zu diesem letzten Morde, aber auch das Maß der Langmut erschöpft. Gerade der Tod Franz Ferdinands schuf das, was die Mörder in Belgrad verhindern wollten: ein entschlossenes, tatbereites, kraftvolles Österreich-Ungarn.

Die Kriegserklärung
1914

Die Kunde von der grauenhaften Mordtat in Sarajewo, der nicht nur der zukünftige Herrscher Österreich-Ungarns zum Opfer gefallen war, sondern auch eine unschuldige Frau, erregte in ganz Europa und weit darüber hinaus, in der ganzen gesitteten Welt, Abscheu und Empörung. Besonders im Deutschen Reiche, wo das Volk den Kaiser mit dem Erzherzog Franz Ferdinand in inniger Freundschaft verbunden wußte, erkannte man die Bedeutung des Verlustes, und in der Monarchie äußerte sich die Empörung gegen die vermutlichen Anstifter des Attentats, gegen die Serben, in derart vehementer Form, daß die Regierung Gewaltmaßregeln aufwenden mußte, um Ausschreitungen in Kroatien und Bosnien zu verhindern. Selbst in Ländern, deren Sympathie wir politisch nicht erhoffen durften, wandte sich der Unwille gegen die Verbrecher, und der Präsident Poincaré erklärte ausdrücklich unserem Gesandten, er hoffe, daß die serbische Regierung alles tun werde, um der österreichisch-ungarischen bei der Verfolgung des Komplotts hilfreiche Hand zu bieten. Alle Monarchen sandten zur Bestattung des Erzherzogs Vertreter, und einhellig war das Empfinden, daß ein solcher frevelhafter Mord kraftvolle Sühnung erheische.

Die Stimme ganz Europas sprach. Nur in Serbien war ein seltsames, ein verlegenes Schweigen. Längst war die Nachricht durchgesickert, daß die Bomben des Čabrinović aus dem königlich-serbischen Arsenal in Kragujevac stammten, daß Princip in Belgrad Schießunterricht genommen habe. Aber das offizielle Serbien schwieg, und in einem Interview erklärte der serbische Polizeipräsident, einen Mann namens Milan Ciganović habe es nie in Belgrad gegeben, obwohl er ihm selbst zwei Tage vorher einen Paß ausgestellt hatte. Besser erkannte man die wirkliche Stimmung, die mühsam zurückgehaltene Freude, aus dem Verhalten der Leute und der Zeitungen. Die verschiedenen Konsularbeamten erzählten übereinstimmend in ihren Berichten (die im österr.-ungar. Rotbuche[34] veröffentlicht sind), mit welchem Jubel die Nachricht von dem gelungenen Attentat in ganz Serbien aufgenommen wurde und wie diese Tat dem Fest zur Feier des serbischen Sultanmörders Obilić zu einer unerwarteten Steigerung verhalf. „Die Leute sollen sich vor Freude in die Arme gefallen sein", berichtet der Belgrader Gesandte, und der Konsul in Nisch meldet: „Es war eine Pein zu beobachten, wie eine förmlich fröhliche Stimmung sich der Gäste der Lokale bemächtigte, mit welcher sichtlichen Genugtuung man über die Tat debattierte und wie Ausrufe der Freude, des Hohnes und Spottes aufflatterten." Die Zeitungen versuchten in den ersten Tagen die Gründe des Attentates mit anarchistischen Tendenzen zu verschleiern, aber bald begannen sie, von einem „Verzweiflungsakt des jungen Märtyrers" zu sprechen und eine „Provokation" darin zu erblicken, daß der österreichisch-ungarische Thronfolger sein Kronland gerade an dem Tage eines serbischen Volksfestes zu besuchen sich erlaubt hatte. Je sichtlicher aber die Spuren der Untersuchung nach Belgrad hinwiesen und je gewisser es selbst den Voreingenommensten werden mußte, daß dieses

---

[34] *Österreichisch-Ungarisches Rotbuch*: Wird auch als „Die Wahrheit geben" bezeichnet; Sinn dahinter war es, alle Aktenstücke und Vorgänge des Staatsamtes zu veröffentlichen.

Komplott von offiziellen serbischen Kreisen angestiftet war, um so wahnsinniger und verzweifelter wurden die Beschuldigungen. Bald war es – wie die „Tribuna" in Belgrad schrieb – die österreichisch-ungarische Kriegspartei, die diesen Mord „bestellt" hatte, bald behaupteten sie, man suche durch „unmenschliche Torturen" von den Mördern belastende Geständnisse zu erpressen, und ein Blatt ging in seiner Schamlosigkeit soweit – ohne darum der Konfiskation zu verfallen –, den lächerlichen Irrwitz in Druck zu geben, der Mörder Princip sei der Sohn der Gräfin Lónyay[35] und von ihr gedungen, um den Tod des Kronprinzen Rudolf an seinem Mörder, den Erzherzog Franz Ferdinand, zu rächen. Solche wahnsinnige, mehr von der Angst als aus Wut ersonnene Beschimpfungen ließ das offizielle Serbien zu, zwei Wochen nach der fluchwürdigsten Ermordung eines kaiserlichen Prinzen und seiner wehrlosen Gattin.

Aber noch immer wartete man in Österreich-Ungarn. Immer noch hoffte man, die serbische Regierung werde der unseren die peinliche Pflicht ersparen, Mörder und Hehler auf ihrem Territorium suchen zu müssen und selbst mit dem Angebot einer Untersuchung den unausweichlichen Forderungen zuvorkommen. Aber keine Geste ließ den Wunsch nach freundschaftlicher Auseinandersetzung vernehmen: Im Gegenteil, bei der feierlichen Einbringung der Leiche des Erzherzogs in Wien mußte der serbische Gesandte von der Polizei genötigt werden, einen sichtbaren Trauerflor zu hissen. Ein einziges Zeichen offenen, herzlichen Bedauerns hätte genügen können, um einen Vergleich anzubahnen, aber das störrische, trotzig-beharrliche

---

[35] *Stephanie von Belgien*: Gattin von Kronprinz Rudolf; verliebte sich nach dessen Tod in Elemér Lónyay von Nagy-Lónya und Vásáros-Namény; 1864 – 1945.

Schweigen mußte die Vermutung bestärken, die serbische Regierung fürchte eine Untersuchung, weil sie in zu hohe Kreise hinaufführen könnte und das endlich unwiderleglich zu beweisen, was im Friedjung-Prozeß und jenem zu Agram durch die Geschicklichkeit der Beteiligten mißlungen war: daß die verbrecherische Agitation gegen Österreich-Ungarn trotz aller gegenseitigen Versprechungen offiziell von den niedern wie von den höchsten Kreisen des Königreiches Serbien gutgeheißen, gefördert und sogar systematisch organisiert werde.

Endlich wußte man in Österreich-Ungarn den wahren Wert der serbischen Versicherungen und war nun entschlossen, ohne Bedenken eine Tat zu fordern, die Aufrichtigkeit der freundnachbarlichen Beziehungen verbürgte. Die ganze Monarchie war wach geworden, man wußte jetzt, daß nicht diplomatische Zwistigkeiten uns von dem Balkankönigreich schieden, sondern ein unversöhnlicher, bösartiger, mörderischer Haß. Sie hatten auf das Haupt des Reiches gezielt, aber sein Herz getroffen: Eine einhellige Erbitterung bemächtigte sich aller Kreise, seit man gesehen, daß jene verbrecherische Wut nicht vor dem Hause des greisen Monarchen Halt machte, und noch nie so sehr wie diesmal konnte die Diplomatie, die Armee der leidenschaftlichen Einheit des ganzen Millionenreiches gewiß sein. Kein Minister, kein Herrscher hätte es verantworten können, nicht Sühne zu fordern für eine so meuchlerische Tat: Aber die Friedensliebe des Monarchen ließ es bei einer gelinden bewenden, und die Forderung, die an Belgrad gestellt wurde, entsprach nur den billigsten Anforderungen der Justiz: ihr den Zugang zu gestatten zu den Schlupfwinkeln, in die jene Anstifter der festgenommenen Mörder geflüchtet waren. Es durften jetzt nicht mehr biegsame Worte als Sühne gegeben werden, sondern sichere Garantien, die allen Winkelzügen und Verschleppungen, allen Intriguen und Gehässigkeiten ein dauerndes Ende machten. Nicht Österreich-Ungarns, sondern Serbiens Sache war es nun, den unleidlichen Zustand ein für allemal zu beenden.

Am 23. Juli 1914 überreichte der k. und k. Gesandte Freiherr von Giesl im Auftrage der österreichisch-ungarischen Regierung der königlich serbischen Regierung die folgende Note:

„Am 31. März 1909 hat der königlich serbische Gesandte am Wiener Hofe im Auftrage seiner Regierung der k. und k. Regierung folgende Erklärung abgegeben:

‚Serbien anerkennt, daß es durch die in Bosnien geschaffene Tatsache in seinen Rechten nicht berührt wurde, und daß es sich demgemäß den Entscheidungen anpassen wird, welche die Mächte in Bezug auf den Artikel 25 des Berliner Vertrages treffen werden. Indem Serbien den Ratschlägen der Großmächte Folge leistet, verpflichtet es sich die Haltung des Protestes und des Widerstandes, die es hinsichtlich der Annexion seit dem vergangenen Oktober eingenommen hat, aufzugeben, und es verpflichtet sich ferner, die Richtung seiner Politik gegenüber Österreich-Ungarn zu ändern und künftighin mit diesem letzteren auf dem Fuße freundnachbarlicher Beziehung zu leben.'

Die Geschichte der letzten Jahre nun und insbesondere die schmerzlichen Ereignisse des 28. Juni haben das Vorhandensein einer subversiven Bewegung in Serbien erwiesen, deren Ziel es ist, von der österreichisch-ungarischen Monarchie gewisse Teile ihres Gebietes loszutrennen. Diese Bewegung, die unter den Augen der serbischen Regierung entstand, hat in der Folge jenseits des Gebietes des Königreiches durch Akte des Terrorismus, durch eine Reihe von Attentaten und durch Morde Ausdruck gefunden.

Weit entfernt, die in der Erklärung vom 31. März 1909 enthaltenen formellen Verpflichtungen zu erfüllen, hat die königliche serbische Regierung nichts getan, um diese Bewegung zu unterdrücken. Sie duldete das verbrecherische Treiben der verschiedenen, gegen die Monarchie gerichteten Vereine und Vereinigungen, die zügellose Sprache der Presse, die Verherrlichung der Urheber von Attentaten, die Teilnahme von Offizieren und Beamten an subversiven Umtrieben, sie duldete eine ungesunde Propaganda im öffentlichen Unterricht und duldete schließlich alle Manifestationen, welche die serbische Bevölkerung zum Hasse gegen die Monarchie und zur Verachtung ihrer Einrichtungen verleiten konnten.

Diese Duldung, der sich die königlich serbische Regierung schuldig machte, hat noch in jenem Moment angedauert, in dem die Ereignisse des 28. Juni der ganzen Welt die grauenhaften Folgen solcher Duldung zeigten.

Es erhellt aus den Aussagen und Geständnissen der verbrecherischen Urheber des Attentates vom 28. Juni, daß der Mord von Sarajewo in Belgrad ausgeheckt wurde, daß die Mörder die Waffen und Bomben, mit denen sie ausgestattet waren, von serbischen Beamten und Offizieren erhielten, die der ‚Narodna Odbrana' angehörten, und daß schließlich die Beförderung der Verbrecher und deren Waffen nach Bosnien von leitenden serbischen Grenzorganen veranstaltet und durchgeführt wurde.

Die angeführten Ergebnisse der Untersuchung gestatten es der k. und k. Regierung nicht, noch länger die Haltung zuwartender Langmut zu beobachten, die sie durch Jahre jenen Treibereien gegenüber eingenommen hatte, die ihren Mittelpunkt in Belgrad haben und von da auf die Gebiete der Monarchie übertragen werden. Diese Ereignisse legen der k. und k. Regierung vielmehr die Pflicht auf, Umtrieben ein Ende zu bereiten, die eine ständige Bedrohung für die Ruhe der Monarchie bilden.

Um diesen Zweck zu erreichen, sieht sich die k. und k. Regierung gezwungen, von der serbischen Regierung eine offizielle Versicherung zu verlangen, daß sie die gegen Österreich-Ungarn gerichtete Propaganda verurteilt, das heißt die Gesamtheit der Bestrebungen, deren Endziel es ist, von der Monarchie Gebiete loszulösen, die ihr angehören, und daß sie sich verpflichtet, diese verbrecherische und terroristische Propaganda mit allen Mitteln zu unterdrücken.

Um diesen Verpflichtungen einen feierlichen Charakter zu geben, wird die königlich serbische Regierung auf der ersten Seite ihres offiziellen Organs vom 26./13. Juli nachfolgende Erklärung veröffentlichen:

‚Die königlich serbische Regierung verurteilt die gegen Österreich-Ungarn gerichtete Propaganda, das heißt die Gesamtheit jener Bestrebungen, deren letztes Ziel es ist, von der österreichisch-ungarischen Monarchie Gebiete loszutrennen, die ihr angehören, und sie bedauert aufrichtigst die grauenhaften Folgen dieser verbrecherischen Handlungen.

Die königlich serbische Regierung bedauert, daß serbische Offiziere und Beamte an der vorgenannten Propaganda teilgenommen und damit die freundnachbarlichen Beziehungen gefährdet haben, die zu pflegen sich die königliche Regierung durch ihre Erklärung vom 31. März 1909 feierlichst verpflichtet hatte.

Die königliche Regierung, die jeden Gedanken oder jeden Versuch einer Einmischung in die Geschicke der Bewohner in was immer für eines Teiles Österreich-Ungarn mißbilligt und zurückweist, erachtet es für ihre Pflicht, die Offiziere, Beamten und die gesamte Bevölkerung des Königsreiches ganz ausdrücklich aufmerksam zu machen, daß sie künftighin mit äußerster Strenge gegen jene Personen vorgehen wird, die sich derartiger Handlungen schuldig machen sollten, Handlungen, denen vorzubeugen und die zu unterdrücken sie alle Anstrengungen machen wird.'

Die serbische Regierung verpflichtet sich überdies:

1. jede Publikation zu unterdrücken, die zum Haß und zur Verachtung der Monarchie aufreizt und deren allgemeine Tendenz gegen die territoriale Integrität der letzeren gerichtet ist;

2. sofort mit der Auflösung des Vereins ‚Narodna Odbrana' vorzugehen, dessen gesamte Propagandamittel zu konfiszieren und in derselben Weise gegen andere Vereine und Vereinigungen in Serbien einzuschreiten, die sich mit der Propaganda gegen Österreich-Ungarn beschäftigen; die königliche Regierung wird die nötigen Maßregeln treffen, damit die aufgelösten Vereine nicht etwa ihre Tätigkeit unter anderem Namen oder in anderer Form fortsetzen;

3. ohne Verzug aus dem öffentlichen Unterricht in Serbien, sowohl was den Lehrkörper als auch die Lehrmittel betrifft, alles zu beseitigen, was dazu dient oder dienen könnte, die Propaganda gegen Österreich-Ungarn zu nähren,

4. aus dem Militärstand und der Verwaltung im allgemeinen alle Offiziere und Beamten zu entfernen, die der Propaganda gegen Österreich-Ungarn schuldig sind und deren Namen unter Mitteilung des gegen sie vorliegenden Materials der königlichen Regierung bekanntzugeben sich die k. und k. Regierung vorbehält;

5. einzuwilligen, daß in Serbien Organe der k. und k. Regierung bei der Unterdrückung der gegen die territoriale Integrität der Monarchie gerichteten subversiven Bewegung mitwirken;

6. eine gerichtliche Untersuchung gegen jene Teilnehmer des Komplottes vom 28. Juni einzuleiten, die sich auf

serbischem Territorium befinden; von der k. und k. Regierung hiezu delegierte Organe werden an den bezüglichen Erhebungen teilnehmen;

7. mit aller Beschleunigung die Verhaftung des Majors Vojislaw Tankosić und eines gewissen Milan Ciganović, serbischen Staatsbeamten vorzunehmen, welche durch die Ergebnisse der Untersuchung kompromittiert sind;

8. durch wirksame Maßnahmen die Teilnahme der serbischen Behörden an dem Einschmuggeln von Waffen und Explosivkörpern über die Grenze zu verhindern; jene Organe des Grenzdienstes von Sabac und Loznica, die den Urhebern des Verbrechens von Sarajewo bei dem Übertritt über die Grenze behilflich waren, aus dem Dienste zu entlassen und strenge zu bestrafen;

9. der k. und k. Regierung Aufklärung zu geben über die nicht zu rechtfertigenden Äußerungen hoher serbischer Funktionäre in Serbien und im Auslande, die, ihrer hohen offiziellen Stellung ungeachtet, nicht gezögert haben, sich nach dem Attentat vom 28. Juni in Interviews in feindlicher Weise gegen Österreich-Ungarn auszusprechen;

10. die k. und k. Regierung ohne Verzug von der Durchführung der in den vorigen Punkten zusammengefaßten Maßnahmen zu verständigen.

Die k. und k. Regierung erwartet die Antwort der königlichen Regierung spätestens bis Samstag, den 25. d. M., um 6 Uhr nachmittags."

Beigelegt war dieser Note ein ausführlich erläuternder Bericht, der die einzelnen Tatsachen schilderte und auch den europäischen Mächten zur Einsicht übermittelt wurde. Ein noch reichhaltigeres Rundschreiben erging an alle Gesandten in den verschiedenen Staaten, das mit Einzelheiten die ganze verbrecherische Propaganda darstellte und auf jeden Einsichtigen unbedingt überzeugend wirken mußte.

Einige Vorzeichen hätten in Belgrad als Warnung dienen können. Mehrmals war Graf Berchtold nach Ischl gereist, um dem Monarchen Bericht zu erstatten, auch der Ministerpräsident Graf Tisza hatte sich eingefunden. Aber in Belgrad heuchelte man Unwissenheit, mimte man Ahnungslosigkeit. Man wußte, daß Sühnung dort gefordert werden mußte, aber man arbeitete an einer Dupierung der Welt: Man bereitete im Voraus schon ein Erstaunen über die Anschuldigung vor. Man ging keinen Schritt Österreich-Ungarn entgegen, man wollte sich – wohlvorbereitet wie man war – überraschen lassen. Aber man hatte lang genug in Wien gezögert, und das Unausweichliche mußte geschehen.

Durch die letzte Forderung der Note, die restlose Erfüllung der österreich-ungarischen Wünsche innerhalb von achtundvierzig Stunden erheischte, war diesem Dokument der Charakter eines Ultimatums verliehen. Man kannte jetzt schon zu gut die raffinierte serbische Technik der Verschleppungen und Winkelzüge, das Hinausschieben auf Wochen und Monate unter dem Druck der russischen Drohung, die militärische Gegenmobilisationen und damit ungeheure Kosten verursachte. Der Alp mußte endlich abgewälzt werden, ein redliches Ja oder Nein die Antwort geben auf die nur zu berechtigte Forderung der Regierung: Es war jetzt an Serbien, zu entscheiden, ob es die verbrecherisch-ehrgeizige Politik der Karageorgević mit den Waffen verteidigen oder ehrlich und loyal mit der Nachbarmonarchie in Frieden leben wollte.

Auf die serbische Bevölkerung wirkte die feste, entschlossene Maßnahme wie ein Donnerschlag. Sofort wurden zwar von den erfahrenen Regisseuren die Kulissen des vergangenen Jahres wieder aufgestellt: die Straßendemonstrationen mit den Freiwilligen, die Wutartikel der Zeitungen, die Reden in den Versammlungen. Aber im Volke selbst war ein dumpfes Erschrecken: Man fühlte zu deutlich, daß diesmal der Entschluß ein unbeugsamer war. Und das Land war von zwei Kriegen belehrt, wie teuer ein Volk den verbrecherischen Ehrgeiz einzelner Diplomaten zahlt, sie hatten die Krone der Karageorgević mit tausendfachem Gewicht an Blut erkauft. Aber die Hehler, Mörder und Anstifter fürchteten für sich, und in jenen Kreisen schmiedete man den Krieg, um sich selbst zu schützen. Ein Weltbrand war diesen Ehrgeizigen nicht zu viel, um ihre kleinen Gelüste nach Ruhm und Volksgunst zu befriedigen. Geplant war natürlich ein Ausweichen. Man wollte nach orientalischer Taktik verzögern, hinausschieben, bis aus Sibirien und der Mongolei die russischen Millionenheere gekommen seien und auf unsere Grenzen drückten.

In Wien und in der Welt war man sich klar, daß die Antwort an uns nicht von Serbien, sondern von Rußland gegeben würde. Hartwig, der emsige Mittler, war zwar in diesen Tagen der Erregung einem Schlaganfall erlegen, aber das ganze Auswärtige Amt war nur eine Filiale der Petersburger Sängerbrücke. Serbien hatte sich Rußland in einer Art moralischer Vasallenschaft ergeben, auf sein Kommando war es im Jahre 1908 eingeknickt, auf seinen Befehl hatte es gegen die Türkei losgeschlagen. An Rußland allein war es, Nachgiebigkeit oder Trotz in Belgrad spielen zu lassen. Nicht nur an den König Peter war die Frage gestellt, ob er sich endlich von den verbrecherischen Elementen seiner Umgebung offen und deutlich lossagen wollte, sondern auch an den Zaren, ob die russische Politik gesonnen sei, die kleinen Balkanstaaten auch dann noch in Schutz zu nehmen, wenn sie den Mord und die Bomben als Argumente benützten.

Europa erkannte sofort den Ernst der Situation. Zwischen den Kabinetten begannen fieberhafte Verhandlungen: Der deutsche Kaiser eilte von seiner Nordlandreise zurück, Poincaré von seiner russischen Reise. Wie mit einem Ruck brach die Sorglosigkeit der Optimisten zusammen, die den Gewitterzeichen nicht Glauben geschenkt und auch jene letzte Mahnung aus Sarajewo überhört hatten. Wer diese Tage des Fiebers und der Erwartung erlebt hat, dem wird sie niemand ins Gedächtnis zurückzurufen brauchen, sie gehören dem Unvergeßlichen eines jeden Lebens.

Der Angelpunkt der Situation lag, das war offenkundig, in Petersburg. War man dort entschlossen, die Sache zwischen Österreich-Ungarn und Serbien austragen zu lassen, so brauchte man die Nachgiebigkeit des Balkanstaates nicht zu besorgen, und der Friede war gerettet. Behielt aber dort die slawophile Kriegspartei die Übermacht, so war diese Angelegenheit – jeder fühlte dies sofort – der Weltkrieg. Alle Verantwortung lag in den Händen des Zaren und seiner Ratgeber.

Schon der Empfang, der unserem Botschafter in Petersburg bei der Überreichung der Note von dem Minister Sasonow zuteilwurde, ließ keinen Zweifel, daß dort längst für den Krieg entschieden war –, was wenige Tage später die seit Wochen bereits eingeleiteten militärischen Vorbereitungen noch zwingender erwiesen. Sasonow zeigte wenig Verlangen, sich die Note vorlesen zu lassen und erklärte kategorisch, Österreich-Ungarn suche nur – Österreich-Ungarn, dem sein Thronfolger von serbischen Revolvern ermordet worden war – einen Vorwand, um das kleine Land zu überfallen. Das Verlangen der russischen Regierung um Aufschub der Frist mußte natürlich abgelehnt werden: Es war von der Militärpartei gestellt, damit Österreich-Ungarn wieder unter dem Druck der ganzen russischen Armee zu verhandeln genötigt und aus Sibirien inzwischen neue Armeekorps herangeholt werden könnten. Vergebens wandte sich die deutsche Regierung an die englische, französische und italienische mit der Bitte, sie möchten Rußland veranlassen, an den Verhandlungen teilzunehmen, ohne vorher zu mobilisieren, damit nicht wieder jener unerträgliche Druck auf ganz Europa laste. Aber Englands Absicht war es nicht, Deutschland und Österreich-Ungarn eine schwere Stunde zu ersparen. Sie sollten wieder ins kaudinische Joch einer diplomatischen Niederlage, gedemütigt sollten sie werden, wenn sie wagten, eine Provokation zu erwidern. Im Geheimen hatte Grey schon in Petersburg und Paris Rücksprache gehalten, und statt Unterstützung fand Österreich-Ungarn nur Schürung und Widerstand. Die Mächte antworteten mit Gegenvorschlägen, Österreich-Ungarn möchte auf einem Kongreß seine Sache verfechten. Aber man wußte schon zu gut, daß diese Kongresse Rußland nur Zeit ließen zu rüsten und dann mit der Hilfe der Bundesgenossen den berechtigten Anspruch des Zweibundes – denn Italien erkannte den Dreibund nur dort an, wo er seine Interessen schützte – zu vergewaltigen.

Rußland wollte den Konflikt und tat darum alles, Serbien den Nacken zu steifen. Noch ehe die von Österreich-Ungarn gestellte Frist abgelaufen war, erschien im Petersburger amtlichen Organ die folgende Note: „Die kaiserliche Regierung, lebhaft besorgt durch die überraschenden Ereignisse und durch das an Serbien von Österreich-Ungarn gerichtete Ultimatum, verfolgt mit Aufmerksamkeit die Entwicklung des österreichisch-ungarischen=serbischen Konfliktes, in welchem Rußland nicht indifferent bleiben kann." Gleichzeitig sandte der Zar an König Peter ein Telegramm, in dem er ihm mitteilte, daß Serbien „für alle Fälle auf seine Unterstützung zählen könne".

Nun war dem Verbrechen von Sarajewo vor aller Welt die russische Sanktion gegeben, und es war nicht zu zweifeln, daß in Belgrad Österreich-Ungarns Forderungen abgelehnt werden mußten. Freilich blieb man dort der alten Praktik treu, selbst den hartnäckigsten Widerstand mit dem Schein der Loyalität zu umkleiden. Vor der Welt mußte so getan werden, als sei Serbien zu völliger Nachgiebigkeit bereit und wünsche nur in einigen unwesentlichen Punkten kleine Korrekturen, damit man später sich als das unschuldige Opfer eines brutalen Angriffs ausgeben könnte. Daß man sich aber in Belgrad über die gänzliche Unzulänglichkeit der Antwort vollkommen klar war, bewies die Tatsache, daß drei Stunden, ehe die Antwort dem Gesandten überreicht wurde, schon die allgemeine Mobilisierung in ganz Serbien anbefohlen war und die gesamte Garnison in Marsch-Ausrüstung die Stadt verlassen hatte. Pašić wußte, daß seine angeblich so loyale Antwort eine Kriegserklärung an die Monarchie war. Es ist grauenhaft auszudenken, daß in jenem kleinen elenden Konak von Belgrad Europas Schicksal entschieden wurde, daß die Hände, blutbesprengt von dem des eigenen Königs, nun jenes Blut von Hunderttausenden und Millionen fordern sollten. Ein Wort, ein einziges loyales Wort hätte alles Unheil verhindern können, ein Wink, eine Bewegung, und die grauenhafte Furie wäre nie entfesselt worden. Aber dieser Konak war voll finsterer Erinnerungen, dort war gegen Fürsten und Reiche, gegen einzelne und Völker zu oft gefrevelt worden, als daß diesmal das Gefühl der Verantwortung hätte Einhalt gebieten können. Der entscheidende Kronrat hatte gesprochen –, Serbien warf die brennende Lunte in das Pulverfaß.

Zwei Minuten vor dem Ablauf der gestellten Frist, zwei Minuten vor 6 Uhr am 25. Juli 1914 wurde endlich die

Antwort überreicht. Ein Blick genügte unserem Gesandten, um zu sehen, daß sie unzulänglich war. Es stand darin der heitere Satz: „Die königliche Regierung sei durch die Behauptung, daß Angehörige Serbiens an der Vorbereitung des in Sarajewo verübten Attentats teilgenommen hätten, schmerzlich überrascht" –, eine Überraschung, die seltsam aufrichtig war, nachdem die Bomben aus den Arsenalen von Kragujevac stammten und nur im Einverständnis mit königlich serbischen Offizieren hatten ausgefolgt werden können. Die Regierung hätte ferner „erwartet zur Mitwirkung bei den Nachforschungen über dieses Verbrechen eingeladen zu werden", aber eben diese Regierung lehnte glattweg ab, die Untersuchungen in Serbien unter Kontrolle der österreichisch-ungarischen Amtsorgane führen zu lassen – denn ohne diese wäre jede Untersuchung durch die Identität von Richtern und Verbrechern eine Farce geworden –, sie erklärte sich außerstande, den Angriffen der Presse Einhalt zu gebieten und gab außerdem jeder Annahme undeutliche und dehnbare Form der Auslegung (wie im Österreichisch-ungarischen Rotbuch genauer dargestellt wird). Selbstverständlich reiste unser Gesandter sofort ab, ebenso der serbische Gesandte in Wien. Die Beziehungen waren abgebrochen. Und man wußte: Mit unserem Gesandten verließ auch die letzte Hoffnung auf den Frieden das erschreckte Europa.

Aber dennoch: Zwei Tage noch wartete Österreich-Ungarn. Noch war es Zeit, die Serben zum Einlenken zu bewegen. Um Rußland jeden Vorwand zu nehmen, hatte Graf Berchtold vertraulich mitteilen lassen, Österreich-Ungarn sei um des Friedens willen bereit, die Integrität und Souveränität Serbiens zu wahren und sich mit einer Entschädigung für die Rüstungskosten – die schon zum dritten Mal notwendigen – zu begnügen. Er teilte Sasonow mit, dem der eine Punkt des Ultimatums, man möge die Untersuchung mit Hilfe österreichisch-ungarischer Organe führen, bedenklich schien, die österreichisch-ungarischen Beamten sollten nicht dem eigentlichen Gerichtsverfahren, sondern nur den Voruntersuchungen – *„aux recherches"* – beigezogen werden. Aber Rußland, offenbar durch geheime Zusicherungen Greys gestützt, blieb intransigent. Es wollte eine Demütigung Österreich-Ungarns vor dem Balkan, vor der ganzen Welt. Nach dem Ultimatum noch sollte Österreich-Ungarn verzichten und sich in die Knie beugen vor dem serbischen, dem russischen Willen.

Zwei Tage noch zögerte Österreich-Ungarn. Noch nach jener Entschließung sollte Serbien ein gütlicher Rückzug ermöglicht sein. Deutlicher und finsterer erhob sich von Tag zu Tag am Horizont die furchtbare Wetterwolke des europäischen Krieges. In Wien und allen Städten zeigten patriotische Demonstrationen gefestigten Willen zu jedem Opfer. Aber das Serbien der Karageorgević zögerte nicht, eine Welt in Flammen zu setzen für seine ehrgeizigen Ziele. Auch diese Frist, die ungeforderte, die freiwillig von Österreich-Ungarn gegebene, ließ es störrisch verstreichen. Und erst am 28. Juli 1914 unterschrieb der Friedenkaiser Franz Joseph schwerer Hand die Kriegserklärung und jenes denkwürdige Manifest:

„An Meine Völker!

Es war Mein sehnlichster Wunsch, die Jahre, die Mir durch Gottes Gnade noch beschieden sind, Werken des Friedens zu weihen und Meine Völker vor den schweren Opfern und Lasten des Krieges zu bewahren.

Im Rate der Vorsehung ward es anders beschlossen.

Die Umtriebe eines haßerfüllten Gegners zwingen Mich, zur Wahrung der Ehre Meiner Monarchie, zum Schutze ihres Ansehens und ihrer Machtstellung, zur Sicherung ihres Besitzstandes nach langen Jahren des Friedens zum Schwerte zu greifen.

Mit rasch vergessendem Undank hat das Königreich Serbien, das von den ersten Anfängen seiner staatlichen Selbständigkeit bis in die neueste Zeit von Meinen Vorfahren und Mir gestützt und gefördert worden war, schon vor Jahren den Weg offener Feindseligkeiten gegen Österreich-Ungarn betreten.

Als Ich nach drei Jahrzehnten segensvoller Friedensarbeit in Bosnien und der Hercegovina Meine Herrscherrechte auf diese Länder erstreckte, hat diese Meine Verfügung im Königreiche Serbien, dessen Rechte in keiner Weise verletzt wurden, Ausbrüche zügelloser Leidenschaft und erbittertsten Hasses hervorgerufen. Meine Regierung hat damals von dem schönen Vorrechte des Stärkeren[36] Gebrauch gemacht und in äußerster Nachsicht und Milde von Serbien nur die Herabsetzung seines Heeres auf den Friedensstand und das Versprechen verlangt, in Hinkunft die Bahn des Friedens und der Freundschaft zu gehen.

Von demselben Geist der Mäßigung geleitet, hat sich Meine Regierung, als Serbien vor zwei Jahren im Kampfe mit dem türkischen Reiche begriffen war, auf die Wahrung der wichtigsten Lebensbedingungen der Monarchie beschränkt. Dieser Haltung hatte Serbien in erster Linie die Erreichung des Kriegszweckes zu verdanken.

Die Hoffnung, daß das serbische Königreich die Langmut und Friedensliebe Meiner Regierung würdigen und sein Wort einlösen werde, hat sich nicht erfüllt.

---

[36] Die Hofschranzen, die diesen Text verfasst haben, hätten gut daran getan, das Wort Marie Ebner-Eschenbachs zu beherzigen, das da lautet: „Das Recht des Stärkeren ist das größte Unrecht." (Anm. K. G.)

Immer höher lodert der Haß gegen Mich und Mein Haus empor, immer unverhüllter tritt das Streben zutage, untrennbare Gebiete Österreich-Ungarns gewaltsam loszureißen.

Ein verbrecherisches Treiben greift über die Grenze, um im Südosten der Monarchie die Grundlagen der staatlichen Ordnung zu untergraben, das Volk, dem Ich in landesväterlicher Liebe Meine volle Fürsorge zuwende, in seiner Treue zum Herrscherhaus und zum Vaterlande wankend zu machen, die heranwachsende Jugend irrezuleiten und zu frevelhaften Taten des Wahnwitzes und des Hochverrates aufzureizen. Eine Reihe von Mordanschlägen, eine planmäßig vorbereitete Verschwörung, deren furchtbares Gelingen Mich und Meine treuen Völker ins Herz getroffen hat, bildet die weithin sichtbare blutige Spur jener geheimen Machenschaften, die von Serbien aus geleitet und ins Werk gesetzt wurden.

Diesem unerträglichen Treiben muß Einhalt geboten, den unaufhörlichen Herausforderungen Serbiens ein Ende bereitet werden, soll die Ehre und Würde Meiner Monarchie unverletzt erhalten und ihre staatliche, wirtschaftliche und militärische Entwicklung vor beständigen Erschütterungen bewahrt bleiben.

Vergebens hat Meine Regierung noch einen letzten Versuch unternommen, dieses Ziel mit friedlichen Mitteln zu erreichen, Serbien durch eine ernste Mahnung zur Umkehr zu bewegen.

Serbien hat die maßvollen und gerechten Forderungen Meiner Regierung zurückgewiesen und es abgelehnt, jenen Pflichten nachzukommen, deren Erfüllung im Leben der Völker und Staaten die natürliche und notwendige Grundlage des Friedens bildet.

So muß Ich denn daran schreiten, mit Waffengewalt die unerläßlichen Bürgschaften zu schaffen, die Meinen Staaten die Ruhe im Innern und den dauernden Frieden nach außen sichern sollen.

In dieser ernsten Stunde bin Ich Mir der ganzen Tragweite Meines Entschlusses und Meiner Verantwortung vor dem Allmächtigen voll bewußt.

Ich habe alles geprüft und erwogen.

Mit ruhigem Gewissen betrete Ich den Weg, den die Pflicht Mir weist.

Ich vertraue auf Meine Völker, die sich in allen Stürmen stets in Einigkeit und Treue um Meinen Thron geschart haben und für die Ehre, Größe und Macht des Vaterlandes zu schwersten Opfern immer bereit waren.

Ich vertraue auf Österreich-Ungarns tapfere und von hingebungsvoller Begeisterung erfüllte Wehrmacht.

Und Ich vertraue auf den Allmächtigen, daß er Meinen Waffen den Sieg verleihen werde.

F r a n z J o s e p h *m. p.*"

Der Friede war nun verloren, aber noch war es nicht der Weltkrieg geworden, die furchtbarste Katastrophe der Menschheit. Noch glimmte nur ein Funke, ein einzelner loser Balke an dem herrlichen Bauwerk, das die Jahrtausende Kultur aufgerichtet, noch konnte ein energischer Griff, ein gemeinsamer Wille die aufzüngelnde Flamme niedertreten, noch die entsetzliche Gefahr beschränken. Österreich-Ungarn und das Deutsche Reich taten ihr Bestes. Unsere Truppen wurden zurückgehalten, die Operationen mit Absicht verlangsamt, nur um den Großmächten Zeit zu geben, Serbien aufzurütteln und zu veranlassen, einen verlustlosen Frieden zu schließen, ohne Krieg geführt zu haben. Nochmals meldete unser Botschafter in Petersburg, Österreich-Ungarn begehre keine Gebietserweiterung und garantiere die uneingeschränkte Souveränität des Balkanstaates; Deutschland, und vor allem sein Kaiser, bekräftigten mit ihrem Einfluß und ihrer makellosen Ehre dies Versprechen, auch Italien – wir wissen heute, daß es uns diplomatisch nur unterstützte, weil es sich militärisch zum Verrat noch nicht gerüstet fühlte – suchte zu vermitteln, aber in Petersburg war man taub. Man wollte dort nicht den Frieden, Iswolski lechzte nach einer Demütigung Östereich-Ungarns, nach einer Satisfaktion. Reuig, beschämt, gemaßregelt und verhöhnt, mit beschmutztem Prestige sollte die Monarchie aus diesem Konflikte hervorgehen, sklavisch sollte unsere Macht einknicken vor Rußlands erhobener Faust. Der Großfürst Nikolaj Nikolajewitsch [Romanow], ehrgeizig, die langjährige Ungnade des Hofes durch die Bewunderung der Nation wettzumachen, gierig nach dem verheißenen und nur durch den Krieg zu erlangenden Titel des Generalissimus, hungrig nach Unsterblichkeit, wenn auch nach einer herostratischen, peitschte die Kriegslust auf. Um ihn rottete sich die alte slawophile Garde, die pravoslawe Kirche, alle Mächte, die ungestüm die Russifizierung der Welt anstrebten. Ihrem Ansturm gelang es, bei dem Zaren die Mobilisierung durchzusetzen. Ungeheure Truppenmassen wurden an die Grenze des Reiches geworfen und die gefährlichen Vorbereitungen auch gegen Deutschland gewandt.

Mit Besorgnis hatte die deutsche Regierung die russische Kriegspartei die Führung der Politik ergreifen gesehen und sofort erkannt, daß bei gerüsteten Heeren auf die Dauer ein Zusammenstoß schon wegen der unerträglichen Kosten und vor allem durch die Leidenschaften der Völker unvermeidlich war. Die Siedehitze mußte zur Explosion führen, umso mehr als von Paris und London geschäftige

Hände immer wieder Öl ins Feuer gossen. Da entschloß sich der Kaiser zu einem großherzigen Schritt, er wandte sich persönlich an den Zaren, dem er in den schwersten Krisen des russischen Reiches als Freund und Berater zur Seite gestanden hatte und wies ihm den ganzen Umfang der Gefahr. Mit bewegten Worten legte er ihm nahe, die Mobilisierungen rückgängig zu machen, die lange mit falschen Ehrenwörtern des Kriegsministers verschleiert worden waren. Der Zar antwortete ausweichend. Er versprach, kriegerische Akte zu verhindern, solange die Verhandlungen über Serbien mit Österreich-Ungarn andauerten, aber deren Dauer und Erfolg hing einzig vom Gutdünken des Minister Sasonow ab, der nur zweierlei wollte, erstlich Zeitgewinn und dann den Krieg.

Für den Krieg arbeitete der Großfürst und die Armee, für den Zeitgewinn sollte inzwischen England sorgen. Sir Edward Grey hatte auf den Vorschlag Deutschlands, England solle tätig mithelfen, eine Lokalisierung des Krieges zu erwirken, nur den alten heuchlerischen Gegenvorschlag, das Allerweltsmittel, die Konferenz. Dort sollte das Spiel von Algeciras von neuem beginnen, Österreich-Ungarn und Deutschland von der Mehrzahl überstimmt oder zum Kriege gezwungen werden, den bis dahin die Gegner in Ruhe vorbereiten könnten. Die Flotte war inzwischen geheim mobilisiert worden, die Kabel in ihren Händen, Frankreich, England, Rußland hielten ehern zusammen, der Treulosigkeit Italiens war man gewiß, so war dies anscheinend friedliche Angebot in Wirklichkeit die Vorbereitung einer mörderischen Pression. Und vor allem ein Eingriff in die Souveränität Österreich-Ungarns, das seinen mit Blut zu führenden Krieg durch Papier sich entwinden lassen sollte.

In Frankreich war die Presse gleich lichterloh seit dem Tage der serbischen Note. Iswolski hatte mit der goldenen Stimmgabel den Zeitungen den Ton angegeben, dazu bliesen die Fanfaren der Revanche. Englands war man sicher, obzwar es sich kühl und unabhängig gebärdete, aus seiner Versenkung reckte sich der gestürzte Minister Delcassé empor, und der emporgekommene Provinzadvokat, der Präsident Poincaré, die Augen noch geblendet von den Prächten des Zarenpalastes in Zarskoje-Selo[37], sah sich schon in der Glorie des ersten Carnot, des *„organisateur de la victoire"*. Der Tanz war zwar erst für 1916 angesagt, aber die Ungeduld wollte die Stunde nicht versäumen. Auch hier wurde die Mobilisation angeordnet, und die französischen Aeroplane surrten neugierig und drohend ins südliche Deutschland hinein.

Jedoch Frankreich ist ein demokratisches Land, in dem nicht die russischen Großfürsten und ihre Söldner allein über Krieg und Frieden entscheiden können. Eine starke Gruppe hatte dort immer erkannt, daß mit Deutschland besser und leichter im Frieden zu leben sei als im Krieg, eine Gruppe, die sich nicht von den Truppenparaden des Zaren blenden ließ und nicht gewillt war, für den Dreizack Englands zu kämpfen. Ihr Führer, Jean Jaurès, selbst von seinen Feinden als unbestechlicher, ehrenhafter Charakter anerkannt, merkte rechtzeitig den Unwillen der führenden Politiker, die Verwicklung zu lösen, er merkte, wie sie im Gegenteil die Fäden zwischen Rußland und Frankreich hastig verknoteten, um beide Nationen an diesem Seile in den Krieg zu reißen. Energisch forderte er die Minister auf, nicht ehrgeizigen Umtrieben, sondern dem wahrhaften

---

[37] *Zarskoje Selo*: Heute Puschkin; bis 1918 Царское Село, Zarskoje Selo (Zarendorf).

Vorteil Frankreichs und der ganzen Menschheit zu dienen. Seine Ansichten fanden in den Couloirs der Kammern Zustimmung, mit Besorgnis sahen die Revanchehetzer und Trabanten Iswolskis ihren Plan gefährdet und zitterten um die Majorität. Am nächsten Tag drohte ein gefährlicher Artikel Jaurès in der „Humanité" – so gab es nur ein Mittel, das Gewissen Frankreichs zum Schweigen zu bringen, den Einzigen, der hinausschreien wollte, daß hier ein Komplott leichtfertig gegen den Weltfrieden geschmiedet wurde. Das Mittel war eben von den Karageorgević erprobt worden – der Browning. Am 31. Juli abends wurde der gefährliche Anwalt des Friedens heimtückisch ermordet, und heute hat die französische Regierung noch nicht gewagt, den Mörder vor ein öffentliches Gericht zu bringen. Der Bote könnte die Auftraggeber verraten, und die freuen sich heute – oder freuen sich schon nicht mehr – ihres Erfolges, des Weltkriegs.

Noch einmal wandte sich Deutschland an Rußland mit befristeter Frage, ob es die Rüstungen einstellen wolle und an Frankreich, wie es sich im Kriegsfalle verhalten würde. Aber der so geschäftige Telegraph wurde auf einmal stumm. Sie schwiegen –, Deutschland sollte ja die Last aufgehäuft werden, den Krieg eröffnet zu haben, den sie herbeigeführt. Verhandeln wollten sie nicht, so mußte gehandelt werden. Am 2. August erklärte Deutschland, in äußerster Gefahr, durch den einheitlich vorbereiteten Angriff der drei Mächte ungerüstet überfallen zu werden, den Krieg, zwei Tage später kalkulierte Sir Edward Grey kühl vor dem englischen Parlament, England würde, wenn es friedlich bliebe, nur wenig geringer leiden, als wenn es am Kriege teilnehme, das Geschäft sei also einzuleiten. König Eduards Reisen mußten nun mit dem Blute Europas bezahlt werden, auch an Österreich-Ungarn wurde die Rechnung gesandt für jenen Besuch in Ischl, wo der König Eduard vergebens versucht hatte, uns als Hehler und Mittäter des Attentats auf den europäischen Frieden zu kaufen.

Nun war die Stunde gekommen. Und während Italien, wie immer, wenn es die wirkliche Entscheidung galt, verlegen zur Seite trat, rafften sich die drei mächtigsten Staaten Europas Söldner und Helfer von aller Welt. Belgien, Japan, Montenegro, aus aller Welt wälzten sie Hörige und Kauftruppen gegen Deutschland und Österreich-Ungarn, eine Vielzahl, die erdrückend gewesen wäre, zählte nicht in den Stunden des Krieges auch der moralische Wert, das Kraftvertrauen und die kulturelle Überlegenheit des Einzelnen wie des Volkes und seiner Führer mit. Aus der verbrecherischen Anmaßung eines der kleinsten europäischen Staaten war die größte Katastrophe der Weltgeschichte geworden, die Blutsaat von Belgrad und Sarajewo war furchtbar und fruchtbar aufgegangen. Das Herz Europas, Deutschland und Österreich-Ungarn, mußten sich und ihre Existenz in Waffen behaupten gegen fast alle Nationen des Erdreichs. Aber diese höchste Not hatte auch eine höchste Kraft in ihnen gezeigt, eine Anspannung und einen namenlosen Heroismus, der Taten vollbrachte, wie sie Europa noch nie gekannt und der diese Zeit in Ewigkeit überdauern wird als das wertvollste Vermächtnis für die Späteren, als die vielleicht überhaupt erhabenste Leistung eines Volkes in der Weltgeschichte.

Nachwort
von Klaus Gräbner

Ob Stefan Zweig bewusst denselben Titel wie Fontane für seinen „Roman aus dem Winter 1812/13" gewählt hat oder dieser von der Militärverwaltung vorgeschrieben wurde, in deren Auftrag diese Arbeit entstanden ist, wir wissen es nicht. Wir wissen überhaupt sehr wenig über „Vor dem Sturm", die den Auftakt zu „Die Geschichte des großen Weltkrieges mit besonderer Berücksichtigung Österreich-Ungarns" mit dem Titel „Unteilbar und Untrennbar"[38] die Deutsch-Österreichisch-Ungarische Waffenbrüderschaft dokumentieren soll. Stefan Zweig gehörte wie die Literaten Rudolf Hans Bartsch, Erwin Rieger, Alfred Polgar und, eine Zeitlang, auch Rainer Maria Rilke der „Literarischen Gruppe" des Kriegsarchivs an. Dort war er gelandet, da er auf Grund seines Gesundheitszustandes für den Dienst an der Waffe nicht geeignet war; aber seine staatsbürgerliche Pflicht befahl ihm dort zu dienen, wo er dem Lande am nützlichsten war. Allein die Vorstellung, jemand könnte durch seine Hand getötet werden, war ihm unerträglich, wie er auch in seinem „Testament des Gewissens" („Ich betrachte es als meine moralische Pflicht, den Mord zu verweigern ..."), das er am 28. November1917, sein 36. Geburtstag, an Romain Rolland übergeben hatte, festhielt.

---

[38] Leitung: Emil Woinovich von Belobreska und Max von Hoen; Hrsg: Alois Veltzé, Wien 1917

Weder ist in den großen biografischen Werken, angefangen bei Erwin Rieger, Richard Specht, Friderike Maria Zweig über Donald A. Prater, Gert Kerschbaumer und Oliver Matuscheck, noch bei den Herausgebern wie Richard Friedenthal, Dieter Simon und Knut Beck davon die Rede. Auch nicht im „Zirkular", das eine Untersuchung von Klaus Heydemann über „Zweig im Kriegsarchiv" enthält. In seinem Tagebuch aus dieser Zeit und in den Briefen erwähnt Zweig dieses Werk, und ich sage bewusst: ‚Werk', mit keinem Wort. Lediglich in einem Brief vom 12. Juli 1915 an den Militärbeamten und Dichterkollegen Franz Karl Ginzkey erwähnt Stefan Zweig das „bekannte Buch", für das er diesen geschichtlichen Abriss verfassen musste. Dass er dies mit Bravour tat, versteht sich von selbst.

Wer mag ermessen, wie viel Kraft es Stefan Zweig gekostet hat, diese Arbeit zu verfassen. Wie oft mag ihm der Vers von Matthias Claudius durch den Kopf gegangen sein:

's ist Krieg! 's ist Krieg!
O Gottes Engel wehre,
Und rede Du darein!
's ist leider Krieg –
und ich begehre
Nicht schuld daran zu sein!

Hier die Arbeit im ärarischen Sinne, dort der „Jeremias", das Anti-Kriegs-Drama: dazwischen immer wieder kleinere Arbeiten wie „Die Legende der dritten Taube", „An die Freunde im Fremdland", die keinen Zweifel über seine wahre Gesinnung zuließen. Das wurde von der Presse auch so gesehen: Sein Nachruf auf den französischen Sozialistenführer Jean Jaurès (er wurde Opfer eines Attentates) wurde in einem deutschnationalen Blatt als „einen drei Spalten langen Wortbrei" gebrandmarkt. Man wusste also genau, wo die unsicheren Kantonisten zu suchen waren.

Aber, trotz aller Fremdenfeindlichkeit, gründete Paul Zifferer, der spätere Kulturattaché der Österreichischen Botschaft in Paris, eine in französischer Sprache gehaltene „Revue d'Autriche", wozu Stefan Zweig den Beitrag für Heft 3 „La nouvelle génération dans l'art autrichien" beisteuerte, ein Unterfangen, das im 2. Weltkrieg unmöglich gewesen wäre.

Der Herausgeber dankt der mutigen Verlegerin, Frau Mag. Nadja Rösner-Krisch, herzlichst für die Möglichkeit der Veröffentlichung und Frau Laura Rösner für die wundervolle Begleitung und Kommentierung dieses wichtigen Textes.

Bamberg, im Januar 2018